Trade Like a Pro

Founded in 1807, John Wiley & Sons is the oldest independent publishing company in the United States. With offices in North America, Europe, Australia and Asia, Wiley is globally committed to developing and marketing print and electronic products and services for our customers' professional and personal knowledge and understanding.

The Wiley Trading series features books by traders who have survived the market's ever changing temperament and have prospered—some by reinventing systems, others by getting back to basics. Whether a novice trader, professional or somewhere in-between, these books will provide the advice and strategies needed to prosper today and well into the future.

For a list of available titles, please visit our Web site at www.Wiley Finance.com.

Trade Like a Pro

15 High-Profit Trading Strategies

NOBLE DRAKOLN

WILEY

John Wiley & Sons, Inc.

Published by John Wiley & Sons, Inc., Hoboken, New Jersey.
Published simultaneously in Canada.

For general information on our other products and services or for technical support, please contact our Customer Care Department within the United States at (800) 762-2974, outside the United States at (317) 572-3993 or fax (317) 572-4002.

Wiley also publishes its books in a variety of electronic formats. Some content that appears in print may not be available in electronic books. For more information about Wiley products, visit our web site at www.wiley.com.

Library of Congress Cataloging-in-Publication Data

DraKoln, Noble.
  Trade like a pro : 15 high-profit trading strategies / Noble DraKoln.
      p.   cm. – (Wiley trading series)
  Includes index.
  ISBN 978-0-470-28735-4 (cloth)
  1. Investments.   2. Investment analysis.   3. Financial risk management.
4. Stockbrokers.   I. Title.
  HG4521.D698   2009
  332.6–dc22
                                                    2008036346

Printed in the United States of America.

10   9   8   7   6   5   4   3   2   1

To my friend, Mike Moone

Although you're gone, your wisdom and presence are still felt.
Thanks for all your support when you were here
and the good word
you have been putting in for me in the hereafter.

Contents

Preface

I n 2000, approximately nine years ago, I released my first book, *Futures for Small Speculators*. This book was meant to be a repudiation of all of the misinformation that investors were receiving from brokers and the industry. I was angry at how many and how often investors were losing their money trading. I realized that losing was the norm for them and when they *did* make money, they had a difficult time replicating their success. Since then I have put out six publications—this being the sixth—and while my anger has subsided, my hope is still to see investors readily able to trade successfully.

This book is a logical extension of the book, *Winning the Trading Game*. That book broke down the three components of successful trading: money management, technical analysis, and risk management. After it was completed, I realized that to clarify the distinction between risk management and money management, I would have to write another book. I knew this book would have to break down as many risk management techniques as possible—in clear concise terms—with as many chart examples as I could muster. I also needed to point out to stock investors, forex investors, and futures investors that risk management transcends trading genres, and in order to trade like professionals, they need to cross those barriers without hesitation.

Things have changed so much in the industry in the last decade, with new exchanges, the weakening dollar, the growth of China and India, and the creation of new tradable instruments like contracts for difference (CFD). All of this change means more opportunities to profit. The old way of looking at futures as too risky or of trading stocks with 100 percent cash has become more fluid. This book is designed to help you make that adjustment.

This book has 15 risk management strategies in two parts. There are nine basic strategies, originally discussed in *Winning the Trading Game*, and now, in *Trade like a Pro*, analyzed more in depth. In addition, there are six advanced risk management strategies, that build on that knowledge.

Finally, this book shows you how to put the two sets of strategies to use to improve your odds of success.

While this book can teach you techniques on how to manage risk, it really cannot make you money, nor can it lose you money. Only your intelligent reaction to the markets can do that and these tools are designed to help you make those intelligent decisions. You still need to have a trading plan, trading goals, a well-kept trading journal, and a sound money management plan, win or lose.

Your dedication to the craft of trading is constantly tested by the demons of fear and greed. It is always tempting to go for a magic bullet, but if it exists—I have yet to find it. Trading is difficult and requires a set plan, built around discipline and perseverance. My book helps you erect and maintain that plan and face the losses that occur with confidence.

Good fortune and good luck in all of your trading endeavors.

Acknowledgments

This book was very difficult to complete in the face of my personal adversity. Like so many other people I was affected by the economic downturns in the real estate market as well. Couple that with the responsibilities that come with being a single father and I could have been overwhelmed at any time. My faith in God not only sustained me, but helped me thrive. I definitely want to acknowledge and thank God for his presence in my life and the constant blessings I have received, which includes all of the wonderful people that have strived to help me both professionally and personally.

As a single father, I really would like to thank my two sons, Alex and Zach. When I am writing, they may as well be writing too since they are directly affected by it. I appreciate their love and their patience in dealing with my odd writing hours and intense work schedule. I also want to thank Lori for being a part of this process, again. You are so loving, supportive, and encouraging. Just by having you around, you definitely made the writing process go easier. I also want to thank my mom, Celestine. You have made me smile and laugh throughout the process and your calls to check up on my writing helped get me to the finish line.

I also want to thank Meg Freeborn and Emilie Herman. Editors extraordinaire! You both have made my writing shine. Not being a writer by trade has meant a lot of reliance on your notes and recommendations on how to improve the manuscript, all of which have helped the quality of my writing.

Without question, I must also acknowledge one of my favorite places to write, Portfolio Coffeehouse. I have been writing there since 1994. Many of my articles, large sections of my books, and a significant amount of my ideas have come while sitting there sipping on a cup of black tea. Thanks.

Finally, I'd like to thank all of my colleagues, clients, customers, supporters, and friends for your constant prayers and well wishing. Your encouragement and positive energy is greatly valued.

PART I

Designing the Trade

T he next few chapters lay out a set of ideas and concepts that help you make the transition from a retail trader to a professional one. Professional traders approach the market with three distinct differences that their retail counterparts don't have to consider.

First, the majority of professional traders are working for someone else. This means that they have what is known as a fiduciary responsibility to their clients. They must, at all times, act in the best interest of their clients at all times. This means that when choosing between risk and rewards, managing risk takes precedence in order to preserve the client's principal.

Second, professional traders don't get paid unless their clients get paid. While this can be stressful, it is the only way to keep the professional traders focused on what's important—making their clients money. This philosophy creates a spirit of cooperation in which everyone wins. If the client doesn't make money, then the trader doesn't make money. This is a simple philosophy that should be embodied in all forms of investing.

Finally, professional traders are looking for returns that are meant to beat stock and bond returns, not necessarily to break the bank. For anyone who has ever played baseball, you know that you don't hit for the fences every time you are up at bat. In fact, you always take into consideration what has happened before and what will happen after your turn. That might require you to be conservative or loose with your playing, depending on the situation. Trading is no different. Historically stocks have returned 12 percent annually and bonds have returned 7 percent; any program that beats these returns is considered a success.

The ability to set aside greed is one of the professional trader's biggest assets. If done correctly, setting realistic goals does not hinder opportunities; it simply diminishes the need to take unnecessary chances for unlikely rewards.

When a retail trader recognizes that he has a fiduciary responsibility to himself, pays himself from his profits, and makes greed take a backseat to the reality of the situation, he has taken some solid steps to trading like a professional.

CHAPTER 1

From Retail Trader to Professional Trader

October: This is one of the particularly dangerous months to invest in stocks. Other dangerous months are July, January, September, April, November, May, March, June, December, August, and February.
—Mark Twain

W hen it comes to the futures and forex markets, it is important to understand the difference between trading and investing. The fast-paced nature of these markets, the high degree of leverage, and the limited nature of the contracts (from a few days to a few months) make it difficult to invest in them for the long haul. It takes a significant amount of active involvement in these markets to have even a chance at being successful. This means that as an investor you have two mental transitions to make. The first transition is your ability to change a buy-and-hold mentality to a buy-and-hold-as-long-as-I-need-to mentality. The second transition is to make the leap from approaching the market like a retail trader to approaching the market like a professional trader. Let's tackle the first transition.

Investopedia defines a trader as "an individual who engages in the transfer of financial assets in any financial market, either for themselves, or on behalf of someone else." It further states that "the main difference between a trader and an investor is the duration for which the person holds the asset. Investors tend to have a longer term time horizon where as traders tend to hold assets for shorter periods of time in order to capitalize on short-term trends."

While all investors who make the transition to futures and forex believe that they are traders who focus on profiting from short-term trends, it

3

quickly comes to light that they really do not know how to do it properly. In my last book, *Winning the Trading Game,* chapter after chapter was devoted to dispelling classic stock market beliefs and busting various myths that can be fatal to would-be traders. While the transition from investor to trader is not easy, it can be accomplished through planning and a constant vigilance of your mental attitude.

The second mental transition is a lot more difficult. Taking the leap from the mentality of a retail trader to that of a professional trader is one of the most difficult, yet rewarding, transitions any trader can make. While there is nothing inherently more difficult about being a professional trader, there are several factors, both personal and market oriented, that the retail trader needs to take into consideration.

It is often said that the difference between amateurs and professionals is that professionals get paid for their work. It is the same in the trading industry. The professionals are typically paid a salary plus a bonus based on their performance. While for many of them this setup is well-deserved, for others, not so much.

From a December 18th, 2007, news report on Bloomberg, Goldman Sachs announced a bonus pool of $12.1 billion, up 23 percent from the prior year. Some of the top officers were expected to receive bonuses in excess of $60 million, with average compensation per employee to reach $661,490. What makes Goldman Sachs significant is that they are one of the few investment banking firms that generate a significant portion of their revenue from their own in-house trading operations. This is no small feat for a company with a market capitalization of over $74 billion.

Your average retail trader is lucky if he can put together $50,000 to trade, much less the $9 billion that Goldman Sachs has allotted in its own fund, GS Capital Partners. This type of disparity between the Goldman Sachs's of the world, professional traders, and you, the retail trader, leads many to believe that the leap from retail trader to professional trader is not only difficult, but impossible.

This is the wrong way to think. If simply the amount of trading capital available to professional traders is what separates them from retail traders, then we wouldn't see so many so-called professional firms having difficulties. In just the past few years we have seen two huge fiascoes. We have seen a $6 billion meltdown occur at the Amaranth hedge fund in the natural gas market and a $7 billion loss at Société Générale SA, each of them collapsing because of the actions of just one of their traders. These were both preceded by the well-publicized collapse of Barings Bank at the hands of Nicholas Leeson in 1995. These large losses prove time and time again that it's not just the amount of money you have to work with that makes you a professional.

In each one of these public debacles it is clear that the "traders" working for these companies were far from professional when it counted the most. Their motivations, financial attitude, and psychological makeup made them operate more like amateurs with access to a lot of money, as opposed to professional traders with a strict agenda and plan. These problems were further exacerbated by the lack of basic corporate checks and balances.

In this chapter we explore what it takes to transition from a retail trader to a professional one. We gain insight into professional traders' motivations, financial savvy, and the psychological differences from most retail traders. Successful professional traders are supposed to operate with constraint and discipline and have loss minimization at the forefront of their market trading strategy. We look to replicate this mindset for retail traders. Finally, we review the impact that outside accountability to regulatory bodies, clients, and peers plays in keeping the professional trader honest and the significant amount of pressure on professional traders to simply do things right.

By mimicking the same high level of responsibility that professional traders feel, retail traders can accurately assess their strengths and limitations while developing the necessary attitude it takes to trade in this increasingly competitive market environment. By taking a proactive role in acting like a successful professional trader, you can make a realistic assessment of whether you should be trading or if you should hire a professional trader to work for you.

There is little doubt that the market is becoming more saturated every day. With trading competition going global and a huge breadth of contracts strewed across every time zone, you need a competitive edge. To not only survive, but thrive in this ever-changing environment, it is imperative that you, the retail trader, take a page out of the professional trader's handbook and ultimately tighten up your approach to the markets.

TRANSITIONING FROM RETAIL TRADER TO PROFESSIONAL TRADER

They say "money can't buy happiness," but the appropriate extension to that is "nor can it turn you into a professional trader." As a retail trader, the secret to transitioning to a professional trader is not about how much money you bring to the table but a combination of your motivation, how you deal with the money you have, and your mindset. From the outset you must ask yourself the million-dollar question, "Are you more interested in being right or being profitable?" The stage is set for your ultimate success or failure depending on how you answer this question, and your answer will guide your motivations, how you manage your capital, and how you mentally approach the market.

Many retail traders assume three things about professional traders that are simply not true. First, they assume that almost every trade that professional traders pick is a winner. Second, they assume that it takes a lot of money to be a professional trader. Finally, they assume that professional traders are secretly doing something that can't possibly be done by retail traders.

None of these assumptions is correct and in fact we see time and time again that it isn't the number of winning trades you pick, how much money you have, or your privileged access to contracts that makes the difference—it is how you behave.

Motivation

So are you more interested in being right or being profitable? Answer carefully.

When asked this question, many people's knee-jerk response is to say "profitable." What makes this strange is that they oftentimes do the opposite. They would rather pick the right market direction, regardless of how fruitful the move itself may be. Then they will find any reason to support their market-picking prowess; while the market is prepared for a reversal or has actually gone in the opposite direction.

What motivates you more, being right or being profitable? This is a crucial question you must not only ask yourself, but also listen to your heart's answer intently in order to make the transition from retail to professional trader. The majority of retail traders are conditioned to believe that being right about the market's direction is the same as being profitable. Every advertisement on TV and trading system touts the percentage of successfully picked trades. Whether they are real world results or hypothetical scenarios (which are more likely), many gurus do their best to optimize the results of the system they are promoting in order to boost the number of successful picks over the number of losing ones.

You only notice a kink in any of these programs when you run the numbers yourself. While the programs appear to be highly successful, it quickly becomes apparent that there is a schism between the number of successful picks and the actual amount of money made. In black and white you can see that when the system fails, it really fails. Although there are allegedly fewer losing picks than winning ones, the amounts of the losses can add up to being greater than any individual win. You soon realize that not only are there significantly more losses than wins, but if you were to incur them at the wrong time in the system your account would be wiped out, and you could never realize the potential pyramided profits that the programs tout.

The Commodities Futures Trading Commission and the National Futures Association have developed regulations to make sure that these programs state "past results are not indicative of future returns" and clearly show the difference between hypothetical and actual results. Nevertheless, the average retail trader consciously or subconsciously equates the number of times that a system successfully picks the market's direction with how successful the system is at making money, which are not necessarily the same thing.

The need to correctly pick the market's direction can quickly deteriorate into an almost obsessive fixation with beating the market. There is a need to anthropomorphize the markets into a person or entity that has feelings and emotions and that you are attempting to outwit. In this way you make the markets into your own personal archvillain. Somehow, by your wits alone, you can become more clever, faster, or insightful than your foe, the amorphous unemotional market you are attempting to beat. This is simply not the case. The market makes you money and the market loses you money, on its own terms, in its own ways. No matter how successful you are at picking the market, it can switch direction at any time. That alone makes it important to fixate on the success of the trade itself, not necessarily on how well you picked it.

A trader who fixates on market picking gets only one thing—that warm fuzzy feeling of being right—while missing the fact that the success of a trade comes from the ability to manage the trade itself. The constant insistence that you be right about every trade you pick is a common mistake of retail traders. The approach to being right about the market's direction over being profitable rarely leads to success. In fact, it does quite the opposite; it pits the trader against the very system he hopes to make money from. The constant struggle ends up clouding the trader's judgment and driving him to treat the market as an adversary that must be battled as opposed to an ally that he is sharing opportunities with.

Needing to be right about the market's direction rather than being profitable is not the domain of just the retail trader. Professional traders can find themselves on the wrong side as well, focusing on getting the market right as opposed to being profitable.

Following are some examples of traders who chose being right over being profitable.

In 1974 Dany Dattel of Herstatt Bank lost a total of $360 million (unadjusted for inflation) trading the USD/DEM. Clearly one of the first, if not the first, currency trading meltdowns, Dattel's actions led to the collapse of Herstatt Bank, originally founded in 1792 (Borse Online, www.graumarktinfo.de/gm/grauestars/firmen/dickedinger/: Herstatt-Bank:Dany-Dattel-und-die-DM-Deals/493304.html).

In 1994 Robert Citron drove one of the most prosperous counties in the nation into bankruptcy. Citron used derivatives to support his bet that interest rates would not increase. If not for the fact that he was using the county's money, his mistake would not have been noticed. Instead Citron lost his interest rate bets to the tune of $1.7 billion. Orange County, California, had to file bankruptcy and cut back on various municipal services for years in order to recover, solely because of Citron's actions ("The California Wipeout," *Time*, www.time.com/time/magazine/article/ 0,9171,982029,00.html).

The need to be right about the market's direction is an endemic disease of the industry. While we would hope that traders and companies would learn from mistakes made a decade or two ago, we still see the same patterns repeating themselves, from Amaranth Advisors losing big in the natural gas market, Barings Bank taking a nose dive in the Nikkei futures market, to Société Générale losing the most money to date, trading European Index futures. In each instance the management was willing to turn a blind eye to the activities of their traders as long as they kept getting the right picks, but they were quickly ready to abandon them and label them rogue traders when they were no longer picking the right markets. Instead of putting the necessary safeguards in place that would protect the banks or hedge funds from loss, management operated with the belief that it was good enough to have someone who could pick the right trade.

This was just such a case at Amaranth Advisors. In 2005 their trader Brian Hunter had made enormous profits, to the tune of $3 billion, in natural gas market spreads. The impact that Hurricane Katrina had in halting the Gulf region's ability to refine oil played a significant part in Hunter's success. While he had successfully called the market in 2005, when he attempted to do it a second time he got it all wrong. The spread trades that he had set up for 2007 and 2008 quickly deteriorated, and Amaranth lost $6.5 billion. The need to be right about the market's direction led Hunter to purchase and hold illiquid contracts far past their prime.

Had Amaranth's positions simply been on the other side of the market, they would have made $6.5 billion. Had they used a proper hedge to protect themselves against being wrong, they may have only lost a fraction of the $6.5 billion that put them out of business. Had Amaranth simply prepared for the possibility of their trade picker not being right about the markets this time, the story would have ended completely differently. This is the benefit of having 20/20 hindsight ("Betting on the Weather and taking an Ice Cold Bath," *New York Times*, www.nytimes.com/2006/09/29/business/29insider.html?_r= 1&oref=slogin).

The same thing happened to Barings Bank. Nicholas Leeson originally made trades that were quite profitable for Barings. The first set of profits he racked up accounted for 10 percent of the bank's entire annual income. In hopes that he could duplicate his success, he was allowed to execute riskier and riskier strategies, while at the same time secretly hiding various losses that he was accumulating. While the fraud is inexcusable, Barings was suffering from the same fixation that Amaranth was, being right about the market's direction as opposed to being profitable (*Rogue Trader* by Nicholas Leeson, Little Brown and Company 1996).

Most recently in the news we have seen Société Générale lose the equivalent of $7.1 billion. Jerome Kerviel has been painted as a rogue trader who acted on his own in racking up the largest losses in history. As of this writing, more information is coming out about Kerviel's "rogue trading." If Kerviel is to be believed, two tidbits of information stand out: first, his aggressive trading style was practiced by all the traders at the firm and was tacitly encouraged by the management's turning a blind eye to it; second, in the previous year, Kerviel, using similar, if not the exact same, tactics had made the bank $2 billion. If it is found to be true that his trading activity directly led to $2 billion being added to Société Générale's bottom line, then his trading activity will be seen in a completely different light, and Société Générale will be seen as more of an accomplice to this debacle than a victim ("Rogue Traders a Nightmare Scenario for Finance CEOs," ABC News, http://abcnews.go.com/Business/story?id=4205767&page=1).

By no stretch of the imagination can anyone believe that the men caught in these situations acted professionally. While they operated under the auspices of professional traders, they behaved like amateurs. If major banks and hedge funds, with billions of dollars on the line, can make the mistake of believing that being right about the market's direction takes precedence over being profitable, how can the average retail trader avoid it? More importantly, what does it mean to be profitable in the markets? And is being right about the markets that bad?

Choosing Being Profitable Over Being Right

Lefty Gomez, baseball Hall of Famer, said it best: "I'd rather be lucky than good." The failure of many retail traders is their insistence that being right is good trading; this leads them to ignore the fact that their terribly successful trade was simply the luck of being at the right place at the right time.

Separating being right from being profitable takes a mental shift in what you believe trading is truly all about. It is easy to let your ego get wrapped up in enjoying how smart you are and in knowing the right answer to any problem. All throughout school, from grade school to graduate school, we are rewarded for picking the right answer, whether it's multiple choice or free response; as long as we write down the right answers for the teacher or professor we guarantee ourselves that we will get the "A."

Our society doesn't encourage playing it safe or any form of mediocrity. If you write a paper that is less than stellar, or you are a "C" student in school, it is assumed that you aren't living up to your potential. That type of behavior is simply not tolerated. Being normal or average in any way is considered a shame.

Add up all of the constant positive reinforcement you get when you get things right, the rejections of mediocrity, along with a constant diet of the perseverance pop psychology that we are all subjected to ("No guts, no glory," "No pain, no gain," "It ain't over until the fat lady sings"), and the surprise is not that traders have failed in the past; it's that more of them haven't failed a lot worse.

As long as you are motivated by the need to successfully pick the market's direction you will be plagued by the inability to trade like a professional. In fact, you will be committing the same mistakes that Hunter, Citron, Dattel, Kerviel, and Leeson all committed against their employers. Your mistakes may not make headlines like theirs did, but you will be doing it to yourself, a type of rogue trading. You will work at cross purposes against your desire to be profitable in your trading. The goal is to strive to be profitable at all costs and sometimes that can be accomplished in the most simplest of ways.

Being profitable over being right doesn't mean you don't want to choose markets well; far from it. Every trade has three potential scenarios: profit, loss, and breakeven. If you have only one possible scenario, profit, in mind when you start you have negated two-thirds of your potential outcomes. This in turn eliminates how much preparation you put into protecting yourself against the other two scenarios.

Yet this is exactly what happens when traders choose to be right. By fixating on the end goal of profits at all cost, a type of tunnel vision envelops the trader. All new information about the situation, new twists and turns of the market, as well as fundamental shifts in supply and demand, are ignored or thrown out the window leaving the trader with a fixation on his original goal rather than having the flexibility to change.

> *A penny saved is a penny earned.*
>
> —Ben Franklin

The decision to be profitable over being right can lead a trader into making a different set of choices about how he interacts with the markets. By deciding to be profitable, plans are put in place to protect yourself from one trading potential—loss—and to help you bring about another trading potential more often—breakeven, or as close to breakeven as possible.

When it comes to trading futures and forex there is a professional class of traders: Commodity Trading Advisors (CTAs). This class of traders is similar to the mutual fund managers of stocks. They have more strict reporting requirements than their Hedge Fund counterparts, but are able to be involved in various highly aggressive investment arenas, futures-forex-OTC and options, that their stock market counterparts wish they could participate in. These CTAs are what is considered the gold standard of commodities and forex trading.

Regulated CTAs, as a rule, must write down their strategies, have a specific risk of ruin structure, and halt their trading at specific loss levels. On top of all that, they have various reporting requirements and must show that they can produce a return if they claim they can. The statistics that surround the success of this group can be practically underwhelming.

It is said that out of ten trades they may have six trades that are losers, two trades that are marginal winners or breakeven, and two bona fide home runs. Where their success lies is not in their winners. It is in their ability to minimize the losses on the six losing trades, and, more importantly, their ability to have any breakeven trades at all. By keeping themselves well guarded on those eight trades, they set themselves up for the home runs to find them. When the professional traders maintain and preserve as much capital as possible, it keeps the odds of success within their grasp.

The success of CTAs comes from their ability to waste little precious time in the trading dead ends. Knowing when to admit they're wrong, quickly, is an essential trading skill, oftentimes more important than being right about the market's direction. By minimizing the need to be right, they are able to focus on the trades that aren't being successful and take the necessary corrective action to end the trade or turn it into a breakeven trade.

This is what is meant about being profitable—trading to control the most probable outcome loss, and letting the profits take care of themselves. While it might not be the most glamorous approach to trading, it is the most empowering way to approach it. Focusing on being profitable frees you from the need to always be right when picking the markets to trade, it helps you prepare for the potential losses, and lets the potential profits take care of themselves.

Money

What does money mean to you?

Does money mean freedom, opportunity, nothing, everything, choice? Your relationship to money will be reflected in your trading. Whether you hold on to losing trades or cut your losses quickly will be a clear example of what the capital you are trading with represents to you. If you are chasing trades, cutting your profits short, or pyramiding your contracts with little or no safety net, you are acting out your hidden money desires.

When retail traders come to trading they have one goal in mind: Make as much money as possible. There is no question in their mind that they are in the ideal environment that will help all their dreams come true. The problem with pinning such high hopes on trading is that how they approach the money they bring to trading will be directly affected in their trading. There is a precarious balance of caring too much and caring too little.

On the one hand, if you care too much about the money you bring to the markets, it makes it difficult to make trades. You become afraid that every trade you take will wipe you out. Once you finally enter the markets you assume that the trade you are in has got to pan out—so you hold on to it a little too long and you lose some, if not all, of your money on the trade. You chase markets so you don't miss out on opportunities, even if they are long past.

Caring for your capital too much can be fatal. It is a quick road to disaster. Yet many retail traders do just that. It all stems from the simple fact that they aren't bringing risk capital to the table. The money that they are using for trading is money they really can't afford to lose. So they operate from a deep fear of losing all their capital. This inevitably leads them to bringing their fear to life.

The combination of caring for your capital too much and the fear of losing it is prevalent in trading. No one is immune to it. Even traders at large institutions, as we discussed earlier, get caught on this negative money cycle. The trick is not to ignore that these emotions can influence you, but to recognize that these feelings may be overwhelming and you won't be able to simply trade through them. You may actually have to halt your trading to gain perspective on the situation.

Caring too little for your capital is the other side of the same coin. When you care too little for your capital, you operate as if you were in Las Vegas. You are willing to take every bet no matter how long the odds are, hoping for your long shot to come in. This approach to money foments a belief in the big score. Trading and treating the markets as one giant slot machine, with each pull of the trade trigger you are looking for the out-of-the-ball-park return, with little regard to the process and 100 percent focus on the outcome.

This is the type of trader who constantly gives his profits back to the market. This is the type of trader who will constantly fund his trading account with little realization that it isn't the market that keeps losing him money; it's his approach. This is the type of trader who will eventually give up trading with a lot of good war stories, but will claim that trading is rigged.

The quickest way to trading burnout is caring too much or caring too little for your capital. Each approach can be an exhausting way to trade that leaves you drained, dazed, and confused at how you got to where you are in your trading. In order to trade like a professional trader, you have to take a different approach to what the markets mean to you in relation to the capital you put in and what you hope to achieve.

Demo Trading

As a trader sometimes there is a need to reboot. Professional traders are never afraid to reinvent themselves. They will come up with new systems or new trading tactics when they become aware that their trading results have halted. They will run various computer and back testing models. The simplest way for retail traders to accomplish the same result is to halt their trading and shift from live trading to paper trading.

While it is not a secret that the market can move up, down, or sideways, it appears to elude retail traders that they don't always need to be trading. They can be short, long, or flat the market. Being flat the market is a valid position. While you may not be making money, you are also not losing money. This special flat time can be spent paper trading or demo trading online.

Demo trading has the ability to help you practice the proper trading techniques and build your confidence. Many traders abandon their demo trading once they open a real account, and this is the exact opposite of their professional counterparts. By maintaining both concurrently you will be able to catch yourself when you are making mistakes, move over to your demo trading account, improve your trading, and switch right back over to real trading without breaking stride.

As long as you stay a student of the markets it becomes difficult to get caught in the trap that the money you are working with is in control of your actions. The money becomes a tool to your needs that you neither care too little nor too much about. You are working toward your end goals without the frantic desire to be right, just profitable. Successful hunting requires that we practice shooting at targets just as often, if not more often, than we shoot at actual game.

Trading with the Right Amount of Capital

As a trader you are fighting with whether or not you are trading with the right amount of capital that can help you achieve your goals. The stark naked truth is that you are not trading with enough capital. The majority of retail traders should not be utilizing all of the leverage available to them in futures and forex trading. In forex trading the leverage can be as high 500 to 1. This is far beyond what the average retail trader should be working with when he gets started. When it comes to futures trading you can be trading as high as 50 to 1.

These high levels of trading leverage are a leading contributor to a retail trader's rapid demise. It is difficult to turn down the leverage but a sense of balance must be achieved. For traders who are afraid that they will lose their money, they are trading at leverage far and above what they can handle. This is a dangerous position to be in. It makes your mistakes a lot more critical. When you lose, you lose big, while at the same time making it difficult for you to get your trades right because you are fixated on the fact that you might lose all or most of your money.

For those who care too little for the capital they are trading with, the huge fluctuations in their account's capital have to be managed. The easiest way to find a balance is to come up with a strategy to adjust the leverage when you are trading as a way to reflect your actual trading streak and to help you retain your profits as you trade along.

There are different ideal account amounts bandied about in the trading world. They range from 5 to 10 percent of your overall investments to as little as a few hundred dollars. The old adage used to be that you should trade with enough capital that when you go to bed at night you can sleep, but not sleep well. If you can't sleep at all you are trading with too much money; if you can sleep like a baby you are trading with too little.

On the surface this advice seems to be a little vague, but it is still quite appropriate. There are many factors that go into what makes trading comfortable for you. If you have too much money on the line you will find yourself at a trading disadvantage; if you have too little you find yourself at a trading disadvantage.

Finding a balance between the two requires that you understand how much the actual value of the futures and forex contracts are and add the necessary capital to your account that will not wipe you out in one trade, but will also not diminish the capital returns you were going for when you entered the markets.

There is no magic number. You can cut your leverage in half by doubling the amount of capital committed to your trade or you can put up all of the money for the contract. No matter how you do it, realize that the leverage that you are able to use is not set in stone, and that is the maximum leverage available. Manipulate the leverage to your liking.

Psychology

Understanding why you do what you do as well as how you will treat your operating capital is important. Just as important is understanding what is going on behind the scenes of your mind. There are emotions of fear and greed to overcome. They can make you operate and act in ways you don't really want to. They can bounce you around in a reactionary state, forcing you to go from a bad choice to an even worse choice. Controlling these two emotions is difficult and the only way to really do it is to be aware of them when they arise and to have a plan on how you will trade regardless of them.

There is another emotion that is just as insidious but probably twice as bad as fear and greed. On the surface you can comprehend fear, a self-preservation instinct, and greed, our need to attain more. But when these two emotions fuse together to fuel the emotion of *ego*, watch out.

WordNet defines ego as "an inflated feeling of pride in your superiority to others."

Dealing with this type of ego in your trading is dangerous and is the place where retail traders get stuck in their transition to trading like a pro. We touched a little bit on how the ego wants to be right about the markets as opposed to being profitable. There is also a need for the ego to want to prove its superiority, but this is difficult to do when you are dealing with an amorphous entity like the markets.

Bizarre things begin to happen. The ego can force you to engage in irrational behavior. You may attack the markets when you lose money; this is known as revenge trading, which is usually counterproductive to your goals of being profitable. Since the markets have no memory of what happened yesterday, today, or tomorrow, the logical solution for any trader is to come to the markets with a clean slate. The ego, which feels slighted, will look for a way to get the market back for every little transgression.

The ego doesn't stop there; once it has decided that the position it has taken regarding a market is the right one, it will look for every piece of supporting evidence, no matter how small, all of which may be contrary to what is happening on the screen right in front of your eyes.

The ego also likes to feel like it can outsmart what is happening, so it will often take an outright contrarian view of the markets and their direction to show its superiority over the industry or its peers.

Finally, the ego will tell you that you are smarter than the system you created. It will tell you that you are the creator so you are better than the rules, trading plan, and back testing that you may have conducted in order to get where you are. It will make sure you don't trust the paper trading you have done to get where you are now, and that real trading is somehow different.

The ego is the ultimate enemy of the trader, because it will tell you that you are good and you will forget that your successes have been all about luck. The ancient Roman philosopher Seneca said, "Luck is what happens when preparation meets opportunity." By being properly prepared for the trade (win, lose, or breakeven), when an opportunity arises you will be there to take advantage of it.

The ego requires that it make everything happen. Somehow the ego believes that only its most aggressive actions take precedence, while sometimes trading simply needs the right set of circumstances for the opportunity to appear. If the ego is allowed to run amok there may never be enough capital left over to be able to take advantage of the various opportunities that come your way.

The ego can make it difficult for the retail trader to succeed. The best way to combat your ego is to have a plan and a way to document your activity. The ego needs to know the difference between the facts and its opinion of the facts. This is a crucial distinction that can only be brought to light with due diligence. As time progresses, the ego begins to know what the truth is and its own effects become diminished.

This is one of the most difficult situations to overcome, but once accomplished can make your transition to pro style trading seamless.

SUCCESSFUL PROFESSIONAL TRADERS

The shift from retail trader to professional trader is not easy. Although developing strategies and techniques to make the transition can be difficult, it is not impossible to develop the proper makeup to emulate. While there have been several major professional trader blowups, those instances have been the exception, not the rule. Professional traders break up their approach to the markets in three components: discipline, loss control, and planning.

Discipline

There are several great books discussing the minds of professional traders. One of the earliest books that attempted to give a glimpse into this rarefied world is *The Merchant Bankers* by Joseph Wechsler (Little Brown, 1966). This book breaks down every major banking family throughout history. What makes the book particularly relevant to today's environment is a small anecdote regarding a young banker.

A new young banker executed a trade to impress the partners. Soon the position began to lose. Instead of getting out of the position right away, the young banker held on to it. As the trade continued to collapse, to the tune of 1 million pounds, the young banker, wringing his hands, finally decides to approach one of the managing partners. As he begins to relate his tale of loss and is on the verge of handing in his resignation, the partner stops him and asks him why he didn't come to him sooner when the loss was manageable. The young banker had no response.

The partner tells the young banker that he could have put the company in serious jeopardy, and then reveals a secret to him. He had been watching the young banker all along and had already put the necessary protective trade in place, so that what looked like a 1 million pound loss for the young banker was actually a small profit because the partner had already put a counter hedging position into play earlier.

How many times have we been the young banker, caught in a losing trade, not getting out when the losses are manageable, all the while spiraling down in flames of deeper despair? Unfortunately, there is no benevolent trading partner looking over our shoulder ready to correct our mistakes to protect us from ourselves. We must divide our psyche up and be both the young banker willing to take a chance and the managing partner able to see the devastating results that a potentially big loss can have on us and our account.

Professional traders, CTAs, are required by law to be disciplined at all times in their trading. They must operate as the managing partner 24/7 because of the obligations that they have taken on. CTAs who are disciplined enough to consistently apply the same techniques to their trades, no matter what the market is doing or the number of trades they have executed, are the ideal role models for retail traders who are willing to take their trading seriously. Transitioning from the young banker, wringing your hands in fear, requires that traders take the responsibility of sticking to their trading rules and risk management strategies, just as CTAs do every day.

CTAs from the outset have a set of rules that cover entries, exits, and risk levels that they must adhere to in order to optimize their success and minimize their losses. Adhering to these parameters requires a high level of discipline and focus that comes from multiple layers of responsibility. They have a responsibility to their investors, regulators, and even their families. What makes the successful CTAs unique is that they don't profit unless their clients profit. This is what encourages CTAs to stick to their plan, particularly if they believe it has worked in the past and can continue to work in the future.

Retail traders must have a mental paradigm shift and see themselves just like the CTAs. Identical to the setup that CTAs have, the vast majority of retail traders are only paid when there is a profit. Therefore, retail traders can benefit from treating capital that they place in the markets the same way that CTAs do. It is important that CTAs and retail traders both optimize every opportunity by consistently adhering to their trading plan and strategies.

This is the only way to succeed in the long run. The more faith you can develop in your trading plan the easier it is to be disciplined to follow it. The essential discipline also comes from the ability to be your own inner trading manager; in spite of your hopes that a trade may succeed, the proper preparation to protect yourself from loss long before the situation becomes dire is important.

Loss Control

It is no secret that when it comes to trading losses, the better you can control them, the easier it will be for you to chase down potential profits. As losses rack up you need more and more spectacular returns to recover and then get into the green.

When the trading losses are unleveraged and straightforward, as in stock trading, a 10 percent loss represents a need to gain 11 percent just to get back to even (90 percent × 111 percent = 100 percent). If your leverage is as high as 5 to 1 then that same 10 percent loss represents a 50 percent loss. This means that you need a return of at least 200 percent (50 percent × 200 percent = 100 percent) just to get back to breakeven.

This means that your need to minimize your losses as quickly as possible becomes imperative, if you hope to achieve any success. CTAs typically attempt to control their loss at a fixed percentage of no more than 2 percent on any given trade. For accounts in the millions that can easily be done. For smaller accounts, depending on the market and amount of leverage you use, that can translate into as little as a 10 percent to as much as a 20 percent move in your actual account.

CTAs' conscious decision to minimize their losses dovetails directly into how they calculate the success of their trading programs. When CTAs set out to calculate their potential losses, they always attempt to find the worse possible scenario of their trading program. They do this by calculating their drawdowns and their maximum drawdowns.

Drawdown is defined as the peak-to-trough decline during a specific record period of an investment, fund, or commodity. A drawdown is usually quoted as the percentage between the peak and the trough.

The *maximum drawdown* is the largest drawdown experienced by a strategy during a given time period (both definitions are from Investopedia).

The drawdown and the potential maximum drawdown are numbers that are consistently used by CTAs to help refine their trading programs and to develop loss management strategies to help them protect themselves, while at the same time maximizing their potential for trading returns. The various percentages that can be developed by running multiple scenarios and measuring possible drawdown amounts can be tremendously helpful, but are not meant to be the gospel of your trading.

While on the surface these drawdown percentages can seem to be an efficient way to determine how bad a program can fail you, there are a few flaws. The primary one is that "past results are not indicative of future returns," so while past drawdowns can be calculated, shifts in supply and demand can alter how future drawdowns and yet unseen potential maximum drawdowns can occur. It becomes very important to understand how the CTAs manage their losses while they are trading, not just pay attention to what they do when the worst case scenarios pop up; it is less important to know how they react to the markets when a fundamental shift in the marketplace has already occurred.

In spite of the problems that relying on drawdown calculations have, retail traders rarely incorporate an understanding of how much of a return on their investment they need when they lose, nor do they understand the potential maximum drawdown facing them when they trade a market. This is a huge oversight on their part that needs to be corrected.

Professor Thomas A. Hieronymous, an agricultural economist and the grandfather of farm marketing through futures, conducted a study on speculative (retail) trading accounts in the late sixties. Professor Hieronymous came to a few disturbing conclusions in this study. The first assessment he made was that 92 percent of the one-time traders would lose their money, never to be heard from again. He then narrowed down his field of what he called regular traders to those with more than 10 trades in a year and losses or gains that exceeded $500. That left him with a total of 462 trading accounts to analyze. In this group of accounts 298 had losses and 164 accounts showed a profit.

Based on this data the statistics for retail accounts are not promising. Ninety-two percent of one-timers lose their money, then of those who are left, two thirds of them have losing trades, and one third of them make a profit. While these figures were compiled back in 1969 (excerpted from *The Futures Game: Who Wins? Who Loses and Why?* by Richard J. Teweles and Frank Joseph Jones), they still have relevance today.

Just as we looked at the effects that leverage has on the increased need for an account to do exceptionally well after a loss, and we have developed an understanding on how knowing your drawdown percentages can play a factor in mitigating those losses, it is no wonder that the average retail trader would rather shoot from the hip than figure out these key numbers ahead of time. The problem with the shoot-from-the-hip approach is that it is hazardous to the long-time survival of retail traders.

Another study, The Rockwell Study, followed a period of 18 years. Beginning with 1947, it was observed that small speculators (retail traders) lost in 11 of their 18 trading years, their average loss being $15.1 million and their average profits reaching $23.7 million. The large speculators, on the other hand (CTAs—the pros), show a profit in 15 of their 18 trading years. Their average yearly profit was approximately $13 million and their average annual loss is only $3.4 million. The large speculators had over twice as many winning years.

Another study was conducted by Bard Barber, UC Davis, and Terrance Odean, UC Berkeley. In their 2004 white paper entitled "Do Individual Day Traders Make Money?" they analyzed the accounts of 130,000 investors in

Taiwan, the twelfth largest financial market in the world, from 1995 to 1999. Based on their research they discovered that in a typical six month period more than eight out of ten day traders lose money. The core reason for the traders' losses revolved around their basic inability to cut their losses and ride their profits.

Even though the study itself focused on day trading stocks, it clearly showed the lack of success of retail traders in the largest statistical group sample ever compiled. While day trading stocks and commodities/forex may have few similarities as trading instruments, the way in which stocks are day traded parallels the time constrained nature of futures and forex trading. It can be assumed that the sense of urgency found in futures and forex contract expirations along with their leverage component is very similar to day trading, and had the study been conducted on futures and forex, it most likely would have yielded similar if not worse results than Odean's study.

The reality is that for the past 60 years, from 1947 until the present, retail traders from all genres of trading have consistently lost more and done worse than their professional counterparts. This can be primarily attributed to their completely different (or lack of) approach to controlling their losses. If retail traders would take a similar view of loss to that of their professional counterparts, they would not only improve their trading, but actually turn trading on its ear.

Planning

The success of professional traders is not by accident—it is by design. By focusing on mitigating the various ways that they can lose money, they develop the necessary plans for success. Their stop losses and protective strategies take into account their account value, drawdowns, maximum drawdowns, and leverage. By combining each of these components together, a clear picture of their risk versus reward comes into focus.

Professional traders are constantly developing plans and contingency plans that incorporate various ways to minimize their losses. Since futures and forex is known as a zero sum investment, losers pay the winners directly, the professional traders step up to the plate to make sure they give themselves as many genuine opportunities to transfer wealth to themselves, as well as minimizing the transfer of wealth away from themselves.

This requires a fundamental understanding of all of the players (hedgers, large speculators, and small speculators), as well as the tools at their disposal (cash, OTC, forex, options, and futures). By watching the footprints of their competitors and utilizing every tool in their arsenal, professional traders are light years ahead of retail traders in protecting their day-to-day survival.

The great news is that the techniques that professional traders use easily found and, in fact, if you ask them nicely, they will give you the documents necessary to see behind the scenes in their programs. Then it is a matter of incorporating what they do right into your retail activity to help you get to the next level.

Outside Accountability

While professional traders have different motivations, attitudes toward money, and general psychological makeup from their retail counterparts, it took an act of Congress to get them there. In 1936 the Commodity Exchange Act was implemented as a response the U.S. Supreme Court's decision to declare the original Future Trading Act as an unconstitutional use of the Congress's taxing power. In 1974 the act was amended to create the Commodity Futures Trading Commission (CFTC), an independent agency of the U.S. government.

By creating the CFTC Congress effectively replaced the Commodity Exchange Act. In 1982 the CFTC appointed the National Futures Association (NFA) as a self-regulatory body that deals with licensing, auditing, and monitoring CTAs and professional traders who exceed various maximum contract reporting requirements.

Professional Traders are forced to keep their records transparent to the NFA and the CFTC, both organizations that take their fiduciary responsibility very seriously. Various companies that have been shut down for engaging in unfair practices can be seen every day on the CFTC web site.

Professional traders are not able to set up shop unless they take several precautionary steps. First they must file disclosure documents. The disclosure documents are the professional CTAs' way of revealing their trading secrets, past results, hypothetical results, and responsibilities to their clients. The disclosure document is the number-one stepping stone for retail traders to gain insight into how professional traders trade the markets.

Which markets CTAs trade, whether they buy or sell options, if they have a long or short strategy, the number of contracts traded per particular cash amounts, monthly and maximum draw, commission fees, along with the maximum losses that are used to halt trading for a client, are disclosed. Since the CTA has a legal responsibility to their clients and prospective clients in following their disclosure documents to the letter, a lot of information can be revealed.

Retail traders have none of these outside responsibilities. Their successes, losses, and strategies need not be revealed or monitored by anyone.

With zero required accountability, it is no surprise that retail traders fail in their fiduciary responsibility to themselves. The majority of them lack a written trading plan and feel that a stop loss is money management and risk management all wrapped up into one.

Is it any wonder that 92 percent of first-time traders lose all of their money?

Professional Traders, on the other hand, are constantly being monitored by the government, and many of them take the next step and become monitored by private parties such as Barclays and Autumn Gold. These sites rank CTAs according to their annual returns. In much the same way that the scientific community keeps itself honest through peer review, the private monitoring sites allow other CTAs and potential clients to compare similar money managers to each other.

You can see how the various CTAs who trade currencies, S&P, and the like compare against others in their asset class, as well as how they rank in their overall returns against all CTAs. Those who are doing well must send you their disclosure document just as readily as the ones who are not doing well. This type of research becomes invaluable in helping you determine the realistic returns that you can receive in your trading program and to discover what professionals are doing it right and which ones are doing it wrong.

TIGHTENING UP YOUR APPROACH TO THE MARKETS

When making the transition from operating like a retail trader to operating like a professional trader, retail traders need to go from being haphazard in their approach to taking control of their trading destiny. It is easy to become a trading statistic that falls by the wayside. What isn't easy is developing the necessary winning attitude that will help you make the mental transition to trading like a pro.

This will require that you step outside yourself and take a critical look at your strengths, weaknesses, opportunities, and threats (SWOT) to your trading capital. Writing up a formal SWOT analysis as the first step to developing your trading plan is an empowering act. It has the ability to clarify your trading thinking and allows you to build on your strengths and opportunities while minimizing the impact of your weaknesses and threats.

A proper SWOT analysis will not only help you perfect your approach to the markets, it is essential for you to establish realistic trading goals. Trading goals can be established on a monthly, quarterly, and annual basis.

These goals should encompass not only profit goals, but the number and amount of drawdowns

Forming your own trading club or joining an established trading club can also help you tighten your approach to the markets. It will help you develop accountability while eliminating lonely trader syndrome. This type of peer review forces you to be honest with yourself and your trading results. This will make it easier for you to make your transition to a professional trader.

CHAPTER 2

Markets and Margin

*The one who adapts his policy to the times prospers,
and likewise . . . the one whose policy clashes with the
demands of the times does not.*
— Niccolò Machiavelli, *The Prince*

The futures and commodities market was originally established in the United States in the late 1800s. The original intent was to help smooth out major price fluctuations that occurred when there were either shortages or surpluses in the marketplace. At the time, international commerce on the scale that it has reached in the past two hundred years was unfathomable. Today, trillions of dollars in raw materials and finished goods traverse the globe at a frenetic pace.

While the United States was not the first to lead the world in the industrial revolution, it became the key architect in the development of the world's international commerce that we enjoy today. The United States' influence has brought about a financial model that is being emulated across the globe. Countries all over, such as the economically motivated European Union, as well as India and the politically communist but economically capitalist China, are developing their market economies as quickly as they can. While these countries are important, they are just the tip of the iceberg in the number of countries working hard to build up their burgeoning market economies.

In the wake of this robust global economic growth, the once-humble beginnings of the U.S. futures and commodities exchanges have taken on a new role. As raw materials from various countries must compete against one another, currency rate fluctuations, and the economic reality

of interdependent economic policies, futures and commodity exchanges
have popped up all over the globe. Commodities contracts such as soybeans, oil, and gold, once dominated by the U.S. exchanges, the Chicago
Board of Trade (CBOT), the Chicago Mercantile Exchange (CME), and
the New York Mercantile Exchange, have found themselves sharing space
and multiple time zones with newly formed exchanges in India, China, and
Dubai.

Where once the U.S. exchanges held a virtual monopoly in offering
commodity and futures exchange contracts, they are now faced with fierce
competition from various exchanges in other countries and the entrance
of new players onto their domestic soil. As opposed to being leaders, they
are now pressed into taking a reactionary role. Where once their contracts
set the tone in volume and price discovery, many other similar contracts
are beginning to gain prominence worldwide and are dictating price and
market relevance.

In the midst of all of this is the trader. Whether retail or professional,
the growth of the 24-hour global trading marketplace is playing a significant role in determining everyone's long-term success. The trader's ability
to adapt to information, both technical and fundamental, as well as his ability to be serviced in multiple marketplaces are becoming more and more
relevant. There is no special secret to trading in this new environment; it
simply becomes more important that you be able to process information,
while at the same time being able to protect yourself from activities occurring halfway across the world while you sleep.

In this chapter we explore the recent merger of the CBOT and CME
and what it means to the everyday trader's activities. We also take a look
at the various new exchanges popping up across the United States and
abroad. In addition, we look at the future of single-stock futures (SSFs) in
the United States and their international counterparts, contracts for difference (CFDs), and discover which one is more relevant.

Next, we look at the impact that the over-the-counter (OTC) forex market has on the exchange-traded currency markets, if any. We also discuss
the revolutionary importance of the Standard Portfolio Analysis of Risk
(SPAN) risk management system and the natural interaction of the spot,
futures, and options markets. We take an honest look at the difficulties
of trading these various markets in real time and in back-testing, both of
which are important in order to develop the necessary tools to succeed.

Finally, we highlight the five key markets that will be used as examples
throughout the book (S&P 500, gold, oil, euro, and corn). While these are
not the only markets in the world to trade, many of these are traded in multiple arenas and time zones and are affected on a global scale by policies
and regulations that do not originate in the United States.

EXCHANGES

In the spring of 1848, little did the original 83 merchants of the Chicago Board of Trade know that they would forever change the world. From this humble beginning the asset class of derivatives has exploded. Nobel Prizes have been awarded to mathematicians who have come up with formulas to predict the behavior of option derivatives. Companies have come and gone, almost taking entire economies with them, trying to beat derivatives. Countries that once banned commodity trading are now jumping on the bandwagon. All of this activity has forced commodity exchanges to grow from trading just agricultural products to trading a wide array of financial, climate, and currency products that could not even have been imagined 160 years ago.

The success of the derivatives asset class is fueled solely by traders worldwide wanting to participate in markets that they could not afford otherwise. The versatility of the commodity exchange model has moved it so far from its original roots as to almost confuse those who are familiar with agricultural commodities and stocks into believing that the products being presented to them are somehow different from what they have been trading all along. This is not the case.

Since the inception of the forward contract, there have been two markets for it. There have been the standardized contracts, what we know as futures contracts, and the customized contracts, what we know as over-the-counter (OTC) contracts. Whereas the liquidity of the standardized contracts has always been guaranteed by the exchanges themselves, the OTC market was thought to be nearly illiquid because of its customization. Since two counterparties are agreeing to an arrangement with very specific criteria, it was thought that it would be difficult to find anyone else who would be willing to accept the same terms. The OTC markets, realizing the dilemma, decided to take a page out the commodity exchange handbook and simply standardize the sizes and increments of their custom contracts. Consequently, they have added a tremendous amount of volume to their activities. OTC forex trading is a prime example of that; it currently trades approximately $2 trillion worth daily, all between counterparties with no central pricing exchange.

The far-reaching effects of the commodity exchange model have quite literally changed the world. Largely because of passage of the Commodity Futures Modernization Act of 2000 (CFMA), there are exchanges all over the world that will allow you to trade on various future events, like presidential elections, greenhouse gas emissions, and the weather. The Commodity Futures Modernization Act paved the way for OTC trading of energy credits and electronic energy trading, along with the development of single-stock futures. There are exchanges that have tapped into these simple expansions of power in new and amazing ways. They have developed ways to minimize traders' losses by stylizing their product offerings through so-called binary futures and binary options, along with developing all-electronic trading markets. No matter what the product is or how it is administered, the same elements always apply: The contracts are leveraged, the product traded is not the actual product, and the product is primarily designed to manage unseen risk.

Exotic Exchanges

The CFMA has led to many exchanges popping up that do not fit the traditional mold. Some are recognized members of a trading exchange, while others are traded OTC. Whatever the case, they do not fall in line with what is traditionally traded, yet they have an impact on what occurs in today's trading environment and may actually be what retail traders have an opportunity to trade in the future. At one time the OTC forex market was considered solely the domain of banks and major corporations protecting themselves from import and export risks. Today it is commonly traded by retail investors and is a major contributor to the U.S. $500 trillion OTC market.

TradeSports Ltd./Intrade   TradeSports Ltd. was originally founded in 2000 in Dublin, Ireland, as an online web site with the express purpose of letting speculators choose whether or not future outcomes will come to pass. Within five years the site had accrued more than 50,000 members and had monthly trading volume of almost four million trades. In order to make sure it was not limited to being just a sports betting site, TradeSports separated its sports-related trading site from its nonsports markets by acquiring Intrade. The Intrade.com web site offers traders the ability to speculate on the outcomes of presidential nominations, U.S. recession figures, as well as the Dow Jones final close for the year. Each position is simple: If you buy (go long), you think the event will happen; if you sell (go short) you think the event won't happen. In order to facilitate a better understanding of the odds, the sites have developed a simple 0 to 100 system, with 0 being 0 percent likelihood of an event occurring and 100 being 100 percent likelihood of an event occurring. Any figure in between 0 and 100 represents the market's overall sentiment at that time. When I originally wrote the manuscript for this book the web site predicted that there was a 72 percent likelihood of the United States going into a recession in 2008 and that Barack Obama had an 82 percent likelihood of winning the Presidential Election. As we now know, the web site was right in both instances.

While this exchange is exciting, it is an OTC exchange that acts as the go-between for various counterparties and is not without controversy. Since the contracts are customized, the wording can be very strict and if not followed closely you can be left a little confused about whether you can receive your payout.

Although rare, one contract stands out clearly. In July 2006 North Korea gave out a press release stating that it could successfully fire ballistic missiles outside of its airspace. At the time, Intrade had a contract that revolved around this potential outcome. Those who had bought a contract (they believed that the outcome could occur) felt that they should be paid out. The fine print of this contract, however, stated that two stipulations had to occur simultaneously: First, North Korea had to be able to fire ballistic missiles outside of its airspace; and second, this had to be confirmed by the U.S. Department of Defense. The U.S. Department of Defense never confirmed the test, which led to the Intrade buyers not being paid out on their contract purchases.

In 2005 Intrade applied to the Commodity Futures Trading Commission to become a recognized exchange in the United States.

HedgeStreet   In 2004 HedgeStreet became the first Internet-based futures/derivatives exchange. The goal was to provide a forum where speculators and retail investors could protect themselves by hedging against major economic events and price movements. In an attempt to differentiate itself from the typical options and futures contracts, HedgeStreet chose two innovative products, binary options and capped futures. Each product was chosen for its ability to minimize the losses of the retail traders who decided to invest in what they called "hedgelets."

Binary options were not completely new, but HedgeStreet was the first exchange to build its entire business model around them. Binary options are simple yes/no contracts, similar to Intrade's will/won't setup. You are paid out only if the final price is above the strike price. You receive a flat $10 for getting it right and nothing if you get it wrong. The capped futures have a variable price payout, but it is capped at an upper limit, and losses are limited to a predetermined floor.

Although both products are exciting, HedgeStreet has had difficulty in developing volume, liquidity, market makers, and the right set of products to present to the public. As of this writing, it has been acquired by IG Group, a major binary option player in the United Kingdom.

Chicago Climate Exchange   The Chicago Climate Exchange (CCX) is the brainchild of Richard Sandor. Through his efforts, major corporations, states, municipalities, universities, and farm bureaus have joined together to create the only voluntary, legally binding greenhouse gas reduction exchange in North America.

CCX has developed a market in six greenhouse gas emissions: carbon dioxide, methane, nitrous oxide, sulfur hexafluoride, perfluorocarbons, and hydrofluorocarbons. Since its inception in 2003, it has reached two monumental milestones: First, it has committed its members to reducing aggregate emissions by 6 percent by 2010; and second, it has accumulated an aggregate baseline of 226 million metric tons of carbon dioxide equivalent (credits), which is equal to the United Kingdom's total allocation.

Like any effective exchange-traded market, CCX has started at the base—the market makers, those companies that are in need of greenhouse gas credits, and those capable of qualifying for greenhouse gas credits—and brought them together. That means that in the not-too-distant future retail traders will be able to participate in the trading of greenhouse credits themselves or at the very least some form of derivative of the greenhouse credit program.

New U.S. Exchanges

The futures and commodities market took 160 years to develop in the United States. In just the past eight years, since the passing of the CFMA, the entire culture has been turned on its ear. What were once considered foregone conclusions about the exchanges—member-owned exchanges, floor brokers, and open-outcry trading—are quickly becoming a thing of the past.

In November 2002 the Chicago Mercantile Exchange (CME) became the first commodities exchange to be listed as a public company. In much the same way that agricultural commodities account for less than 30 percent of the active contracts traded, electronic trading has begun to replace open-outcry trading. Floor brokers have had to either adapt to a changing environment of trading from a screen (as opposed to gaining their cues from other traders on the floor) or leave the business altogether. In the midst of all of this change, more and more foreign entities have succeeded in gaining a foothold in the U.S. commodities exchange markets. This has led to a pan-global trading environment, the likes of which we had never seen before.

While some of these exchanges are not 100 percent new, they have been retooled and revamped in such a way as to be unrecognizable from the original. Oftentimes they provide the only way that foreign entities can come into the United States and hope to succeed in developing a relationship with the retail market. Make no bones about it: They are changing only the name, not everything else that has worked for them in the past; electronic platforms, OTC quoting, and access to international markets are just a few of the things that are here to stay.

U.S. Futures Exchange The U.S. Futures Exchange, LLC, was originally called Eurex US. It was established by Eurex, quite literally the world's largest derivatives exchange. In 2006 alone Eurex executed more than 1.5 billion contracts. It has established trading and clearing relationships all throughout Europe and Asia. What has made the exchange so powerful over the years is its ability to deliver trading and clearing fully electronically. As a pioneer in the electronic arena, Eurex felt that it could easily expand its global reach into the United States. After only a few years in the U.S. market, Eurex sold 70 percent of its stake to the Man Group. The two have teamed up to make a second go of the U.S. market, utilizing Man's extensive U.S. introducing broker (IB) and retail network.

ICE Futures U.S. (ICE/NYBOT) The Intercontinental Exchange (ICE) is a direct product of the CFMA. Founded in 2000, the exchange's original intent was to provide an around-the-clock transparent OTC derivatives energy exchange. It quickly outpaced its competitors and expanded into the futures business through the acquisition of the International Petroleum Exchange. With the development of its electronic platform, ICE has succeeded in moving its entire energy futures contracts electronically. Continuing its progressive move forward, in 2007 ICE acquired the New York Board of Trade (NYBOT).

Before 1998 the New York Board of Trade didn't even exist. Just like ICE, it is an amalgamation of multiple exchanges that have merged over the years. A combination of the Coffee, Sugar, & Cocoa Exchange, Inc., founded in 1882, and the New York Cotton Exchange, founded in 1870, NYBOT became the premier exchange for the soft commodities in the United States. While the currently retooled NYBOT still maintains an open-outcry pit concurrently with the new electronic offerings, ICE's drive to make its energy contracts fully electronic will most likely be repeated.

ICE's experience in international markets located in the United Kingdom and Canada as well as its OTC business provides an unparalleled level of access and a robust amount of information for U.S.-based traders. As traders begin to understand the quotes and utilize the platform, they will see opportunities for arbitrage and an unparalleled level of service that didn't exist in the old limited open-outcry format.

NYSE Euronext With the express goal of being the world's number one equities exchange, the New York Stock Exchange (NYSE) acquired Euronext N.V. Euronext has a huge array of financial products and services spread out over five countries. It currently operates five derivatives exchanges and six cash equity exchanges; combined with the might of the NYSE, this group will be able to offer trading in security and futures products 21 hours a day. While they are currently focused on dominating the equities market, they have the infrastructure and the capability to branch out into the futures and commodities markets at a moment's notice and dominate the domestic environment with a slew of offerings never seen before.

CME Group: The Last U.S. Exchange?

The competition worldwide is getting cutthroat. In order to have any chance at competing in this global environment, U.S. exchanges have had to look toward consolidation in order to survive the monolithic power of mergers like the NYSE Euronext and the aggressive move by Eurex to enter the U.S. market. While this activity looks exciting on the surface, the move of the big fish to eat the little fish leads to many casualties. The floor brokers and traders are clearly seen as being impacted by these consolidation moves, which are driving the markets to become electronically traded, but all of the support staff is being adversely affected as well, many of whom have been doing their jobs for years with little prospect of being properly retooled and retrained at this point.

The most high-profile merger of commodities exchanges has been the CME and CBOT merger. This merger has brought together under one roof the United States' two oldest exchanges. The combined power of these two exchanges will allow the CME Group to compete in today's new environment. It will be able to reduce costs, transition to electronic trading, and use the might of the merged exchanges' combined capital to acquire competitors, like NYMEX, and to increase its ownership position in joint venture partners, like the Singapore Exchange (SGX).

From humble beginnings, the CME and the CBOT not only have made themselves relevant for the twenty-first century, but they also are considered serious players. Smaller exchanges, such as the Kansas City Board of Trade and the Minneapolis Grain Exchange, will find it difficult to continue their exchange life quietly and without disruption. There is no doubt that in the near future they will be absorbed in some form or fashion in order to stay competitive.

Critical Worldwide Commodity Exchanges

At an unprecedented speed since the 1990s, futures exchanges have been popping up around the world in the most unlikely places. From China and India, both countries that banned futures in the 1950s, to places like Dubai, futures exchanges are exploding. This worldwide growth in the development of the commodities markets has been a major contributing factor to the global renaissance in commodity prices. As countries all over the world begin to use the futures markets as a form of price discovery, disparities in the value of goods around the world quickly begin to dissipate. Large profit margins, which were once the domain of aggressive importers and exporters willing to traverse the world to find bargains, are becoming more difficult to find as electronic markets are linked up around the world.

China In China there are two prominent commodity exchanges. There is the Dalian Commodity Exchange and the Shanghai Futures Exchange. They each comprise 50 percent of the Chinese marketplace in terms of dollar volumes in trading. In the Dalian exchange alone the total trading volume for 2007 reached U.S. $1.67 trillion. The Futures Industry Association recently reported that the Dalian exchange has been the dominant futures exchange for the past eight years. With only 110,000 investors in a nation of 1 billion people and a growing middle class, the Dalian exchange is poised to be the largest exchange in the world. Currently, the exchange has been limited to trading soybeans, soy meal, soy oil, corn, palm oil, and linear low-density polyethene. These limits have been put in place by the Chinese government in large part to control the rampant fraud and unscrupulous behavior that existed in the early years of the reintroduction of commodity trading in China. The Dalian Commodity Exchange has stated on its web site that it intends to release a hog/pork belly futures contract, a coal futures contract, and a commodity index futures contract within 2008. The Dalian exchange also plans to launch options on its actively traded soybean and corn futures contracts.

Dubai The only question is "What took them so long?" Dubai, one of the jewel cities of the United Arab Emirates, has finally established its own gold, commodities, and energy exchanges. With only 6 percent of its revenue generated from oil, Dubai has a long history of encouraging free trade in the region. With multiple free trade zones in media, technology, and manufacturing, Dubai is one of the most ethnically diverse and business-friendly cities in the world. Established in 2005, the Dubai Gold and Commodities Exchange is fast becoming one of the region's most important exchanges. Located right in the middle between Europe and the East, this exchange helps provide for the continuous trading that a 24-hour marketplace needs in order to thrive. As of this writing, the market trades in gold, silver, euro, British pound, Japanese yen, Indian rupee, and fuel oil futures. The exchange is expected to develop product offerings in steel, jet fuel, and cotton.

A second exchange, the Dubai Mercantile Exchange, is set to be the first energy exchange of the Middle East. Created as a joint venture of Tatweer, NYMEX, and the Oman Investment Fund, it is poised to be an international competitive powerhouse for the region.

India The Multi Commodity Exchange (MCX) is extending its footprint across the globe. While operating an exchange in India, it is also a significant partner of the Dubai Gold and Commodities Exchange. Based in Mumbai, the exchange has taken a policy of working with both the spot and futures markets in key agricultural products. This has led it to retaining 72 percent of India's market share. With India being the number one importer of gold worldwide and currently importing over 3,000 tons of silver annually, it is not surprising that MCX ranks number one and number three in silver and gold futures trading. Couple that with India's consumption of 2.4 million barrels of oil a day (according to www.cia.gov), and it is no wonder that MCX is number two in the world for natural gas futures contracts and number three for crude oil futures.

Brazil The Brazilian Mercantile and Futures Exchange (BM&F) is the fourth largest exchange in the world, according to the Futures Industry Association. It is also the number one exchange of Latin America. With an average daily volume of 1 million contracts and its recent partnership agreement with the CME Group, the exchange is poised to play a significant role in all of North America. Without a doubt it is a major player in the futures market, providing futures contracts on gold, feeder cattle, live cattle, arabica coffee, robusta coffee, cotton, crystal sugar, corn, and soybeans.

WHAT DOES THIS MEAN FOR THE MARKET?

With the constant merger of exchanges from around the world, new and more interesting products are constantly being created. There is a greater effect of settling commodity prices in China or Brazil and how they impact the opening of commodity prices in India or the United States. The rules and regulations for stocks, commodities, and indexes quickly become the concern of an international marketplace.

Various forms of trading and contract types that are considered over-the-counter in one country, that may be illegal in another, and that may be caught in limbo in yet another country are still owned by the same corporation. This brave new trading environment leads both to a world of opportunity and to a world of land mines and problems, both legally and logistically.

As the CME Group aggressively begins to flex its financial muscle in the acquisition arena, industry operators become increasingly skeptical and worried about the implications of a monolithic, all-encompassing exchange. The CME Group, NYSE Euronext, the U.S. Futures Exchange (formerly Eurex US), and ICE face a multitude of hurdles in offering their exchange and clearing services. Banks and industry experts are wising up to the consolidation efforts. They are beginning to see that the concentration of both clearing and exchange services may lead to higher pricing for them in the long run.

Where once before traders could rely on competition to minimize their transactional costs, it has become apparent that when one group owns 10 percent in one exchange, owns 35 percent of another exchange, and is about to acquire another, the competition that allowed them to search for the best price possible is slowly evaporating. Add to the simmering rebellion from the banking and brokerage community the fact that many of these acquisitions involve exchanges that were once involved exclusively in either stocks or futures, but rarely both, a recipe for disaster is on the horizon. So while the push to merge and develop one worldwide electronic exchange is an inevitable conclusion to all of this activity, the regulators are light-years behind in how best to operate in this cross-border community.

New products are constantly being developed all across the globe, and either various rules and regulations will have to be adjusted to accommodate them or a whole generation of regulators will need to be retrained in their auditing duties. Cash markets all around the world are being affected by stock and commodity exchanges in far-flung regions simultaneously using price discovery to determine the true value of various underlying assets. In this environment, a growing schism of what activity is acceptable or not acceptable and what regulator or regulators have jurisdiction over what is happening is on the horizon.

A prime example of this regulatory schism is the contracts for difference (CFDs) and the single-stock futures (SSFs) fiasco that occurred in the United States. An antiquated law, the Shad-Johnson Accord, separated the joint efforts of the stock and futures markets for almost two decades. By the time the Commodity Futures Modernization Act of 2000 had kicked in to allow SSF trading, the rest of the world had already passed it by. Currently South Africa hosts the world's largest SSF exchange at 700,000 contracts daily, which dwarfs the 26,000 contracts traded by the last SSF exchange in the United States, OneChicago.

In contrast, CFDs are experiencing tremendous growth. They are utilized in at least 12 different countries, with more countries joining daily. Unfortunately, since the U.S. Securities and Exchange Commission maintains strict regulations on OTC trading of financial instruments, the products cannot be offered in the United States, although traders outside the country can purchase CFDs of U.S. companies and indexes. How U.S. regulators will react to the pan-global commodity exchanges that will want to increase revenues by offering CFDs to their customer base is unknown, but the question will arise a lot sooner than later.

Contracts for Difference (CFDs)

Contracts for difference (CFDs) grew out of the unique tax regulatory environment of the United Kingdom. They were developed as a way to avoid unnecessary taxes for companies or money managers that wanted to hedge against the risk in their portfolios. Soon after their creation they jumped over to the retail sector like wildfire. The elegance of the concept has driven its acceptance across the globe and has paved the way for a simple solution for traders to participate in shares, currencies, and commodities anywhere in the world.

Known by its other name, leveraged share trading, CFDs allow the creation of a contract between two private parties. The buyer and seller simply agree to pay each other the difference between the current value of an asset and its value at contract time. With this simple contract any investor can speculate on the price of stock shares, commodity prices, or index values without being required to actually purchase the underlying item.

There are three core benefits to end users: First, they can go long or short with few, if any, restrictions; second, they can own a contract that may never expire, unlike futures and options; and finally, they can choose the amount of leverage that they want to have, putting up anywhere from 1 percent to 30 percent of the contract value, depending on the agreed-upon contract or counterparty. This without question is the fastest-growing financial sector. It will quickly dwarf the amount of retail activity that the forex OTC market is currently enjoying.

CFDs are superior to options because there are no "greeks" (beta, delta, etc.) to contend with. CFDs follow the underlying shares one for one with few modifications. There are no long, complex formulas that have to be calculated in order to determine the true value of the CFD or the effects that volatility is currently having on the CFD.

Not only being superior to options, CFDs also beat out SSFs in both liquidity and flexibility. SSFs require that you buy a set number of shares, 100, typically at a fixed rate of 20 percent of the contract value and at an inflated price to the underlying share because of various interest rate costs, but with no ability to share in the dividend payout of the stock itself.

All is not roses with CFDs, though. Much like any OTC market, forex trading being a prime example, the broker is the market maker. How he makes his money is through a commission or a spread between the buy and sell price and interest rate charges for carrying a position overnight. This spread can run from a fraction of a percentage point to a flat fee. Whatever the case, associated costs have the ability to become expensive if not watched carefully. There is also the danger that, since the CFDs are traded with little or no regulatory oversight, the assumed liquidity for your position can evaporate overnight. The problems don't end there. CFDs are nonnegotiable contracts. Whichever broker you established the CFD contract with is where your CFD has to stay. Regardless of whether the CFD price spread is tighter somewhere else, you must maintain your position.

While these potential issues with CFDs are real, there is no precedence of brokers abusing the system. Yet for those who have been afraid to venture into the world of CFD trading, there has been an even bigger move to legitimize the product. With the recent merger of the Sydney Futures Exchange and the Australian Stock Exchange, there is a proposed expansion of their exchange-traded CFDs to include stocks from around the world. If this occurs, they will be the only exchange-traded CFDs in the world, eliminating many of the problems that OTC CFDs incur. Currently the Australian Stock Exchange has an online simulator to help traders learn about CFDs without having to risk their capital or run afoul of their local regulations.

The backbone of the futures and options industry revolves around the ability to offer leverage through margin. In trying to do that effectively, exchanges have been hamstrung by the requirement that the contracts that they have to offer must expire at various intervals (monthly, quarterly etc.). If the CFD makes the leap from stocks to other spot markets, without the problem of having a forced expiration date, what is the true relevance of the futures market and how do CFDs affect the relationship that all of these markets have with options? These are questions that the exchanges, regulators, and shareholders will have to answer.

With that being the case, speculators—longs (buyers) and shorts (sellers)—must put up the exact same amount of margin. When the market goes against the speculator, money is transferred directly from the longs to the shorts during a bear market, and the shorts directly transfer funds to the longs during a bull market. Therefore a margin call is of great importance and if it is not met within the allotted time your position can be liquidated without notice. If the forced liquidation results in losses that exceed the margin amount, the speculator is held liable.

DAISY CHAIN EFFECT

It is important to note that every actively traded market discussed in this book was designed to do one thing and one thing only: operate as insurance for the cash market. The OTC market was developed as a way to customize the protection of commodities, currencies, and shares. Futures were developed to protect farmers against wild fluctuations in supply and demand, along with many other cash markets. Options evolved to protect shares and futures contracts. No matter what the underlying cash market is, whether commodities or equities, every derivative that has grown out of it was originally intended to manage risk or operate as a hedge.

The fact that in order for any of them to work you need liquidity and speculators is the nature of the beast. Based on the level a speculator can afford, there are many places where he can interact, head to head, with the people who ultimately buy and sell the actual cash positions. If a trader has enough capital, he can operate directly in the cash market. However, the OTC market is the closest the majority of traders will come to trading the cash market. The futures market runs third in the daisy chain, and finally you have the options market.

A multitude of different types of contracts are traded in each of these arenas, many of them so complex as to need a PhD in mathematics to understand them, let alone trade them. How these markets interact with one another is based on an amazing dance of credit, faith, history, technology, and rules—each one depending on the other to manage risk and diminish loss, while at the same time making the credit easier along the way so they can expand the number of market participants (speculators).

Cash

Without the cash market, none of the others would exist. Or at least the cash market would like to believe so. The majority of traders experience the cash market in only a few arenas—stocks, precious metals, and currencies. At one time or another on a small to moderate scale they may decide to get involved with any of the three markets out of necessity. Either they are participating in a retirement plan of some sort, or they visit a gold dealer, or they travel overseas. Whatever the case, they then experience the rules of the cash market firsthand.

The cash market is straightforward. When you decide to purchase a share of stock for $1, you receive ownership of a share of stock for $1. The same can be said for investors who are familiar with spot transactions in gold and silver, whether they purchase a few precious metal coins or own several ounces of gold and silver bars. Investment in precious metals is an all-or-nothing deal. Investors who travel may have to exchange one currency for another. Rarely do individual investors purchase cattle, soybeans, or all the companies in an index.

Those who have ever had a cash transaction have experienced one of the most frustrating experiences possible, the spread. Whether it is shares in a company, gold bars, or a foreign currency, the difference between the price you pay and the price at which the seller is willing to buy it back from you are often nowhere near each other. This spread, in addition to whatever other built-in markups there are, is how the cash market makers turn a profit.

This is the danger zone. No one wants to lose their hard-earned capital. So in order to be able to speculate in the cash market but still have an out, the over-the-counter market was developed. Whatever position can be taken in the cash market can be offset or protected in the over-the-counter market for a fraction of the cost.

Over-the-Counter (OTC)

Currently the most popular OTC market in the world is foreign exchange (forex) trading. Trading upwards of $2 trillion a day (hard figures are difficult to come by since there is no central exchange), banks and retail investors rub shoulders in attempting to figure out what the true value of a country is. In the OTC forex market the rules are fairly simple. Two counterparties agree to cross buy and sell particular lots of foreign currencies that must be bought or sold back within a given time. This typically can occur anytime within a 24-hour period. If a position is carried overnight, then interest rate charges may accrue. Contracts for difference (CFDs) operate on the exact same principles as the OTC forex market.

Just like the cash transactions, the difference between the bid and the ask provides a profit spread that the brokerage or bank uses to make its money. In return for the opportunity to earn your business, the brokerage or bank will extend you credit (i.e., margin) to buy and sell currencies throughout the day. While possible, rarely do retail investors choose to put up the face value of a currency contract. They will typically take advantage of the leverage provided in order to increase the returns on their dollars.

For those companies or institutional investors actually holding on to cash positions in stocks or foreign currencies, the leverage of forex and CFDs gives them an inexpensive way to put on a countertrade just in case they have misinterpreted the market's direction.

Futures

The futures market is the OTC market without the need for blind trust. Grown from the world of the OTC forward contract, the futures market provides several key services. The primary service is the centralizing of information. In the OTC market, every bank or brokerage offering contracts is able to set its own spreads and slightly different pricing. In order to get the best bid/ask spread or to discover the best pricing, a consumer (retail or institutional) had to call around. With the prevalence of the Internet, it is an easier task, but it still requires research on the part of the consumer to find the best deals.

The by-product of the centralizing of information is the transparency in pricing and information. Anyone in the world can receive quotes from the exchange and receive the exact same price. Anyone can look at the Commitments of Traders reports and see exactly who is buying and selling what markets and the ebb and flow from the longs to the shorts and vice versa. Another key benefit of the exchanges is that there is no overt bid/ask spread. You have a likely chance to buy or sell at any quote on the screen if you are willing to put in a special order request, such as limits or stop limits.

Finally, unlike the OTC market, you are able to hold on to your contracts for longer time frames, there are no interest rate charges for using margin or carrying contracts overnight, and your liquidity is not solely dependent on just the bank or the brokerage—you have the world.

For those who hold significant cash or OTC positions, the ease of getting in and out of futures contracts and the ability to use margined contracts to do so are attractive prospects when you want to manage your risk.

Options

The last instrument on this daisy chain is the option. There is a reason why the fee you pay for an option is called a premium and fee you pay for an insurance policy is called a premium. While the financial party line talks about options in terms of the "right" versus the "obligation" to own the underlying asset, the reality is quite simple. Options are an inexpensive insurance for the cash, OTC, and futures markets. Whether they are stock options, futures options, or currency options, they all operate with the exact same principles.

For a small fee (a premium), you can purchase an option (put or call) at a specific price, typically the same price at which you got into one of your other positions, and for a set amount of time. The fact that you can purchase options in-, at-, or out-of-the-money is a testament to their ability to help you protect against risk.

Credit (Margin)

What makes this entire system of cash-OTC-futures-options work is the ever-increasing amount of credit that you receive as you work your way through the chain. Let's look at the stock market as a prime example:

$100 in shares (cash) is the same as
$30 in CFDs (OTC)
$20 in SSFs (futures)
$5 in calls (options)
$5 in puts (options)

The same $100 in shares is supported by at least four other products. (There are many more products such as swaps, warrants, and convertibles that are not appropriate for this book, but also extend the credit.) This has created an additional $400 in credit for just $60 in up-front cash. That is almost a sevenfold increase in purchasing power.

On the face of it, economists and major investors like Warren Buffett are consistently worried that this pyramid of easy credit will cause the collapse of our civilization as we know it. If done properly, the interrelationship between each of these markets was designed to make it less risky, not more risky. The worry may be unnecessary. It's like saying that if too many people buy car insurance, whether they drive a car or not, it will destroy the car industry. One need not be in direct correlation with the other.

Whatever the case may be, the current system has a built-in checks and balances. There is a requirement that the options be purchased outright, since they are the least expensive, and that when margin is extended it comes in two forms. In the first stage you are extended what is known as an initial margin. This is a percentage of the contract that brokerage or the exchange has deemed to be appropriate for the market's current volatility levels.

In the second stage of a margin offering is the maintenance margin. The maintenance margin is the absolute minimum amount that trader must keep in his account in order to maintain his position. If the trader cannot keep his account at the maintenance level, then he must put up more money to get back to the initial margin or close his position out. This is known as a margin call.

While the system is far from perfect, it works. If not for the fraud component, major disasters at Société Général and Barings Bank could have been avoided solely based on the various margin calls the traders were receiving on the way down.

Standard Portfolio Analysis of Risk (SPAN)

Whether by design or by chance, in 1988 the Chicago Mercantile Exchange created one of most sophisticated systems for margin calculation around. In light of the fact that the CME is expanding at a rapid rate and acquiring both international and domestic products as part of its stable, the SPAN system will allow the CME to assess account risk in an ever-expanding way.

As excerpted directly from the CME Group web site:

> *SPAN uses the risk arrays to scan underlying market price changes and volatility changes for all contracts in a portfolio, in order to determine value gains and losses at the portfolio level. This is the single most important calculation executed by the program.*

Through its sophisticated calculations the SPAN program takes into account the delta of options, intercommodity spread credits, as well as the amount of volatility affecting the overall account. Based on this calculation, something interesting happens, not just for the exchange, but for the trader as well. When a trader has properly daisy-chained his cash, OTC, futures, and options holdings, margins have a way of almost magically being reduced.

The exchange realizes that the OTC, futures, and options markets were designed as insurance vehicles for the cash market. Through the SPAN system, traders are rewarded for being aware of this. By strategically managing your positions into a way where they are protecting one another and reducing your overall volatility, you can easily find your margin requirements being cut by half or more. Although the CME invented the SPAN margin calculation system, various exchanges around the world have adopted it.

GLOBAL MARKETS

There are so many markets, exchanges, and contracts that you can trade. It becomes an overwhelming task to pick and choose just the right markets and just the right exchanges to interact with. At the same time, the various markets fall into several broad categories: stocks, indexes, interest rates, currencies, agriculture, softs, precious metals, industrial metals, energy, and meats. There are also several exotic categories such as the climate and oils. In this book the goal is to narrow down the universe of markets and to make examples of just a handful. The markets that are represented are meant both to be broad strokes of a category and to reflect the interrelationship that this market has with various other factors in the economy.

By no means is this done to suggest that you trade these markets exclusively or to teach you to trade these markets to riches. They are meant as examples to assist you in selecting your markets to trade. My book *Winning the Trading Game* (John Wiley & Sons, 2008) outlines how to select markets for your own risk, reward, and volatility levels. Reading that book will do a better job of helping you determine what is right for you instead of blindly following the markets that are outlined in this chapter. The goal here is to see you become a trader who can nimbly look at a market and construct a trading approach around it, regardless of what it is.

That being said, five markets were chosen for their robustness, current international importance, and the fact that they are traded across multiple contract types. While not the only markets to meet these criteria, they are the easiest to recognize among a slew of other contracts. The examples in the book revolve around the S&P 500, gold, crude oil, euro, and corn. Many other contracts are also relevant in today's trading environment, including U.S. Treasury bonds, the CAC 40, DAX, soybeans, Japanese yen, silver, and the eurodollar.

The funny thing about trading is that you do not need to be in a market to benefit from the correlative effects of that market's activity. For example, when you short the euro in futures, you are essentially buying the dollar as well; therefore, you do not need to be also be short the yen, for you would be exposing yourself to the same long dollar risk. If you are buying gold, you do not need to also buy silver and double expose yourself to a precious metal long side bias. Or if you are long corn, it is rare that you need to also participate in all of the grain complexes, wheat-soybean. As always, choose the markets you are most comfortable with.

S&P 500

The S&P 500 is one of the most widely tracked indexes. It contains stocks of 500 large-cap corporations. It is a mixture of stocks that trade on the NYSE Euronext and NASDAQ. The success of the S&P 500's ability to gauge the U.S. economy is rivaled only by the Dow Jones Industrial Average. Over 20 years ago the CME launched the first-ever stock-index futures on the S&P 500.

The S&P 500 futures contract was meant to fill a need for money managers and investors with large stock portfolios seeking to minimize their exposure to risk. In 1998 a smaller version of the S&P 500 futures contract was introduced, the Emini S&P 500. One-fifth of the size of the full-size S&P 500 futures contract, the Emini has gained in volume and liquidity over the years. In fact, it is the preferred contract of many institutional traders because of its electronic execution. As of this writing the notional daily value of the traded Emini S&P 500 is over $140 billion. This is a gross exaggeration of the value of the actual shares traded on a daily basis.

The S&P 500 futures contract plays a significant role in determining the opening of price of the actual index on the NYSE. This is due in large part to the fact that the Emini S&P 500 futures contract trades 23.5 hours per day five days a week.

Gold

Metals come in two general categories, precious and nonprecious. The precious metals are gold, silver, platinum, and palladium. They tend to be prized for their jewelry qualities even though they also have industrial and financial applications as well. The two precious metals that sit at the forefront of all precious metals trading are gold and silver. From India to

New York, gold's long precious metals history has given it a seat on several commodities exchanges and has helped it to develop a robust OTC market in the past decade.

With the average mining expense of gold at $238 per ounce, it is a wonder that the price of gold stagnated in the $300 per ounce range for almost a decade. Couple the high cost of mining with the limited supply of gold worldwide, and gold has the potential to continue on a significant bull run. As of this writing the price of gold has exceeded $950 per ounce. The last previous time it exceeded $800 was January 21, 1980; adjusted for inflation that would be approximately $2,398.21.

Crude Oil

The finding and drilling of oil has changed the world as we know it for the past 100 years. Crude oil's impact on the environment, on economies around the world, and on substitute goods will continue to affect the world for another century to come. Energy trading became a significant part of futures in 1978. Energy futures and OTC contracts cover a wide array of energy products from crude oil to electricity, with crude oil leading the pack. OTC energy trading can be directly attributed to the Commodities Futures Modernization Act of 2000. With the liberalization of the futures rules, energy contracts have become quite popular to trade.

The crude oil market has three large players: Saudi Arabia, Russia, and the United States. With over five thousand varieties of crude oil available, it is no surprise that OTC oil futures have played a significant role in reshaping the commodities landscape. The most commonly sought-after crude oil, sweet crude, is also becoming the most difficult to come by. Couple that with limited access to the most touted crude oil alternative, natural gas, and we have an energy market that will be overheated for years to come.

Euro

The OTC foreign exchange market is a several trillion dollars a day industry. Quite literally, more money is moved daily in the forex market than in the U.S. equity market and all of the futures exchanges combined. This market is raw capitalism at work. With a six-day, 24-hour time schedule, it is one of the most exciting places around to put your money, retail or institutional.

Fueling a significant portion of this growth has been the creation of one of the most important currencies in the twenty-first century, the euro. Consolidating the economies of the 15 countries that are members of the European Union, the euro was launched in January 2002. Affecting the lives of over 500 million people, the euro has surpassed the dollar in terms of use and value.

Corn

Corn is one of the most versatile commodities in the world. Whether used for livestock feed or whiskey, sweetener or fuel, corn is a staple in the lives of people around the globe. With over 600 million metric tons being produced worldwide, it is a valuable part of the economy in a number of countries. The United States alone accounted for 280 million metric tons. Couple the agricultural uses of corn with its potential to be used as a fuel additive or fuel alternative to gas, and corn production may be seen as being more in its infant stage. With China currently producing only 131 million metric tons and Brazil at 35 million metric tons, these two countries alone have the ability to expand their corn production, particularly to meet demands of the burgeoning economies.

BECOMING A SOPHISTICATED TRADER

True progress quietly and persistently moves along without notice.
—St. Francis of Assisi (Founder of the Franciscan order, 1181–1226)

The world is changing right before our eyes. The roles of the exchanges, speculators, hedgers, regulators, and products are being affected by a global need to connect. What was once a cloistered club centered in a few select regions has expanded in both amazing and frightening ways. While the United States' prominence as a world power is slowly being economically diffused, it also opens the doors for a new form of economic prosperity.

Part of the success of the retail trader, going into the twenty-first century, is his willingness to evolve not only his approach but his mind-set to what trading is really all about. The trading isolationism to which he has subjected himself is not being mirrored by his professional counterparts. In fact quite the opposite is occurring; a spirit of cooperation in the shared end goal of making money is at the forefront of the professional trader's mind. Your success as a trader will come from your ability to adopt this exact same frame of mind.

The other part of your success as a retail trader will come from sheer luck. The first-century philosopher Seneca came up with the quote, "Luck is what happens when preparation meets opportunity." The opportunities are abundant; what will make all the difference is how you prepare yourself today for the trading world of tomorrow.

WHAT DO THESE CHANGES MEAN FOR YOUR TRADING?

Why does the consolidation of exchanges in the United States, increased activity in exchange trading around the world, new and exotic trading products being invented, and the daisy chain of the various markets that can be traded matter to you, the retail trader? The level of sophistication of your trading needs to transcend the basic goal of just making money. With new and better opportunities, the primary requirement that traders will need is the ability to protect themselves from loss. By focusing on loss protection as your first order of business, you move yourself from the arena of trading dabbler to trading professional.

In much the same way your professional counterparts attempt to maximize their risk management, so will you. It is the badge of the professional to be able to practice or demo trade or back-test trading ideas with the end goal of showing how well he manages risk in addition to returns. A professional trader who has 40 to 50 percent returns but also has a maximum drawdown of 50 percent is far less desirable than a professional trader who shows 20 to 30 percent returns with a maximum drawdown of 5 percent. Why would you expect anything less from yourself?

By knowing all of the tools at your disposal—cash, OTC, futures, and options—and how they dovetail with one another, you begin to improve your odds of success, solely by diminishing your odds of defeat. This can be done in your own demo trading or with skilled back-testing on the right trading platform. However you do it, the goal is to now think outside of the rigid box of short-term profits and look for an overall healthy way to preserve your capital while you pursue the best opportunity possible, no matter what it is or where it is traded.

CHAPTER 3

Some Essentials of Trading

The secret to trading is often thought to be more a function of time frame than a function of skill. In much the same way that university students and alumni promote and defend their alma mater, come hell or high water, so do proponents of the different schools of trading. With almost fanatical zeal, traders will tout the benefits of being a day, position, or swing trader.

One trader will say going home flat is the only way to trade; another trader will say that the trend is your friend. Who's to say either is 100 percent right? As with many things in life, success in trading is not cut and dry. If it were, everyone who attends a trading seminar or reads a trading book would be able to emulate the success of the speaker or author immediately. Each trader has to find his own path to success, using the information that he acquires along the way as a guide post towards his end goal.

George Soros, Warren Buffett, and Richard Dennis are each successful in their own right. George Soros founded the Quantum Fund with the express purpose of speculating. Much of his trading revolved around short-term and opportunistic currency moves, long before he established his non-profit company. Warren Buffett took a different approach. Known as a value investor, Warren Buffett's buy and hold strategy turned many of his shareholders into multi-millionaires. Richard Dennis, on the other hand, used commodity options as a way to trade himself to wealth.

All of these men are considered professional traders, yet each has his own way of doing things, his own strategy for protecting himself from loss, and his own variety of success in trading the markets. It's a lot like professional sports. In professional sports there are no two players that are just alike. You can point to two athletes in the same sport, with similar size, strength, speed, training, and ability. While both are professional athletes and can become hall-of-famers, it could be for entirely different reasons.

This chapter is the most important chapter in the book. It lays the foundation with your choice of approach to the market and utilization of the various strategies presented. Overall, it will help clarify how you operate in the markets. You may discover that you operate just like a professional trader or, that you have a long way to go. It also sets up how your attitude toward trading.

We explore the three common types of traders—day, swing, and position traders—and delineate the advantages and disadvantages of each. We then look at whether or not being a trader focused solely on time is a realistic option when attempting to mimic a professional trader interacting with the markets.

We spotlight the necessary components found in a successfully designed trade: entry, loss target, and profit target numbers. Following, we look at the daisy chain interaction of the cash, futures, and options markets. This sheds light on why the strategies work.

Finally, we look at the essential trade setups of trends and countertrends and explore them in depth. We show how each type of trader can benefit from them, as dependent on their end goals.

Many of the topics that are touched on in this chapter are explained more fully in my earlier book, *Winning the Trading Game*. Nevertheless, it is not essential to have read it in order to understand the concepts presented here. The strategies and ideas that we cover can be incorporated into any trading system or program. By identifying the key components, as presented in this chapter, and utilizing your own system or approach to the market, you benefit from the information.

THREE DIFFERENT TYPES OF TRADERS

Being called a day trader, swing trader, or position trader is both a badge of honor and a title. The majority of traders entering the field come through one of these gateways. Depending on the book they've read or the guru they're following at the time, a trader can feel a sense of belonging.

The problem with being a "time frame specialist" is that it holds you back. While any time frame may earn you money, there are times when the market dictates which time frame is better. By not listening to the market and insisting instead on trading a specific time frame, you lose opportunities for profits and limit your success.

The market is the great dictator of time frame decisions. To ignore the market's rhythms is to make it difficult to let your profits ride and cut your losses as necessary. Being a time frame specialist can limit your chances to manage your losses. Various loss strategies that apply to one time frame can apply to another time frame, if the trader is willing to look beyond his horizon.

That being said, there are three traditional time frame categories that most traders fall into: day, swing, and position. No time frame is superior to another. They each have their own pros and cons. The secret to being a pro in successful trading is to move from one time frame to another seamlessly (if it makes sense), and knowing when it makes sense to do so.

Day Trader

Investopedia defines *day trader* as "A stock trader who holds positions for a very short time (from minutes to hours) and makes numerous trades each day. Most trades are entered and closed out within the same day."

The name could be day trader, scalper, or active trader, but the process is the same. You execute trades intraday in order to achieve your profit goals, with the express purpose of being flat in your trading at the end of the day.

Whether you are attempting to earn a few hundred dollars or even thousands, the practice is to take many small chances throughout the day without risking all your capital. By minimizing how much you are trying for, whether it's a few points on the Emini S&P or a couple hundredths of a cent in currency trading, the belief is that you are risking less and therefore will have much greater longevity than the swing or position traders.

On the surface, this logic is sound. Problems arise when the market significantly moves against you when you least expect it, or when slippage occurs, or when there is a spread involved in the quoted bid ask price. Any of these three situations can diminish how much you are able to make and at the same time how much you are losing.

Couple this with a trader's need to be right about the markets—as opposed to being profitable—and you run into what could be characterized as slow death. Every day the trader is gaining a little, but losing more. As time goes on he finds his account value slowly eroding, until eventually he either has no more trading capital or he can't make any headway.

In the end the demise of the day trader comes about because of two things: time and commissions. Since day trading is supposed to save you money with a diminished time frame, it inversely requires more of your time to monitor, prepare, and participate. For those who simply want to make a little extra money or for those who are looking to supplement their retirement, the commitment can easily far exceed the rewards. Spending

10 to 12 hours a day involved in the markets, while mentally stimulating, can make anyone's retirement feel like a chore.

The second failure of the day trader comes by way of commissions. Now even E*TRADE has jumped on the bandwagon and joined the futures revolution by offering 99-cent commissions. Commission rates are playing limbo around the world, to actively recruit futures and forex traders. The problem is that no matter how low they go, they will always beat the customer. You have to think of the commodities house as a bookie joint. No matter what side the customer is on, long or short or whether he wins or loses, the brokerage makes money. And the dirty little secret of the industry is the fact that the lower the commissions, the more the customers will trade.

Like anything in life, if you think that you are getting a deal for something you buy regularly, you simply buy more of it. That's how Costco and Sam's Club work. Those two companies are continually making record-breaking profits. There is no material difference between how these retail outlets generate business and trading. The perceived discount in trading encourages the traders to trade more. Does this mean that there is less slippage or that the market is less likely to move against you? No! Not only have all your risks stayed the same, but you have increased your exposure to them simply because it seemed cheaper to do so.

One of the most influential studies on the topic, "Do individual day traders make money?" (Brad M. Barber et al., 2004), took a serious look at the day trading phenomena by analyzing 130,000 investor accounts. Their abstract put forth many straightforward conclusions, one of which was, "Heavy day traders earn gross profits, but their profits are not sufficient to cover transaction costs." This is an alarming revelation. If you are solely a day trader, you are not working for yourself: You are working for the brokerage.

The goal of the day trader must be to make a gross profit, with the aim of keeping as much as possible and giving as little as possible back in transaction costs.

Swing Trader

Investopedia defines a *swing trader* as "A style of trading that attempts to capture gains in a stock within one to four days."

The level of research that has been conducted on day trading simply doesn't exit for swing trading. The flexibility of the time frame means that a trader may hold onto a trade for a few days or a few weeks, depending on the end goal.

Like their day trading counterparts, swing traders attempt to gain a few hundred dollars or more and they also attempt to limit their exposure to the markets by minimizing the amount of time spent in the trade. There is the assumption that the market moves in a particular direction, whether up or down, for only a finite amount of time before it retraces or pulls back.

The role of the swing trader is essentially to pick when the move begins and to get out right when the move ends. This ability is akin to being able to pick market highs and lows. The swing trader is looking to find out when the market is going to explode on fundamental or technical information and how much of a profit they can gain while it is moving.

This is nearly an impossible task to undertake. Many swing traders tend to be system or black-box traders. They look for the market to be packaged as a black-and-white scenario of "get in here and exit there." The problem with this style of trading is that its predictive nature can lead to a lot of false entries and exits. You can be fooled by false entry signals or exit trades too early, losing all your profits by chasing the markets to catch that last little move.

If the market could be predicted to behave in a certain way then there would be no need for books, videos, and seminars about trading. We would be better off learning how to read tarot cards or astrological charts. The markets are really a microcosm of human psychology coupled with a dose of insider trading.

With the limited knowledge afforded to the retail trader, it is difficult to pick absolute tops and absolute bottoms. By attempting to trade within these parameters there is a significant need for risk management as opposed to money management in order to protect yourself from the unknown.

The weakness of the majority of swing trading is the belief that stop losses or risking only 2 percent is sufficient risk management. This could not be further from the truth. While less demanding in actual face time in front of the trading screen, swing trading requires a lot of preparation time to determine entry, profit, and loss exits. This preparation time is essential in order to set a trade and forget it. A lack of preparation time along with an insufficient risk plan leads many swing traders to give up.

Position Trader

A *position trader* (trend trader) is defined as "a trader who attempts to capture gains through the analysis of an asset's momentum in a particular direction." What these position traders are looking to do is to make the big bucks, no matter what the day-to-day fluctuations may be. This is similar to buying and holding stocks. The belief is that there are only two ways to make money in the markets: either you can afford to make quick sniper attacks or you catch a trend at its beginning and hold on.

There is sound logic in wanting to be a position trader, particularly in the current commodity bull market. The euro has increased from .89 cents to breaking over $1.50. If you had traded a euro futures contract you would have made $76,250; if you had held onto a euro spot trade you would have made $61,000. The same thing has happened with crude oil. Crude oil, has gone from a price of $12/barrel to breaking over $100/barrel. A position trader that caught that entire move would have made $88,000.

Position trading can have great rewards, as the above examples can attest to. The core problem with position trading is that only with 20/20 hindsight can we see the actual result of buying and holding. During the wild fluctuations of the markets' movements it becomes difficult to maintain a conviction. Long or short, position trading can be unnerving at times.

Rarely does a market simply move straight up or straight down. The peaks and valleys along the way give the illusion that a trend has stopped or a move is reversing itself, only to have it resume unexpectedly. While on the surface these moves may not amount to much more than a few percentage points here and there, the margin leverage makes it difficult to hold onto trades for the long haul. For example, if you trade a market with a 10 to 1 leverage, a 4 percent move against you is the equivalent of a 40 percent loss.

What trader would willingly give up 40 percent gains in order to make just 10 percent? None in their right mind, but that is what is asked of the position trader time and time again. By not knowing if the particular market they are trading has reached its plateau, a position trader must be willing to give up what he has for the possibility of gaining more. This simple fact makes it difficult for small retail traders to be both psychologically and financially prepared to properly hold onto trades for the long haul, even if they know that the market will continue in the direction they expect.

A TRADER'S FOCUS

By highlighting some of the problems of day traders, swing traders, and position traders, it becomes apparent that focusing on time frames in order to define yourself as a trader may not be the most successful way. Each of these time frames is just as capable of producing successful results as another. They should be treated as fluid parts of a whole which can be incorporated at any time, depending on the market's activity, rather than artificial constraints.

Instead of fixating on various time frames, professional traders tend to take a specialist approach. They may specialize in bonds or short selling or a particular strategy, or they may combine all three. The specialist approach to trading allows them to incorporate fundamental information, multiple market time frames, and a specific set of technical analysis tools.

By removing time as the definitive determinant of a trader's success, the market dictates whether you become a day, swing, or position trader. Specialization is liberating in its confinement and teaches you how to read the rhythms and opportunities according to what's most appropriate, not according to your whim. Millions of dollars have been made by stock specialists and traders in the pits in Chicago.

Instead of focusing on a time frame for trading, traders should look to three arenas to specialize: market, buy or sell, and technique. By specializing in one or all of these areas, the time frame has a tendency to take care of itself. The benefits of specialization far outweigh the negative of missed opportunities.

Market Specialist

Retail traders have a tendency to watch too many markets. They want to be involved with gold, oil, S&P 500, cocoa, lumber, euro, and so on, all at one time. This is counterproductive. Their reasoning is that they don't want to miss anything. They simply do not see the material difference between gold and lumber or the euro and the yen. They are all interchangeable when it comes to opportunity.

Two problems arise when speculation is approached in this way. The first is that not all opportunities are created equal. By approaching gold the same way you approach wheat, you are ignoring several key factors. There is a difference in leverage, difference in fundamental factors, and a difference in volatility that affects each market.

The second problem is that you will miss opportunities by trying to watch everything at once. Computers have changed the life of the trader tremendously. Each trade setup can be programmed and the trader can be alerted to the setup. Unfortunately, as often happens, by the time you are alerted to the activity the move is underway and you are effectively chasing the market. Or you can be faced with too many choices, with little chance of discerning which one will actually take off and which one will not. This type of trade cherry picking can be frustrating and adds another layer of decision making that can cause trading hesitation.

The professionals that trade in the pits of the corn market trade one thing and one thing only: corn. The professionals that trade in the pits of crude oil options only trade crude oil options. Many of them successfully earn a living focusing on one market. This can be replicated by retail traders. By focusing on one market, retail traders go from being just a trader to a euro trader or a wheat trader or an oil trader.

By becoming a market-specific trader you liberate yourself. Much like your current (or former) profession, there are trade journals, conferences, magazines, and seminars designed for these specific industries. Each is a fount of information that can give you fundamental knowledge and "public" industry secrets that you would not have access to as an average trader following a few signals.

Couple this additional knowledge with the prescient ability to understand a market's rhythm, solely because you trade it exclusively, and you then begin to approach the same level of market savvy that professionals have. From this level of trading comes the ability to choose a day, swing, or position trade depending on the market's needs, not your own.

Buy or Sell Side Specialist

Who says you have to buy and sell? While it is easy to become caught up in buying stocks, few people ever short stocks. Many stock investors that come to futures or forex trading go to the extreme: they simply buy and sell too much. Since longs and shorts are treated the same when it comes to futures and forex, it is easy to get whipsawed in and out of positions.

If a trader finds himself losing money in his long position, they he may go short; if the short position is losing money, he then may go long. There are no rules against this activity and what many traders find themselves doing is chasing the markets. This constant chase generates commissions for the brokerage, not necessarily profits.

Not all signals are created equal. In a long-trending market, is shorting the best thing to do? In a short trending market, is buying the best thing to do? By limiting trading activity to the market's most probable direction, you can develop a laser-like precision in making your trading decisions. You also learn patience.

All traders operate with a finite amount of capital. Whether it is a few thousand or a few million dollars, successful trading can only be achieved by limiting your trading activity to the opportunities that are most likely to succeed, not by taking every chance that comes your way. Not all opportunities are created equal.

It is said that trading is much like playing baseball, in that the more times at bat the more likely you are to succeed. If you swing at obviously bad pitches you will skew your batting average or even worse—strike out—unnecessarily. The same can be said of trading. Taking every buy and sell signal that comes your way is in no way superior to trading solely longs or solely shorts.

Technique Specialist

Many professional traders come up with one or two techniques that help them trade the markets efficiently. The goal is to help them minimize their losses while at the same time maximizing their opportunity to profit. Sometimes the technique will be something as simple as selling options, other times they can be as complicated as butterfly spreads. No matter what the technique is there are always three components.

First, a trading technique must have a built-in risk management component. Selling options, you might rely on the fact that the majority of options that reach expiration expire worthless (approximately 75 percent). Or, on a spread trade, you limit your downside risk to the difference between a long and a short. Second, a trading technique must be able to be consistently applied to various trade and market setups. Finally, a trading technique takes account of capital appreciation as secondary to capital preservation. This is very important.

Professional traders have a fiduciary responsibility to their clients to preserve their capital, above all else. If they fail in that responsibility it prevents them from collecting incentive fees and will eventually halt their trading altogether. Retail traders should not take their fiduciary responsibility to themselves any less seriously.

Which Is Better: Time Frame or Specialization?

There is a debate as to whether it is better to be a day trader or a swing trader. This debate is rather futile. The market is the best determinant of how long you should be in the markets. No one in their right mind holds on to a losing position simply because they are swing trader, nor will they cut off their profits right in the middle solely because they are a day trader.

Their actions would break one of the core tenets of trading, "cut your losses and ride your profits." That's just common sense. Yet, time and time again, traders break the only rule that makes their trading successful. This is done solely to adhere to an artificial time constraint that the market doesn't put on itself.

Is there any wonder that so many traders have difficulty when it comes to trading? They want to let their profits run, but their day trading system forces them to get out as quickly as possible. Position/trend traders insist that the trend is their friend, but they won't cut their losses because the trend has not "officially" changed. Time frame trading is detrimental in the long run. No market will neatly adhere to the time frame you want to trade. The market will do what it wants and if you are not careful enough to pay attention to it, your trading will be more difficult than it needs to be.

On the other hand, when you specialize in a particular market, market direction, or strategy you give yourself the freedom to trade any time frame based on a different set of criteria. You are fixated on optimizing your profits by managing your risk. Whether a 5-minute chart or a 30-day chart, you make it infinitely easier to enter a trade and cut your losses. This is the key benefit to choosing specialization over time frame.

Pure Trader versus Flexible Trader

If it isn't broke, don't fix it!

If you are happy and successful with the type of trading you're doing then the techniques presented here will be helpful. The intent is not to stop you from doing what works. The goal is to expand your horizon and make your decision-making process more flexible, based on the markets' rhythm, not your own.

Much confusion results when traders attempt to follow market truisms, but feel their hands are tied because of arbitrary time frames. While being a pure trader can be an effective way to earn profits, you must decide whether you want to make living at it or you are only looking to make extra income. Depending on that decision, various time frames may or may not work for you.

Forcing yourself to be a day trader is a difficult task if you are simply looking to earn extra income during your retirement. You may want to travel or take a vacation, and the moment you walk away from the screen is the moment you stop having the market work for you.

On the other hand, if you are trying to earn a living from the markets and are looking for monthly market trading results to pay the bill, swing trades may take too long for you. Whatever the case, you don't have to force yourself to be a different trader than what your lifestyle can accommodate. You can accomplish your goals regardless of the time frame, as long as you keep your eyes on your ultimate profit-making, risk management objectives.

ESSENTIAL TRADING CONCEPTS

There are very few pieces of vital information necessary to effectively use the strategies given here. No matter what trading system or time frame you operate in, you must be able to determine five things at any given time: entry price, loss price, profit price, trend, and counter-trend. If you are lacking anyone of these of bits of information you are better off sitting on the sidelines.

The simple creature that the market is, dictates that it can only move in one of three directions at any given time; up, down, or sideways. Traders have to figure out a way, to the best of their ability, to take advantage of the up, down, or sideways movement. The straightforward approach of the average retail trader requires that they buy when the market goes up, sell when the market goes down, and stay out of the market when it moves sideways.

The problem with the straightforward approach arises when the market doesn't follow the game plan. You go long or short, the market moves in the opposite direction for a little while, then sideways, then back in your direction, and finally collapses into the opposite direction. Until now, the only response for the retail trader was to use a stop to protect them from loss. Yet still traders lose money.

By dissecting a trade into its five core components you give yourself the ability to exploit the market the same way that professional traders do. You go one step beyond stop orders and the need to predict the markets. You are capable of exploiting the entire *daisy chain trading effect* with grace and ease.

Daisy Chain Trading Effect

If there is any secret to trading, it lies with how effectively you manage margin and leverage. The typical approach to margin and leverage is to view it as a dangerous enemy. Whether it is futures, spot forex, or options, the fear of the leverage they provide can be paralyzing. This does not need to be the case.

Futures, spot forex, and options were not created in a vacuum. While they may be traded separately, it was never the intended purpose. Futures and options, along with many more sophisticated instruments, were designed to operate as insurance for the cash market. Whether the cash market is stocks or actual gold and oil, futures and options were created to help protect the owners from losing money.

Time and time again, throughout my books and in my seminars I talk about the daisy chain trading effect. The cash market is protected by futures, which is protected by options, and options protect both cash and futures markets. When the market is looked at in this way a host of opportunities open up. No longer is the leverage or margin your enemy, but a part of your risk management plan.

This feeds directly into trading flexibility. It quickly becomes apparent that opportunities are created by combining the advantages of the various derivatives products with each other and the cash market to maximize returns and minimize losses. In a world in which you use the various forms of leverage and margin together you are able to buy stock shares, but guarantee that your loss won't exceed the strike price of the option, or CFD (for my international readers), that you have put in place to protect yourself. You can combine spot forex trading with futures forex contracts without batting an eye.

This is the approach that professional traders take to trading. Nothing is sacred. You neither attempt to fixate on a time frame, nor do you artificially constrict yourself to one type of financial product. The reality is that technical analysis can be applied in the exact same way, no matter the financial product. So there are few, if any, benefits to being just a commodity trader, or just a forex trader, or just a stock trader.

By being aware of the daisy chain effect and then utilizing it, retail traders develop a proactive approach to the markets. The emphasis shifts from profits to loss management. This is a necessary shift in order to achieve longevity in trading. Developing ways to minimize loss first allows profits to handle themselves. This is the core of the professional trader's approach.

Risk Management Is Not the Same as Money Management   Loss, loss, loss! This is what risk management deals with. Managing your loss. Whether you use stops, limits, or any of the other strategies given, all risk management does is explain how you manage loss. Money management, however, deals with how you handle your money "win, lose, or flat." There is an essential confusion between the two topics. Money management deals with how you treat the money in your account. Risk management deals with what you do when faced with the risk of losing your principal and profits.

Stipulating that the most you will risk on a trade is 5 percent or that you will only commit one-third of your principal to the markets at any given time are both money management rules. They have no bearing on what you do to achieve these goals. But if you say that every time you put on a trade you will use a stop to protect from losing 5 percent of your account value, then you have risk management.

In this way you separate the actions you take to protect yourself from loss, from the amount you are willing to lose. You can adjust the amount from 5 percent to 50 percent, yet still maintain the same set of risk management strategies to get the job done. Knowing the difference is essential to understanding how to react to the markets when your principal is affected by sudden gains and losses.

Five Core Components of a Trade Setup

Now you have become more flexible in your trading. You no longer define yourself in such rigid terms as day, swing, or position trader. You have become more of a market specialist. You have found the few markets that you want to trade and you now find yourself open minded to the daisy chain effect that bears on the markets you watch. Are you ready to get started yet? Not quite.

To develop an effective risk management strategy and to fully utilize the daisy chain effect to your benefit, you must be capable of identifying five core pieces of data. Three of them are lumped together: entry price, loss price, and profit price. These three prices are essential to determining if the risk of the trade is worth the profit potential. The second two pieces of information focus on time. It is essential to determine if you are trading with trend or the counter-trend. Which one you trade will effect the likelihood of you achieving your profit targets and also how quickly.

Entry Price, Loss Price, and Profit Price   No matter what time frame you attempt to trade in there are only three prices that every trader must be concerned with: the trade entry price, the loss target price, and the profit target price. Each one of these components must be determined in advance in order to confidently execute a trade and to decide ultimately what to do, whether the trade is failing or is successful.

In *Winning the Trading Game* we covered various technical analysis tools that help you determine how to effectively come up with the necessary entry, loss, and profit target prices. Knowing these numbers is essential to developing your flexibility as a trader and devising the proper trading strategy to approach the market. These three numbers alone will give you the necessary vision to determine the full potential of a trade.

As with many trading suggestions, finding key prices is simple but not easy. Once established, they reduce your need for guess work. They become the facts and figures you use to design your trade. They illuminate what your potential losses and profits will be. At the same time, it is not necessary to be 100 percent perfect in choosing any of them.

It has been said that W.D. Gann had an uncanny ability for forecasting trades. In 1909 a reporter witnessed 286 winning trades and only 22 losing trades. This gave Gann an accuracy of 92 percent. Too many traders believe they have to have these same types of results in order to be successful. The reality is far from it. Of the three numbers you need to know: entry, loss, and profit; your entry price is the least necessary.

Markets move swiftly, and while you always want to get the optimum entry price, slippage can affect your fill. This phenomenon makes specific entry prices unreliable. It is better to use entry price as a guideline rather than a set-in-stone number. It is more important to know how you will exit a trade. Knowing your potential loss exit price and your profit exit price are essential and should not be afforded the same flexibility as the entry price.

These two prices, loss and profit, are essential in calculating your potential loss and your potential profit. They are the best way to determine if the trade you are thinking of taking is worth the risk. The traditionally acceptable "risk of loss rule" is the willingness to risk one to gain two. While this equation can be effective in assisting traders in estimating what their potential trade success could be, it rarely works out.

It is one thing to know what the numbers are; it's entirely another thing to be able to trade those numbers properly. This flaw is not the fault of the trader—even though traders will typically blame themselves—but more so a fault of the tools at their disposal. The inaccuracy of using stops and limits by themselves makes it difficult to have any sense of control in your trading. With the problem of slippage, missed opportunities of limit orders, and the self-defeating nature of stops, they only get you out when the market has momentum against you. It is no wonder why so many traders are frustrated with them.

With the limitations that stops and limits have, you want to minimize their overall use in your exit prices as much as possible. The more rigid you are in dealing with your exit price, the more likely you will succeed in the long run. This is the place where more emphasis should be placed by the trader, rather than in attempting to discover the best entry price.

Trend and Counter-trend   The trend and counter-trend are two more key components that every trader must be able to successfully identify. If you cannot determine whether you are entering a market when it is trending or counter-trending, how will you know where to place your primary trader?

Knowing whether you are trading the trend or the counter-trend is paramount to which entry and exit prices you choose. If you are following the trend, you will have different time expectations than if you are following a counter-trend. Trends will typically lumber and meander towards their destination in fits and spurts, creating multiple opportunities for anyone to jump on at the appropriate pull back.

Counter-trends typically behave differently. They are swift and aggressive and are actually the retracement opportunities that develop from the actual trend. There is fast money to make and lose during counter-trends. While they may quickly move against the trend, they lose momentum just as fast and turn back around to follow the overall trend once again.

At some point trends and counter-trends converge and switch places. Where once a market moved steadily higher or lower, the counter-trend emerges, acting like a quick-release pressure valve. Then something changes, typically a fundamental shift in supply or demand, which pushes the counter-trend into new territory. It completely changes the rhythm and tone of the markets, thereby setting up new opportunities as the trend.

This yin/yang cycle between trends and counter-trends is important to understand. It dictates how you interact with the markets and what tactics you set out using in order to gain the maximum effect. This is of monumental importance when deciding what time frame you would like to trade in.

In the following figures there are clear examples of the interconnectedness of trend and counter-trend activities. Looking at the daily charts of both the gold and S&P 500 we can clearly see the trends and the countertrends.

In Figure 3.1 we can see that gold has been a long-term up trend from 9/06/2007 to 03/13/2008.

In Figure 3.2 we can see that the S&P 500 is in a long term down trend from 10/01/2007 to 3/10/2008.

Using these same charts we can identify the counter-trends. In Figure 3.3 we can see eight times when the market moves counter, short, to the long-term up trend. Surprisingly, the number of days the market moved counter-trend to the long-term trend were few. An eight-day move in 11/2007 was the longest move of all of the counter-trends.

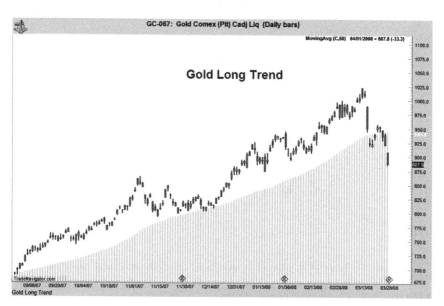

FIGURE 3.1 Gold Long Trend
TradeNavigator.com © 2007. All rights reserved.

FIGURE 3.2 S&P 500 Short Trend
TradeNavigator.com © 2007. All rights reserved.

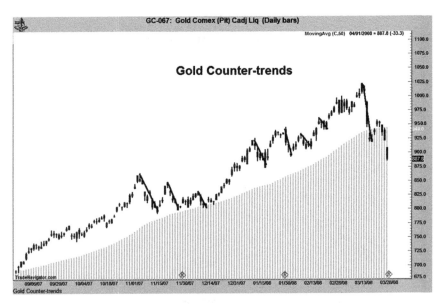

FIGURE 3.3 Gold Long Counter-trends
TradeNavigator.com © 2007. All rights reserved.

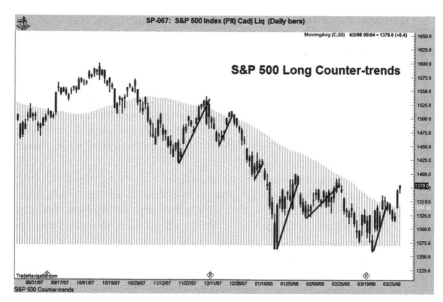

FIGURE 3.4 S&P 500 Short Counter-trends
TradeNavigator.com © 2007. All rights reserved.

Looking at Figure 3.4, we can see that in the S&P 500 market there were only six counter-trends that could be easily identified over the same time frame.

USING THIS BOOK TO ITS FULLEST POTENTIAL

This book, while it can stand on its own, can also be enhanced by your reading *Winning the Trading Game*. If you have a reliable trading system or set of strategies that you feel confident in, you can also use them in conjunction with this book. As long as you can pull together the necessary elements on the chart: entry, loss, profit, trend, and counter-trend, you have a key to unlocking the market's natural behavior and how you should react to it.

There are no short cuts to learning how to skillfully trade the market of your choice. The time invested can be well worth the effort, though. Mix options with futures, right next to stocks with commodity indexes. By knowing essential prices, the direction of the market, and the daisy chain effect, you have an effective tool set that is designed to minimize your losses and maximize your profits.

The basic and advanced strategies presented in later chapters were not invented by me. Professional traders and a handful of retail traders have taken advantage of some of the ideas presented in this book and have met with limited success in applying them in their day-to-day trading.

The reason for the limited success most likely stems from underutilization of the core components discussed throughout this chapter. The lack of success also stems from looking at the world of trading in an either/or scenario: win or lose, in or out. This can be fatal. It leaves little room for the imagination to work and contributes to a lack of control, which leads to irrational trading decisions.

By taking a step back to look at trading through the eyes of the professionals, you should realize that you do not have to adhere to any rigid or arbitrary standards of trading and interacting with the market. You can carve your own path in the markets, with a set of tools designed to help you preserve your capital. By reading further, you continue on a course that strengthens your approach to the market and actually minimizes your losses.

The techniques given are designed to expand your risk management palette. Where novice traders are oftentimes too content to use stops and limits to manage their loss (i.e. risk), there is a risk management world out there, full of choices.

In this book we show you that world. Nine straightforward strategies are presented in familiar settings and you can see how and when to apply the ideas. The last six strategies take a heavy-handed approach toward earning an income in your account while you trade.

Turn some of your bad trades around into potentially profitable ones. These techniques will find their way into your trading and you will see results. At the same time, these tactics are not the Holy Grail. They are meant to be part of an overall trading plan and should complement your short-term and long-term trading goals.

While trading is not easy to do, its individual components are fairly simple to describe—go long, go short, or do nothing. Yet there are so many permutations that it is difficult to pick and choose the right path. By utilizing any one of these 15 strategies you will be restricting the number of permutations to some likely culprits. Learning this alone is worth much more than the price of this book. So sit back and relax and use this book as both a guide and as a reference in your day-to-day trading.

PART II

Basic Strategies

T his section is a breakdown of nine strategies that have been compiled to help minimize your risk and increase your opportunity for success. Risk minimization is of utmost importance to professional traders and should be no less of a concern for retail traders. While none of these techniques is new, it's the context they've been put in that gives them a refreshing new life; this is an important distinction.

In the world of trading there are winners and losers. The winners focus on hedging their trading and the losers don't. Whether you are a professional speculator or a corporation that actually owns the products you are buying and selling, what makes the difference is how you interact with the market when it is moving against you. You can be reactive or proactive; the choice is yours.

For the reactive, a stop is good enough along with the hope that market will move in your direction. For the proactive, a combination of tools is used to exploit inherent market discrepancies. One such market discrepancy is the daisy chain effect. The daisy chain effect highlights the obvious insurance aspects of the market products developed over that last 20 years. By integrating the spot market with the futures market, and then throwing in the options market, an entirely different level of trading sophistication evolves.

This is what the basic strategies in the following chapters are meant to do. They open your eyes to how the spot market is protected by the futures market and how options can protect both the spot and futures market. Taken to its logical conclusion, you can effectively trade both sides of the market's movement, while limiting your exposure to any one side. This is a significant skill when it comes to fast-moving volatile markets.

These strategies have been broken down into four sections dealing with a time frame that each is best suited for. Whether the risk management strategy can best be used for day, swing, or position trading is secondary to understanding the logic of how and why it works at all. With the right risk management strategy you can fluidly switch from a day trade to a position trade and back again. This comes from being willing to not be pigeonholed into a time frame, yet being open enough to know when one is needed.

CHAPTER 4

Holding the Bull and the Bear by the Tails

Prediction is very difficult, especially about the future.

—Niels Bohr

N o one can predict the future with 100 percent accuracy. Even the world's most famous seer, Nostradamus, left much to be desired in his cryptic messages. Predicting the future when it comes to making money is more uncertain. What makes predicting price moves even more difficult is that no matter what the news is, many more influences affect the price that aren't reported and that we don't know about.

Even with the near impossible task of predicting the future, traders still attempt it. It is as if retail traders feel forced or pressured to predict the markets' direction regardless of the likelihood of their prediction's success, which makes the trading more of a matter of "my team is better than your team." If you are long or bullish a market you look to justify your position, if you are short or bearish a market you look to justify your position, and there is no in between.

This narrow view of the market, long or short, pigeonholes a trader in such a way that opportunities are missed. The market moves in only one of three directions (up, down, and sideways) at any given time. The sideways or consolidation pattern occurs 80 percent of the time. So if a trader limits his trading to being long or short he cuts out two-thirds of his market opportunities and he finds himself reacting to the market 80 percent of the time.

This can be a frustrating way to interact with the market. You are constantly on the defensive, from deciding to pick a trade, long or short, or from having to quickly make a decision to jump into a trade once it breaks out from its consolidation pattern. There is a better way to trade.

The secret of professional traders is that they rarely choose a side. They do their best to increase their odds of success by positioning themselves to take advantage of a nascent trend before it develops. The best way to do that is to be ahead of the curve. If you can anticipate where the market is going, you stand to make the most from any developing market trend. Yet if we can't predict the future, how can we anticipate where the market is going? Don't make a choice of being long or short. Be in a position to take advantage of both.

STRADDLE, STRANGLE, AND EXECUTION

Being long and short the market at the same time is practically a revolutionary concept for retail traders, while professional traders have been doing it since the futures market's inception. Somehow the concept has either been lost or is considered a form of trading blasphemy when it is suggested that retail traders incorporate this strategy into their trading. Retail traders often confuse being long and short in the market simultaneously with being *delta neutral.*

Delta neutral is defined in Investopedia as "A portfolio consisting of positions with offsetting positive and negative deltas. The deltas balance out to bring the net change of the position to zero."

The intent of a delta neutral position is to create a net change of zero. This is in direct contrast to the goal of trading both sides at the same time, with the intent to switch over to the winner. So while in the early stages of being long and short the market simultaneously is to diminish your losses, and one may negate the other in the process, holding on to both positions after a trend has clearly been defined is not the intent and is in fact self-defeating.

Throughout the following chapters we look at various strategies that combine long and short positions to give you a distinct advantage over traders that simply pick long or short positions alone, hoping for success. While the strategies in later chapters become more sophisticated, they are still accessible to any trader of any level as long as the goal is to manage risk.

In this chapter we expose how to properly use two long-short strategies. The first strategy we look at is a straddle and the second strategy is a strangle. Both strategies share a few things in common: They incorporate options, they require that you have a long and short option on simultaneously, and they are affected by *delta.*

Delta is defined by Investopedia as "the ratio comparing the change in the price of the underlying asset to the corresponding change in the price of a derivative."

This works in a pretty straightforward way. If you purchase a call and the delta is 0.2, for every $1 that the underlying asset increases, the call increases by $0.20. On the other hand, if you purchase a put, then the delta is quoted as a negative number. As the underlying asset increases in value, the put decreases. A put option with –0.5 decreases $0.50 for every $1 move in the underlying asset.

Delta is one of five risk measurements that are calculated on options. It is only one of three that we talk about throughout the book. The other two are theta, which measures an option's price change based on time sensitivity, and vega, which looks at an option's relationship to volatility.

Straddle and strangle strategies can also be traded in a buy side or sell side fashion. In this chapter we look only at the buy side aspect of both of these strategies. The sell side has the ability to expose a trader to unlimited risk, even though traders can profit from premiums. Since the intent of this chapter and the next several chapters to protect you from risk, not expose you to unnecessary risk, then we do not explore sell side straddles and strangles in this chapter.

The key difference between the two strategies is the price. When you implement a straddle you purchase two at-the-money options. At-the-money options are the most expensive options you can purchase. On the other hand, strangles require that you purchase two out-of-the-money options. Out-of-the-money options typically are less expensive than at-the-money options, but volatility can play a factor in option pricing.

You have a distinct advantage in your trading when you apply either of these two strategies to news announcements and potentially ambiguous governmental data releases.

Historical commodity and futures option data is difficult to come by. Do your best during your demo or paper trading to track relevant option pricing data.

Straddle

Technically, a straddle is considered the purchase or sale of an equal number of puts and calls, with the same strike price and expiration dates. Realistically speaking, a straddle is a way to give yourself a choice. The most difficult part of trading is choosing whether you are going to be long or short; the second most difficult part is giving up that choice once it has been made.

Straddles, like all of the other strategies in the book, teach you to be aware of the rhythm of the market. You learn how to put the reality of the market ahead of your desire to see the market do what you want it to do. This is essential to succeed in trading. When you decide to execute a straddle you are leaving your choice of market direction up to the market itself, as it should be. You then are required to cut off the less profitable position immediately. It is well worth the expense of the straddle to learn both these lessons.

Straddles teach you how to:

1. Let the market decide the direction it wants to go in

2. Cut the losing position immediately

3. Focus on the benefits of risk management, not expense

Don't be fooled into believing that you cannot afford to put on a straddle. If it is the best choice for the situation, then execute it. If you are an active trader or a day trader, a straddle may be the perfect solution for you to achieve your goals. Whether it is a Fed announcement, Consumer Price Index report, or jobless claim numbers, it can be very difficult to get a bead on the market's intended direction. So instead of forcing an artificial or rumored direction on your trading, use a straddle to establish your initial position.

From there you can do one of two things:

1. You can close out the losing position and ride out the profits from the winning position before the end of the day.

2. You can hold on to your winning position and convert it from an active trade to a position trade.

Either way you come out ahead of the person who simply guesses or predicts the market's direction and has a 50/50 shot of getting it right. Does the person who guesses the market's direction have the ability to make more money? Of course! If he guesses right, there is no losing trade that eats away at part of his profits. On the other hand, it is an all-or-nothing proposition. If he guesses wrong, there is no profitable trade to pick up the slack.

The question to ask yourself as a trader is whether you capable of trading with a 50/50 level of certainty or if you want the protection afforded to you that hedging your bets can offer. As with all the risk management strategies throughout this book, this one is not designed for everyone. In fact, not every strategy is designed for every situation.

The straddle works best when it meets at least one of these three criteria:

1. The market has been moving sideways for sometime
2. There is a news, earnings, or government announcement
3. Analysts have talked up the figures of a potential announcement excessively

For those who are new to trading, the last criteria may be a little difficult to understand. Those who have trading experience will comprehend this quickly. Prior to any earnings decision or governmental announcement, analysts will do their best to predict the announcement. They will make estimates weeks in advance of the actual announcement. This has the affect of making the market move. Whether it's right or wrong is secondary to the market's activity.

Once the actual numbers are released, the market has one of two ways to react. It will proceed in the direction of what the analysts predicted or it will show signs of fatigue, because the analysts were in line with what was expected; profit taking will ensue and the market will suddenly move in the opposite direction of what the news portends.

If the news was bullish, but the analyst had already predicted that, and the market had already made gains up until the announcement, then we could see a quick selloff. The identical behavior occurs if the news is bearish. The difficulty occurs in determining when the market will move counter to the news and when the news will simply add to the momentum of the market's direction.

The straddle protects you from what you don't know, or what you can't know as a trader. This is a big feat to accomplish in such a simple package. Yet for all of its positive benefits, the straddle comes with a significant drawback: price. The most effective straddle is accomplished when you are able to purchase a put and call option "at-the-money." Since at-the-money options typically follow the underlying asset practically one-for-one, they can be the most expensive to purchase. This also means that once the market decides on a direction, the losing option begins to erode in value quickly.

In Figure 4.1 we take a close-up daily snapshot of the market. Leading up to the February 27th, 2008, Federal Reserve Board's rate announcement the market is in a fairly sideways motion.

On February 25th, after two days of a weak market, a decision is made to put on a straddle. The consensus is that the Fed wants to lower interest rates to stimulate the economy. The debate is more on how much they will lower it, not whether they will lower it. If rates aren't lowered enough the market will react with weakness; if they're lowered too much, the question is how much inflationary pressure will be put on the dollar in the long run.

The cost of putting on the straddle is (every $1 move in a gold futures contract is worth $100):

$$940 \text{ Call: } 18.30 = \$1,830 \text{ (Delta, .483)}$$
$$940 \text{ Put: } 19.50 = \$1,950 \text{ (Delta, .514)}$$
$$\text{Total value} = \$3,780$$

The numbers in this chapter and others are approximations of option prices and delta values at the time of these examples. There are many sources for options data and they may differ slightly from source to source.

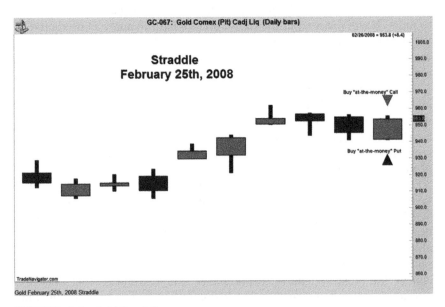

FIGURE 4.1 Gold Straddle
Source: TradeNavigator.com © 2007. All rights reserved.

Throughout the rest of this chapter we follow how the gold market could have been traded around this time frame with a straddle or a strangle.

Strangle

Strangles have all the same benefits of straddles. Strangles work best when the market has been moving sideways, when there is an announcement, and if analysts have talked up or down a position for too long prior to the announcement.

There are three key differences between strangles and straddles. First, strangles are executed using out-of-the-money options, so they are typically less expensive than their straddle counterparts. Second, since the purchased options are out-of-the-money, you expose yourself to the risk of the market not moving at all. That means that you could lose money on both your call and put solely through time erosion. Finally, delta plays a greater role with strangles when making your decision to purchase the proper call and put. You simply do not want to pay too much for an option that moves less than the underlying asset.

Strangles have more flexibility than straddles. Depending on your desired trading time frame, you can purchase out-of-the-money options to either day trade, position, or swing trade with little worry of being forced into a snap decision because of time constraints. This is important if you wish to see a trade slowly evolve past its initial move after the announcement.

Figure 4.2 is the same gold chart we saw in the straddle example. This time we take a longer view of gold's sideways action. We identify support and resistance lines and purchase the corresponding put and call option.

The cost of putting on the strangle is:

960 Call: 8.20 = $820 (Delta, .315)
890 Put: 5.30 = $530 (Delta, .188)
Total value = $1,350

The difference of putting on a straddle and a strangle is a savings of:

$3,780 − $1,350 = $2,430

Even with such a big difference in price there are some serious drawbacks. The options themselves are anywhere from $10 to $50 out-of-the-money, which means that the market must move substantially in either direction before you begin to see the results of the strangle. In the meantime, the loss in value of the option can be significant while the gains are modest

FIGURE 4.2 Gold Strangle
Source: TradeNavigator.com © 2007. All rights reserved.

(as seen by the low deltas), as the market moves towards parity with the underlying asset.

So the savings of $2,430 must be compensated for by the belief that you will be able to make at least half that when the market moves in whatever direction it is going.

Stop-Limit Strangle   Using an option strangle is not the only choice that traders have for taking advantage of potential market volatility. Stop-limit orders can operate in a similar fashion as purchasing a put and a call. For instance, if you did not want to commit any cash to putting on the trade, but you wanted to be poised for any potential movement, you can set a stop-limit order at the same points of support and resistance that you would have otherwise bought options.

There are three drawbacks to using this stop-limit strategy. First, you cannot guarantee that your order will be filled, particularly if the market gaps. Second, the expense of putting on a futures contract or buying shares outright will typically exceed the price of the option. This makes the strategy less expensive in the short run, but more costly in the long run. Finally, by using a futures contract or buying shares directly, you eliminate the benefit of the limited risk that options can afford you. This means that you will need to add a secondary risk management strategy, such as a stop, or purchase a protective option.

Execution

Neither straddle nor strangle is more effective than the other. The single most important factor in choosing either is what you hope to accomplish. When you set out to purchase at-the-money or out-of-the-money options, a myriad of factors come into play.

If it's an option on a futures contract, ask yourself when the underlying asset expires. This directly affects how long you are able to hold on to the option contract. If you are actively trading the option you will want to be aware of the volume so you can liquidate your option as quickly as possible.

Price, while a concern, is secondary to how relevant it is to the trading situation at hand and the goals you have in mind.

GETTING THE RIGHT OPTIONS FOR THE JOB

Understanding option selection, having an idea about delta, and being able to calculate the savings, values, and gains of the various options form the essential foundation needed to utilize any of the ideas presented in this book. By beginning with straddles and strangles you are able to play around with using puts and calls as a risk management strategy without feeling like you are betting the farm. As chapters progress, it becomes increasingly more important that you have a grasp of choosing the right options to work in tandem with your spot, futures, or margined position.

In this section we complete our review of the gold market and its re-action to the Federal Reserve's interest rate announcement on February 27, 2008; we also discuss the S&P 500's and the euro's reaction to various other news announcements and whether putting on a straddle or a strangle is preferable.

Economic Calendars

There is always a debate on whether fundamental or technical analysis is superior. This is a debate best left to amateurs. The market is a complex system that can be influenced by news, supply, and demand just as easily as it can be dissected on the basis of price and time. While many of the news events may have a temporary effect that can last from a few hours to a few weeks, they should not be taken lightly nor ignored.

Various economic news events have the ability to modify how hedgers and professional traders plan out their long-term strategies and approaches to the changing market environment.

This modification can best be seen by looking at the shifting balance of longs and shorts in the Commodity Futures Trading Commission's (CFTC) Commitment of Traders Report (COT). The COT report is designed to show the shifts in various commodity, currency, interest rate, and energy contracts and options. This shift is shown, from week to week, in the fluctuating balance of long and short contract holders. As long and short increase and decrease their holdings, they are constantly reflecting the real world changes in supply and demand.

The COT report is one of many resources used to watch fundamental shifts in the market. Every month there are important economic indicators that have an impact on the markets. When these reports come out the market can behave in unpredictable ways. A tutorial on Investopedia, written by Ryan Barnes, outlines 25 different economic indicators and their impact on the markets. Yahoo! Finance has an economic calendar on their web site that gives the release dates and times of the 25 economic indicators Ryan Barnes overviews, plus many less-talked-about, lower-profile economic indicators.

No matter what economic indicator you follow, when the data is released it impacts to some degree how the people in the know react to it. This means that you can set a straddle or a strangle to take advantage of the impending news that is released. By solely trading in this way you create multiple opportunities to take a proactive stand in the markets that can benefit you no matter which direction the wind blows.

Of the various economic indicators there are five that have a significant impact on how the market moves. The interest rate decisions of the Federal Open Market Committee (FOMC), Consumer Price Index (CPI), Consumer Confidence Index (CCI), Jobless Claims Report, and Producer Price Index (PPI) have a significant impact on how the economic health of a country is perceived. There are also various inventory and weather reports that affect stock indexes and commodity products as well. The goal is to understand these various indicators and to find the ones that work for your trading goals.

Federal Open Market Committee (FOMC)   The Federal Reserve Board has a special branch, the Federal Open Market Committee, that makes key decisions regarding monetary policy in the United States. Seven of the twelve members are the Board of Governors of the Federal Reserve System and the other five are Reserve Bank presidents. The FOMC meets eight times per year to determine interest rates as well as the discount rate, both of which have a direct impact on whether the money supply is tightened or expanded.

Consumer Price Index (CPI)   Consumer Price Index (CPI) is considered one the most definitive economic indicators around. Several other indicators actually use the CPI as a way to determine their own key economic numbers. The anticipation of what the CPI will say leads many Wall Street analysts to actively recommend the buying or selling of the equity markets along with having a direct effect on how investors get involved in the fixed-income markets. The level of impact that the CPI has directly affects how the FOMC will react in deciding if they will encourage a loose or tight money policy.

Consumer Confidence Index (CCI)   Once a month the nonprofit group the Conference Board releases the Consumer Confidence Index (CCI). This information assists the Federal Reserve in determining exactly what the average consumer is feeling about the economy, as far out as six months in advance.

Over 5,000 homes are contacted to take part in a survey conducted by the Conference Board. The survey's sole purpose is to help determine the financial health and spending power of American families. By gathering this data, the Conference Board is able to determine the level of overall confidence that consumers have in the economy.

Jobless Claims Report   Every Thursday at 8:30 A.M. EST the Jobless Claims report is released. This number is meant to show how many first-time filings for state jobless claims are being registered around the country. The data itself is highly volatile. Being a week-to-week indicator based on a four-week sample, states experience high volumes of claims that can easily skew numbers upwards. In order to compensate for the spikes a revised figure is released one week later showing exactly what states had an impact on the numbers.

Producer Price Index (PPI)   The Producer Price Index (PPI) is released by the Bureau of Labor Statistics. It comes out around the 13th of each month. The PPI measures prices at the wholesale and producer level. It accumulates the prior months' data and shows whether prices are increasing, indicating inflation, or decreasing, indicating deflation. Broken up into three parts, it clearly shows exactly what the prices are throughout the production cycle.

With a separate PPI Index for the crude, intermediate, and finished stages of a products life cycle, it is easy to see where inflation is occurring in the production cycle. With all this data, the core PPI number is still seen as the key to understanding the economy. It measures finished goods while simultaneously removing food and energy from the equation. The reason being that food and energy are too volatile to provide accurate numbers when calculating for the real price of finished foods in any given month.

General Economic Indicators   There are many economic indicators that affect commodities across the entire spectrum. From weather predictions to import and export figures, various commodities are positively or negatively affected. Whether you look at crude inventory indicators, the Gross Domestic Product, or wait for Central Banks around the world to make policy decisions, each one can be relevant in setting the stage for your trading decision.

Oil traders are devoted followers of crude inventory indicators, which represent the amount of oil currently being stored for future use. The fluctuations in these numbers gives a strong indicator of whether production is matching consumption, or whether consumption has eased off. The indicator measures the weekly status of U.S. crude oil supplies.

The Gross Domestic Product (GDP) is used by traders to determine the economic health of a country. Strong GDPs have a tendency to buoy stock markets; weak GDPs have a tendency to pull stock markets down. Presented on a quarterly basis, GDP numbers have the ability to set the economic trend for up to four months before any significant change is recognized by the majority of traders. Designed to measure the market value of all goods and services produced, the GDP is a well-balanced view of any country's overall competitiveness in a global economy—as long as it doesn't exceed a 3 percent annual growth rate. If the market moves in excess of that, then investors worry about inflation and potential economic bubbles. Inversely, if an economy has two negative-growth GDP reports in a row, an economy is considered to be in a recession.

Whatever the indicator may be, when it is announced it has the ability to polarize the marketplace significantly. This leaves room for a varied set of trading opportunities for traders familiar with the straddle and strangle strategy.

OPTION TUTORIAL

There are many great books on options investing. Many of them are very detailed in explaining various types of spreads and subtle nuances of options. In this brief tutorial I lay down a basic foundation about options you can use throughout this book.

There are many books and videos available with more details on options investing. See Tables 4.1 through 4.4 to learn about puts and calls, the underlying asset vs. the strike price, interaction of intrinsic value to time value, and a cursory overview of the greeks.

TABLE 4.1 Put and Call Defined

Put	Call
An agreement that gives an investor the right (but not the obligation) to buy a stock, bond, commodity, or other instrument at a specified price within a specific time period.	An option contract giving the owner the right, but not the obligation, to sell a specified amount of an underlying asset at a set price within a specified time. The buyer of a put option estimates that the underlying asset will drop below the exercise price before the expiration date.

Excerpted from Investopedia.com

TABLE 4.2 Options Strike Price and Underlying Asset

	Call	Put
At-the-money option	Price of the asset matches the option strike price.	Price of the asset matches the option strike price.
In-the-money option	Price of the asset is greater than the option price.	Price of the asset is less than the option strike price.
Out-of-the-money option	Price of the asset is less than the option strike price.	Price of the asset is greater than the option strike price.

TABLE 4.3 Option Intrinsic and Time Values

	At-the-Money Option	In-the-Money Option	Out-of-the-Money Option
Call/Put	This type of option derives its value solely from time. Intrinsic value contributes nothing to price.	This type of option finds its time value decreasing while simultaneously increasing its intrinsic value.	This type of option loses time value as the option's strike price gets further from the underlying assets value. There is no intrinsic value.

TABLE 4.4   Option Greeks

Delta	Theta	Vega
This is a measure of the change in an option's price resulting from a change in the underlying asset. Calls have a positive delta from 0 to 100, Puts have a delta range from –100 to 0. At-the-money options typically have a delta of approximately 50. In-the-money options rarely exceed a delta of 80.	This is a measure of the decline of the option time value. As an option's expiration becomes closer the time value begins to rapidly decrease.	This is a measure of the increase or decrease in implied volatility. It successfully quantifies how much an option price will increase or decrease depending on the option's level of volatility.

CAUTION

The trading information that the Greeks provide is purely theoretical. They are designed to give you an idea of what the volatility and rate of change are at the time you looking the screen. If new information comes in, or the mathematical models you are using are not accurate, the projected values can be significantly different than what you had anticipated.

Event-Based Trading Examples

As we've discussed, the various economic indicators have a significant impact on how the market reacts. Within minutes a market that may have been meandering sideways all of a sudden bolts in its chosen direction. In the following examples we look at the tremendous effects that news announcements have on various markets. It will be up to the individual trader to decide if straddle or strangle is the best choice for trading the scenario.

Event 1: Federal Reserve Announcement February 27th, 2008   On January 7, 2005, I wrote an article entitled "America's Silent Mortgage Crisis" and posted it online (www.home-loan-mortgage .info/2005/01/americas-silent-mortgage-crisis.html). At the time it was no secret that interest rates had reached a historical low of 1 percent and that adjustable-rate mortgages would not be able to sustain themselves in the face of any anticipation of a rate increase.

As interest rates increased so did the casual climb in home owner payments, eventually leading up to the fiasco that has been dubbed the Subprime Mortgage Crisis. Attempting to make things right, the FOMC was seen as a driving force in pushing interest rates down in order to stimulate the economy and help people save their homes. Leading up to the FOMC's February 27th, 2008 decision, the market moved relatively sideways for several months. You can see this demonstrated in Figure 4.3.

On February 27th, 2008, Bernanke and the other members of the FOMC clearly stated that they would continue to ease rates in order to stimulate the U.S. economy. All inflationary pressures on the dollar took a backseat to achieving that goal. In Figure 4.4 we see gold react positively to the weakened dollar, moving a total of 566 ticks.

Earlier in the chapter we set up a straddle and strangle for the gold market a few days prior to the FOMC's announcement. Each one had its own capital commitment. While we knew that we wouldn't be holding on to both the call and the put, there was still the initial capital commitment that had to be made in order for the trade to be initialized. That was a total of $3,780 for the straddle and $1,350 for the strangle.

In Figure 4.5 we see the gold market move 566 ticks. With each tick worth $100, a total of $5,660 could have been made on the underlying asset. Since we are dealing with a call option we know that the average maximum delta that an in-the-money option can achieve is 80 or .8 of the actual underlying asset. Based on that number, our hypothetical returns on the runup after the announcement would put us at around $4,528.

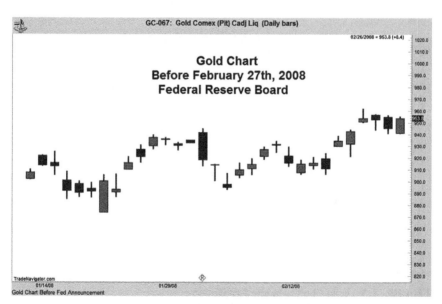

FIGURE 4.3 Gold Chart before February 27th, 2008
Source: TradeNavigator.com © 2007. All rights reserved.

FIGURE 4.4 Gold Chart after February 27th, 2008
Source: TradeNavigator.com © 2007. All rights reserved.

FIGURE 4.5 Gold Chart Straddle Call Option
Source: TradeNavigator.com © 2007. All rights reserved.

FIGURE 4.6 Gold Chart Strangle Call Option
Source: TradeNavigator.com © 2007. All rights reserved.

Risking $3,780 in order to gain $4,528 is not the best risk/reward ratio. And in spite of the fact that we would be releasing the put option as soon as possible, the costs of the loss adds to our overall call expense. In a fast-moving market it could be difficult to get out of the put option without the potential for some significant slippage.

In Figure 4.6 we look at the strangle call option and see a better risk/reward scenario. Putting up an initial $1,350 to catch a move of 397 ticks, $3,970, fits a risk/reward profile of risking one to gain two. Even if you lose 50 percent on the put option value, you only lose $265, for a total real capital commitment of $1,085 (see Table 4.5).

Event 2: Consumer Price Index Release February 20th, 2008

The Consumer Price Index (CPI) was anticipated to move only 0.3 of a

TABLE 4.5 Straddle versus Strangle

	Straddle	Strangle
Initial commitment	$3,780	$1,350
Hypothetical returns (based on .80 delta of an in-the-money option)	$4,528	$3,176

FIGURE 4.7 S&P 500 Chart Prior to CPI Release
Source: TradeNavigator.com © 2007. All rights reserved.

percent; instead it moved 0.4 of a percent. This had a negative effect on the overall U.S. economic outlook and fueled inflationary fears. The best reflection of the CPI's overall impact is the S&P 500 stock index. Representing the top 500 corporations that operate in the United States, the S&P 500 is sensitive to any news, positive or negative.

In Figure 4.7 we see that S&P 500 has leveled off after a steep decline that lasted a month, from 12/26/2007 until 1/15/2008. With the S&P 500 moving sideways, leading up to the CPI's final numbers release, there is an opportunity to put on a straddle and purchase an in-the-money put and call at the 1350 price (see Table 4.6).

TABLE 4.6 Straddle versus Strangle

	Call Strike Price/Premium	Put Strike Price/Premium	Initial Commitment
Straddle	1350/16.70 ($4,175)	1350/13.80 ($3,450)	30.50/($7,625)
Strangle	1400/5.00 ($1,250)	1325/9.00 ($2,250)	14.00/($3,500)

The S&P 500 contract comes in both a full-size contract and a mini contract. The technique can translate to either market. The full-size contract has a value of $25/minimum movement and the mini contract has a value of $12.50/minimum movement and is actually one-fifth the size of a regular contract.

In Figure 4.8 the S&P 500 futures contract penetrates the support line and falls to a low of 1250. This drop comes five days after the initial report, generating a total move of 833 ticks. A short of the underlying asset had the potential to return $20,825. An in-the-money put option had the potential to return 80 percent of that.

If we were to develop a strangle trade based on the same chart, we would use the support and resistance lines to set our buy points for our put and call. In Figure 4.9, we use the support and resistance lines to set up our strangle trade.

This time when the market drops past the put, it gains only 531 ticks for a total $13,275 in the underlying asset. The put has the potential to make approximately $10,620.

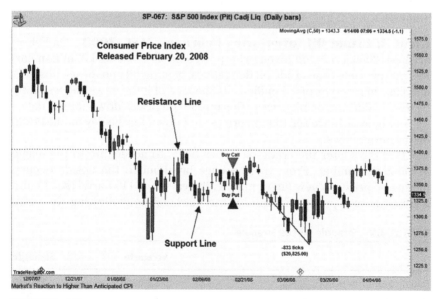

FIGURE 4.8 S&P 500 Breaks Support Line
Source: TradeNavigator.com © 2007. All rights reserved.

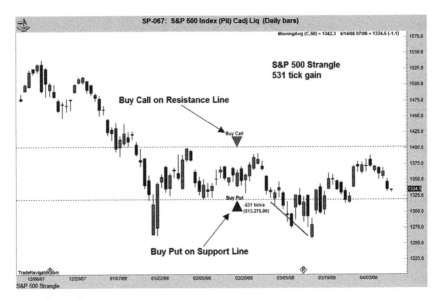

FIGURE 4.9 S&P 500 Strangle Setup
Source: TradeNavigator.com © 2007. All rights reserved.

Whether you execute a straddle or strangle, both of them fall well within an acceptable risk/reward ratio of risking one to gain two (see Table 4.7).

Event 3: Crude Oil Inventories February 21st, 2008 On February 21st, 2008, crude oil inventories posted an increase of 4.2 million barrels. At the same time crude oil derivatives, heating oil and diesel, posted a decrease in reserves of 4.5 million. On the face of it the news had a slightly bearish undertone on oil prices. This pushed oil prices down for the day.

In Figure 4.10 we see that oil prices shot down for the day on the crude oil inventory news.

Two days later the crude oil prices begin to accelerate to the magic $100/barrel number. From there a huge breakout to the upside occurs, driving oil prices to new highs, practically reaching $110/barrel (see Figure 4.11). This is a prime example of the markets' not following the news

TABLE 4.7 Straddle versus Strangle

	Straddle	Strangle
Initial commitment	$7,625	$3,500
Hypothetical returns (based on .80 delta of an in-the-money option)	$16,600	$10,620

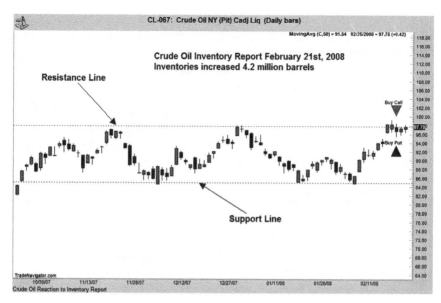

FIGURE 4.10 Initial Market Reaction to Crude Oil Inventories
Source: TradeNavigator.com © 2007. All rights reserved.

FIGURE 4.11 Crude Oil Almost Reaches $110/barrel
Source: TradeNavigator.com © 2007. All rights reserved.

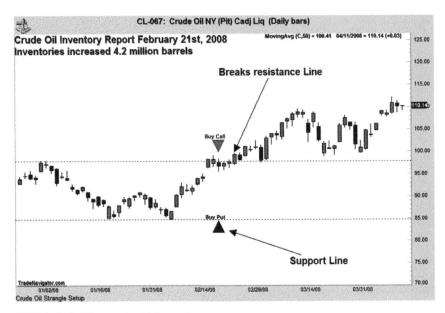

FIGURE 4.12 Crude Oil Strangle
Source: TradeNavigator.com © 2007. All rights reserved.

and why a straddle or strangle can be beneficial in catching some of this unexpected movement.

The movement from $97/barrel to $108/barrel is a significant opportunity to generate $11,680 in profits, if you were holding the futures contract directly. A strangle on the same contract would have you buying a put at the support line, approximately $85/barrel, and at the resistance line, approximately $98/barrel (see Figure 4.12).

In this instance the volatility of the at-the-money options make the prospect of a straddle very unattractive. The strangle is a lot more cost effective for the potential profits that can develop from an unexpected spike. Supply and demand are precariously balanced and those traders who can be nimble enough to ride the crude oil markets effortlessly up and down will gain the most from its aggressive volatility (see Tables 4.8 and 4.9).

TABLE 4.8 Straddle versus Strangle

	Call Strike Price/Premium	Put Strike Price/Premium	Initial Commitment
Straddle	97.50/4.39 ($4,390)	97.50/5.20 ($5,200)	9.59 ($9,590)
Strangle	98/4.09 ($4,090)	85/1.22 ($1,220)	5.31 ($5,310)

TABLE 4.9 Straddle versus Strangle

	Straddle	Strangle
Initial Commitment	$9,590	$5,310
Hypothetical Returns (based on .80 delta of an in-the-money option)	$9,344	$8,576

SAMPLE STRADDLE AND STRANGLE WRITE-UP SHEETS

You can photocopy the following tables or you can make a spreadsheet similar to these two to trade your own events.

Straddle versus Strangle

	Call Strike Price/Premium	Put Strike Price/Premium	Initial Commitment
Straddle			
Strangle			

Straddle versus Strangle

	Straddle	Strangle
Initial commitment		
Hypothetical returns (based on .80 delta of an in-the-money option)		

CONCLUSION

This chapter covers a lot of critical information that is used again in later chapters. Understanding how to select options is a critical skill that you cannot neglect. It will prove the difference between effectively managing your risk and exposing yourself to unnecessary risk if you are not careful. Using straddles and strangles is an easy way to ease yourself into the world of risk management and to learn techniques to protect yourself from being stuck on a market position. Nevertheless, you must still make wise decisions on how you enter the market, and understand what you hope to accomplish once you have done so.

CHAPTER 5

Precision Trading at Its Finest

T he American Heritage Dictionary lists one definition of the word *precision* as "of or characterized by accurate action." In the preceding chapter we looked at straddles and strangles as ways of catching the market's direction, regardless of which direction it is headed. While these strategies are capable of allowing a trader the ability to beat the market at its own game, they don't provide active traders with the most precise way to interact with the markets. That can actually be accomplished by understanding how to use an option contract as a hedge for your trading position.

WHAT IS HEDGE TRADING?

In futures and forex trading there are only two participants, speculators and hedgers. The speculators are out to make money from the simple change in price, whereas the hedgers are out to protect themselves from price changes. Both groups trade on the same exchange, but the key distinction between the two groups is that the hedgers actually own or will own the physical goods. Therefore, they trade the market with the willingness to lose money on the exchange in order to make it up with their actual position. That is hedge trading at its simplest.

The average retail speculator fails to grasp the potential significance that hedge trading can have for them. It is no secret that no one is 100 percent right about the market's direction, but little is done by the speculators to prepare for this eventuality. Stop loss orders, whether mental or actual, are used to stop losses, but no time is spent on how to make money when a trade turns sour. That's where hedging for speculators comes in.

A speculator can look at the market and make a conscious decision to always have a profitable position on if he is willing to concede a small loss on another position—just like the real hedgers do. This type of hedge trading doesn't require a lot of additional effort; it simply requires the willingness to take advantage of the daisy-chain effect of trading.

If you are an active trader, this may also mean that you will need to have a willingness to change your entire approach to trading. You may have to reevaluate it and become a specialist in exactly how you look at the market and what buying, selling, and protecting yourself from loss actually mean to you.

PRECISION TRADING GROUND RULES

When making the transition from a pure speculator to trading the market like a speculator, a set of ground rules must be put in place. The first ground rule is the decision to choose a trend. No matter what time frame you buy and sell in, there is an overall trend that the market is moving in. In fact, as of this writing gold, oil, and the euro had all been on a bullish trend for over four years. During that time there have been pullbacks in the market—counter-trends. Once the market reached certain plateaus the trend would resume. Therefore a conscious decision must be made to actively trade either the trend or the counter-trend.

The best choice is to actively trade the counter-trends; then an option can be purchased as a hedge on the trend. With this trading combination, you operate just like a true hedger. There are two ways to look at this trade. The first way is that you are protecting your counter-trend trades by using an option as a hedge. The second way you can look at it, which is more in tune with why the markets were developed, is that your option trade is following the trend, generating income gradually, and you are protecting that asset, almost like a true hedger's cash position, every time you are actively trading the counter-trend. No matter how you look at it, you are getting the best of both worlds, trend and counter-trend, yet as an active trader you are reducing your commission by almost 50 percent.

The average active trader is constantly buying and selling in and out of the market, attempting to catch a few ticks from a stock index, or a few pips from currencies, or a few cents from stocks—all of them attempting to outperform the market. By using an option as a hedge to follow the trend, there is no need to flip-flop between being either long or short. You are successfully placed in both positions simultaneously. Using options as a hedge is completely separate and distinct from two other option strategies—option-spot or option-futures strategies. In the next chapter we look at the option as a replacement to the stop loss order, and later we look at how to combine a cash or futures position and an option together to create a synthetic option.

Benefits

The options hedge strategy has many great benefits for the active trader; commissions can be reduced, strict trade management strategies can be followed, and trading systems can be properly tested for their viability.

Being able to reduce commissions can justify the risk management strategy alone. Active traders are constantly in and out of the market. If they are actively trading the S&P 500 or some other stock index, racking up several hundred to several thousand trades per month is not unheard-of. There is constant buying and selling pressure, with the ultimate goal of making a fixed daily amount; $500 to $1,000 per day is the typical target.

Reality smashes into any ideal goals that active traders have once they see how much they lose on the losing trades and the amount they rack up in fees and commissions. Regardless of how much or how little they pay in commissions, they can easily find themselves generating twice as much cash activity, in losses and commissions, as they take home as profits. Using an option to follow the trend requires only one commission, and the only loss involved is the erosion of premium. This saves active traders 50 percent of the commissions that they would have usually paid, along with cutting in half their potential for losses in their active trading.

Not all active traders attempt to buy and sell back-to-back. There are some traders who focus on momentum trading only, so on any given day they are only long a market or short a market. While they may not get a reduction in commissions, they will benefit from having the option playing cleanup if the momentum of the day is not in sync with the overall trend of the market.

Another key benefit is the ability to refine entry and exit signals. When the entry is limited to a specific type of situation, in this case counter-trends, trading entry signals can be honed. Whether these signals work or not will quickly become apparent without the trader needing to be wholly committed. This also allows for easier journaling of specific trading strategies.

If all of these benefits aren't enough, futures traders also have the ability to reduce their margins. Whenever they combine options to diminish their risk, regardless of how they do it, margins are reduced at the commission merchant level.

Pitfalls

Picking the right option is the largest pitfall when implementing this option hedge strategy. Years ago a British television game show, *The Weakest Link*, was imported to the United States. Losing contestants were told, "You are the weakest link!" Every time the option as a hedge strategy is proposed, those words ring in my head. The strategy is sound in both theory and practice, but the strike price of the option is essential to its success. That may mean that the average active trader may not be able to afford to use this strategy if the option is expensive or if the option exceeds the price of the underlying asset by too much.

For those active traders who focus on the Emini markets, their commissions and day trading margins can be exceptionally reasonable. As long as a trader is willing to not hold a position overnight, the margin for the Emini S&P can be as low as $250 per contract. The standard Emini S&P contract margin typically runs over $4,000, depending on volatility, when a contract is carried overnight. The day trading margin and overnight margin are tremendously different. This difference allows traders with as little as $2,000 in their accounts to trade the Emini S&P. This has to be taken into account when suggesting to active traders to use options as a hedge for their trading.

There are only two types of options that can be purchased to hedge a position, an in-the-money option and an at-the-money option. Either of these options can follow the trend effectively while the active trader executes counter-trend trades. The primary drawback is expense.

On Friday, July 11, 2008, the September Emini S&P 500 closed at 1239.75. In Table 5.1 we look at two strike prices for the front month, July, Emini S&P 500, 1235 and 1240.

Every one-point move is the equivalent of $50. This means the calls and puts range in price from $750 to $1,025. For an active trader who is enjoying a high amount of leverage in his day trading position, one option is the equivalent of three to four contracts. This can be a significant commitment of capital in a small account.

TABLE 5.1 Option Example 1

	Type	Strike	Cost	Amount
ESN8	Call	1235	20.50	$1,025
ESN8	Call	1240	18.00	$900
ESN8	Put	1235	18.50	$925
ESN8	Put	1240	15.00	$750

TABLE 5.2 Option Example 2

	Type	Month	Strike	Cost	Amount
ESN8	Call	July	1240	18.00	$1,025
ESQ8	Call	August	1240	40.75	$2,037.50

A second problem staring option hedge traders in the face is attempting to figure out exactly which month to purchase options in. In Table 5.2 the underlying futures front month is September, but the first option contract that can be purchased is in July, the next is in August, the one after that is in September.

Although the strike prices are all the same, as each month gets further and further out the built-in time value of the option plays a greater role. In fact, the call almost doubles in value from July to August and increases by more than $500 from August to September.

The same thing occurs when we look at puts in Table 5.3. The price difference between the July put and the August put is such that the latter option is almost triple in value. The price difference between the puts and calls is also pronounced. Volatility is erring on the side of caution by having the puts be slightly more expensive than the calls. This is clearly a reinforcement of a bearish view on the S&P market.

As a trader, a balancing act must be maintained among the strike price, the premium, and the expiration month. It is no secret that options expire earlier than their underlying asset counterparts. This can occur as much as a month before the underlying futures contract. Therefore, it is important to determine whether you are content with having an option as a hedge for protection in just the front month or your hedge position is meant to be set in place in a further-out month and forgotten about. The option will be more expensive, but you will be able to use it as a hedge for a lengthier period of time.

Finally, no matter whether the trader purchases an option for the front month or for a further-out month, he must balance the expense of the

TABLE 5.3 Option Example 3

	Type	Month	Strike	Cost	Amount
ESN8	Put	July	1240	15.00	$750
ESQ8	Put	August	1240	42.25	$2,112.50
ESU8	Put	September	1240	53.25	$2,662.50

option against what his day trading margins are and what the ultimate goal is in protecting himself.

Can you, the trader, use an out-of-the-money option as a hedge? If you do, the difficulty of this option as a hedge strategy becomes compounded. Not only must you pick the right strike price and month, but you must also anticipate where the market will head, as opposed to simply following the trend.

IDENTIFYING MARKET TRENDS

How successfully this technique can be implemented is 100 percent dependent on how well you can determine the trend and the counter-trend. If you are able to exploit this relationship, then all of the other dominoes fall in place. In *Winning the Trading Game* there is a detailed explanation on how to use technical analysis to determine the long-term trend of both the futures market and the forex market. To put it concisely, the 50-day moving average (MA) is a key way to be able to see whether the market is a bullish or bearish market. Once that is determined, then the work of purchasing an option that follows the long-term trend is more than halfway done.

That's when your micro technical analysis tools kick in. They help to determine entries for the counter-trend and when to exit the market once it begins to shift back and follow the trend. That is where your stops or stop limits come in. While there is no love lost between my style of trading and stops, this is one time when I wholeheartedly advocate the use of stops as part of a risk management strategy.

The function of the option as a hedge is to operate as a profit catchall. This technique is versatile for futures, spot forex, and stocks. The objective is to actively trade as you normally would, with the intent of focusing primarily on the counter-trend while your option accumulates value on the trend. Stops must therefore be used liberally to exit the counter-trend positions. There is no need to erode any of the profits that your option accumulates through losses in the counter-trend. More than enough of the premium is being eroded because of decreases in time value and intrinsic value.

This is the simplest way to exploit the insurance nature of futures and options. By working with this strategy, the everyday trader can become enlightened about the true nature of the markets and how capable they are at limiting risk when used in conjunction with one another. The level of impact that that has, coupled with the right timing, trend, and counter-trend, is both the first step and the last step of comprehending what it means to trade like a pro.

In the following examples, the trend and counter-trend are identified for the Emini S&P 500. Multiple active trader time frames are viewed along with their potential optimal returns.

Active Trader Time Frames

There is a dance between the trend and the counter-trend that cannot always be seen. By separating the market's two different directions from one another, active traders can become more effective no matter what their preferred market time frame is. In Figure 5.1 the Emini's trend is identified.

Figure 5.1 is a snapshot of the Emini S&P 500 from April 2008 to July 2008. The gray bars represent a bearish market that sits below the 50-day MA. At the beginning of June 2008 the S&P 500 crosses into the gray bars at around 1375 and ends up hitting a low of 1225 by July 11, 2008. Even if the gray bars weren't visible, there would be little dispute about the market being on a downward slide.

Swing or position traders would have most likely attempted to simply short the market once it crossed the 50-day MA. For active traders the

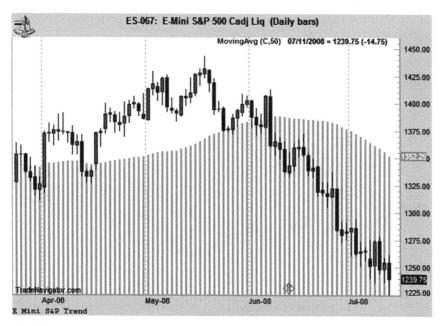

FIGURE 5.1 Emini S&P 500 Trend
Source: TradeNavigator.com © 2007. All rights reserved.

actions would be slightly different. As seen in Figure 5.1, once the market crossed the 50-day MA a put option would have been purchased as a hedge. This way the active trader could pick up any profits from the market's counter-trend moves, while simultaneously catching the moves in the overall trend in the option.

The option that was used as a hedge would accumulate a gain from 1375 to 1225, for a total of 150 points. This would allow the option hedge to accumulate almost $7,500. This would be an enhancement to any active trader's overall profits. Of course this is an ideal scenario, catching the market right when it crosses into a downward trend. As long as the market stays in the gray area, purchasing a put option is the prudent course of action.

There are numerous time frames that active traders watch in order to gain insight into the market's direction. There is a constant search for the optimum time frame, and no two traders are alike. Some of the most common short-term time frames are the 5-minute, 15-minute, 60-minute, and 4-hour charts. Once traders have established that the market's trend is down, they can identify counter-trend opportunities in each time frame.

5-Minute   In Figure 5.2 we see the 5-minute Emini S&P chart. This is one of the shortest time frames in which an active trader can pick and choose signals.

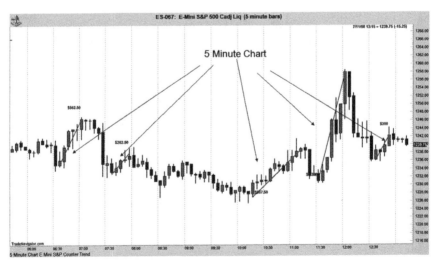

FIGURE 5.2 5-Minute Emini S&P 500 Counter-Trend
Source: TradeNavigator.com © 2007. All rights reserved.

On July 13, 2008, from 6:30 A.M. to 1:30 P.M., there were at least five different opportunities to go long in the Emini S&P 500 based on the 5-minute charts. While there also were opportunities to go short, the put option hedge is in place and there is no need to chase these short opportunities.

15-Minute   From July 11, 2008, to July 13, 2008, we can see multiple opportunities in the 15-minute Emini S&P chart. This is another tight time frame. In Figure 5.3 the long-term downward trend is starting to show itself. Yet there are at least four different opportunities to go long in the counter-trend.

60-Minute   In Figure 5.4 we see three opportunities to go long in the 60-minute chart. From July 8, 2008, to July 13, 2008, three aggressive opportunities to go long appear.

4-Hour   Beginning on June 29, 2008, we see in Figure 5.5 four different opportunities to go long.

It quickly becomes apparent that there are profits to be had in just about any time frame. As long as a trader keeps a level head about his objectives, then trading the counter-trend, with stops in place, becomes an effective strategy. As long as active traders are willing to not have their

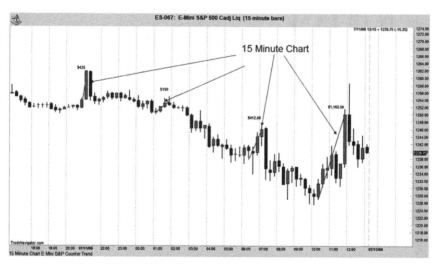

FIGURE 5.3   15-Minute Emini S&P 500 Trend
Source: TradeNavigator.com © 2007. All rights reserved.

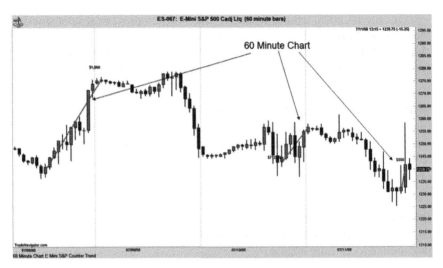

FIGURE 5.4 60-Minute Emini S&P 500 Trend
Source: TradeNavigator.com © 2007. All rights reserved

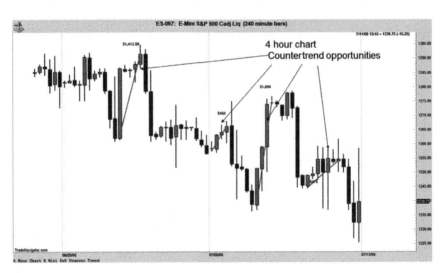

FIGURE 5.5 4-Hour Emini S&P 500 Trend
Source: TradeNavigator.com © 2007. All rights reserved

faces too close to the canvas, they can benefit from taking advantage of the long-term counter-trend.

CONCLUSION

On the Internet and at various trading expos, the Emini S&P is touted as the best market to actively trade. Many traders therefore turn to the Emini S&P to generate daily cash flow. While there is an abundance of liquidity and momentum on any given day in the S&P, the hedge strategy is not limited to the Emini S&P traders. Any market where traders are actively searching for daily or short-term profits (stocks, forex, oil, DAX, Nikkei, etc.) is fair game.

As long as all three components of this strategy are used together—the ability to identify and act on the trend, the ability to identify and act on the counter-trend, and the willingness to use a stop to exit any counter-trend as soon as it loses momentum—then the option as a hedge strategy can be effective.

CHAPTER 6

Trading with Hard Stops

F or swing traders, the object is to buy at a new low and sell at a new high or to sell at a new high and buy back at a new low. Little thought is given to whether the market is in a counter-trend trade or is a resumption of the overall trend. The object is to simply catch a move in the markets that extends beyond the intraday activity. By moving from intraday trading to daily chart trading, swing traders can increase their profit potential, but at the same time the exposure to market fluctuations increases. This exposure can come in the form of unexpected announcements, supply and demand reports, or monthly statistical reports.

Traders are constantly involved in a balancing act of wanting to catch a greater part of a market's trend while at the same time managing their risk. The objective is to be riding the wave of the market's direction on the backs of those in the know. If for some reason the signs have been misread or misinterpreted or if there has been a fundamental shift in the supply and demand of the market, the trader wants to be able to react and get out of the market as soon as possible. On an intraday trading chart, that could be a matter of seconds. On a swing trade, those seconds could translate into days. This is the bane of the swing trader: when and where to get out of a trade that isn't working, but at the same time not exiting too early, before a market makes its move. For years the tool of choice has been the stop loss order.

While in theory the stop loss order makes sense as a tool that can exit a trade when the market is going against a position, it is inherently flawed. There is a better alternative. In much the same way we used options as a hedge in Chapter 5 to protect ourselves against intraday fluctuations of the trend and the counter-trend, we are also able to use options as a type of primary or secondary stop loss in order to maintain our money management rules, without the same worries that a stop loss order invokes.

STOP LOSS ORDER

Success as a trader comes from having two distinct skill sets. The first skill set revolves around the ability to be able to pick the markets that are moving. The book *Winning the Trading Game* discussed that in depth. The second skill set involves the ability to have a realistic backup plan that you can rely on when you aren't able to pick the right direction of a market's movement. This book is designed to help you do that. It seems that for years the only backup plan for traders has been to guess where to place stops or to divine when the market will potentially turn around using a host of technical analysis tools—all of this with complete disregard for the nature of trading.

Over the years, tips and tricks have been suggested on how to get the most from a stop order, most of them conflicting. The varied wisdom has ranged from conservative to reckless:

- Place a stop order when you put in your initial order.
- Put your order in first, and then wait and put your stop order in.
- Never place your stop order in; have a mental stop.
- Use a parked stop order that you can execute at a moment's notice.
- Place a stop order at one and a half times true range to avoid getting whipsawed.
- Don't place a stop order too tight.
- Don't place a stop order too far out.

The list of sage wisdom goes on and on. Every piece of advice is a vain attempt to defeat the inherent nature of the stop loss order. Stops are a good idea. In fact, they are designed to be a circuit breaker when all else fails, and when used in that way stops are effective. However, this circuit breaker behavior is also the inherent flaw of stops. Stops are not a risk management tool; they are a panic button to help you out when all else fails.

On its web site the Commodity Futures Traders Commission defines a stop order as "an order that becomes a market order when a particular price level is reached." This is a significant definition, because it clearly points out that stop orders are a trading fiction. In fact, once they are triggered that is not the end of your trade; it is just the beginning of the end. The order is converted into a market order and once that is filled, your trade comes to an end. Until that time you are exposed to market ineffi-ciencies; whether it's floor traders, market makers, or currency dealers, you are left at their whim to fill your market order at their discretion.

There is no doubt that a stop order is a great tool, on the face of it. You execute a trade, the market moves against the trade, your stop loss order is triggered, and your trade is closed out. The problem arises when the ideal scenario meets the reality of the markets. Using a stop as your primary line of defense lacks both finesse and control, in much the same way that using a hand brake on a car is inferior to using the brake pedal during stop-and-go traffic.

Three Scenarios That Expose a Stop Loss's Weakness

Stop loss orders are simply a tool. There is nothing wrong with them when used properly and with the proper expectations. When a trader works within the confines of the ability of a stop, then the frustration of stop or-ders can be diminished. The simple fact is that when you know what to expect you can't be disappointed.

There are three situations that occur in trading that using a stop loss order can't protect you from: fast-moving markets, consolidating markets, and general shifts in supply and demand.

If the market you are trading experiences any one of these scenarios, then a stop-only approach to trading can and will backfire. In a fast-moving market the stop is triggered, turns into a market order, and you get the worst possible fill, known as slippage.

In a consolidating market, if your stop is too tight the market will hit your stop loss price, turn into a market order, and get you filled; and then the market will turn in the direction you expected all along.

If a fundamental shift in supply and demand occurs, the stop order may be a victim of being placed too far out to compensate for consolidation, and will be triggered into a market order that most likely will exceed any initial money management strategy that was set in place to help protect a trader's account principal in the first place.

The stop loss order has been promoted and marketed as a one-size-fits-all solution, and in the process it has done more harm than good.

Last Resort of a Desperate Trader

Stops, by their very nature, are a reactionary tool. They are triggered only when the worst possible scenario can occur in a trade. By that time it is really too late to do anything.

How can you realistically operate after a stop has been triggered?

If your technical indicators suggest that you reverse your position, then how do you do it without chasing the market?

If you do end up switching your market position, how can you be sure you won't be stopped out again, thereby compounding your losses?

If your technical indicators suggest that you stay in the position, how can you justify ignoring your money management rules that tell you to get out?

Loss of capital, slippage, plus the high degree of uncertainty that a stop loss comes with make it difficult for a swing trader to strictly rely on it as a risk management tool. The stop loss order can only do just that—stop loss—and it doesn't even do that all that well. Unfortunately, stopping a loss is not the same as managing the potential risk of loss. One is proactive, the other reactive. The reactive nature of a stop loss means that it is effective only in times of desperation, when the trader simply can't take the pain anymore. This is not how pros trade, and neither should you.

OPTIONS AS AN ALTERNATIVE TO THE STOP

There is no other way to say it. There is no other way to look at it. No matter how clever you are at placing a stop loss, if it is triggered that simply means that you are on the losing side of the market. This can be frustrating, particularly when swing traders thrive on the exact type of market scenarios that stops are weak in.

Swing traders deliberately seek out fast-moving markets with momentum, consolidating markets with well-defined support and resistance points, and fundamental shifts between trends and counter-trends. The goal of the swing trader is to be there at the beginning of a sudden run in the market, or to exploit the highs and lows of a sideways market just as a market consolidates, or to catch the movement of a market as it transitions from a trend to a counter-trend and vice versa. With this specialized risk comes a need to minimize exposure to being on the wrong side of the market, just in case the unexpected happens.

The use of stops only guarantees the gradual, and possibly sudden, diminishment of a swing trader's capital through slippage and trade loss. There is an alternative to using stop losses, however: options. Whereas stop losses are triggered and force you out of a trade when the market moves against you, options can be triggered into a protective mode when the market moves against them. This can be considered a hard stop.

Anyone who has ever traded realizes that no material benefit is derived from being kicked out of the market abruptly. There is the possibility that the market will turn back your way and it will cost you more in commissions and missed opportunity if you decide to jump back in. If the market doesn't turn back your way, you then have to reevaluate the potential trade and in the process miss out on the market's new direction. If a stop is set too far out, that means that your losses are compounded with excessive slippage. Having the right type of stop in place solves all of those problems.

By using an option as your stop loss order, you switch the dynamic of your interaction from one of being reactive to one of being proactive. The swing trader for once is in control of slippage, market timing, and commission expenses. No more chasing markets, no more false market breakouts, and no more missed opportunities. Well ... mostly. Depending on the size of your account and your trading objectives, options have the ability to operate as both a primary and a secondary line of defense against adverse market moves.

Using Options as a Primary Alternative

In Chapter 5 we looked at an option as a hedge that you can put in place to follow a trend or a counter-trend. Later in Chapter 8 we discuss tying an option directly to a futures or spot position in order to make it a synthetic option position. This chapter sits comfortably between these two option styles.

When a swing trader uses an option as a primary alternative to a stop loss, the intent is to reduce or diminish any exposure to loss while at the same time staying one step ahead of the market. This is directly tied into the money management plan that is already in place. Large money managers will have in place a standing risk of loss that can't exceed 2 percent of their account value, while individual traders may be more liberal, allowing as much as 5 to 10 percent of their accounts to be at risk at any given time.

It is already known that no matter how craftily a stop loss is placed, if the market gains momentum, or during a particularly volatile time in the forex market, a stop loss can be blown through and exceed any preset stop loss amount. A 2 percent loss can become a 3.5 percent loss, or a 10 percent loss can become a 13 percent loss or greater. These extra erosions of capital can quickly lead to an account becoming nontradable in a short period of time.

By contrast, an option can be purchased with a strike price that is close to, if not exactly at, a 2 percent, 5 percent, or 10 percent stop loss. Unequivocally, no matter what the market does, the strike price is fixed. The problems that plagued the stop loss order—slippage, missing out on a market's reversal, or weathering sideways activity—do not affect the protective option. This doesn't mean that the protective option doesn't have its own set of problems. The issues of premium, account size, and delta, discussed in Chapter 4, play a significant role in cutting into profits and changing the dynamics of the trade itself.

Option Premium and Your Account Size

How you use the option as a stop loss tool is dictated by your account size, the markets you trade, and your tolerance for risk. This is usually figured out in advance through your trading plan. The smaller your account, the further out-of-the-money you have to purchase your option. This can work counter to your risk management goal and in fact exceed the 2 percent, 5 percent, and 10 percent maximum account loss you may have set for yourself. In those instances you really have no choice but to use a regular stop loss order.

Those who have followed my recommendation in the past to have three times the margin for a commodity contract will typically have enough capital in their accounts to acquire a protective option. So if you consider yourself an oil trader and an oil contract's margin is $5,000, then you should have $15,000 in your margin account. If you trade spot forex, I recommend you have five times the margin for each contract. So if you purchase a euro contract that requires only $1,000, have $5,000 in the account.

Choosing the Right Strike Price for Your Option

Getting just the right option strike price can be a problem. Each futures contract has its own incremental option numbering. This can make it difficult to obtain an option that is exactly 2 percent, 5 percent, or 10 percent of your account's value.

Let's look back to our $15,000 oil trading account example. If your money management rules cap your losses to just 2 percent, then you can't risk more than $300, a 5 percent loss would be $750, and a 10 percent loss would cap you at $1,500.

Attempting to use a protective option as a hard stop will be difficult at the 2 percent and 5 percent levels. The option strike prices move only in $500 increments. This is in stark contrast to the fact that the underlying futures contract moves in 1 cent increments, which equal $10 per 1 cent move.

If you were to enter a futures oil contract at $100 per barrel, you could put a stop loss order at $300 away from your entry, at $99.70; but if you attempted to purchase a protective option, then you would have to get a strike price of $99.50. This adds an additional $200 to your protective loss.

If you attempt to stick to a 5 percent stop loss of $750, your only choice is to purchase an option with a strike price of $99.50 or $99.00. That would be either $500 or $1,000 away from your entry price. That's either $250 too little or $250 too much.

The only scenario that fits perfectly is the 10 percent ($1,500) risk of loss. If you enter an oil contract at $100, you could then purchase an option with a strike price of $98.50. This would be a perfect match, but it wouldn't make sense to readjust your entire money management strategy to make a perfect match on the strike price. If anything, it is better to err on the side of caution and go with a strike price that may represent a lesser risk of loss than a greater risk of loss.

Delta and Theta Eroding Your Premium   Chapter 4 thoroughly explored delta's and theta's effects on premium. It is important to keep in mind two facts: First, the protective option is meant to protect the overall position against loss, not necessarily to become profitable. Second, the options you will be purchasing will be out-of-the-money; therefore, they will be affected more by delta and theta than an in-the-money option.

Using Options as a Secondary Stop Loss

The second way to use a protective option is in conjunction with a stop. The closer an option is to its underlying asset, the more expensive it will be. It stands to reason that an option placed at a 2 percent loss threshold will be more expensive than an option placed at a 10 percent loss threshold. Whether because of account size, number of contracts placed on the trade, feeling a premium is too expensive, or simply looking for a way to stagger your trades, having a stop loss order in the first position and a protective option as a secondary stop loss can be an advantage.

There are three scenarios that can play out.

In the first scenario, the market is moving quickly. If a there is a tight stop loss order, say at 2 percent, then a trader can exit a losing position immediately, with some slippage. The average retail trader would then attempt to chase the market's new direction by entering a new order and quite possibly end up being whipsawed.

A more relaxing alternative is to have the stop loss order in place at 2 percent and a protective option at 5 percent or 10 percent. The stop loss order is triggered and a loss is booked into your account. Instead of chasing the market, you wait for it to come to your protective option. If the market breaks through the strike price of your protective option, your protective option begins to accumulate profits. If the market begins to turn around at or near the option strike price, you can reenter your original futures or forex position and turn it into a synthetic options position.

In the second scenario, the market is predictably bouncing between a consolidating resistance and support line. As traders we hope for the best, but we prepare for the worst with a stop loss order.

In the final scenario, the market is shifting from a counter-trend to a trend. If your trade is going in the expected direction to the contract's price, then you are trading the trend. Any pullback would be considered a counter-trend. While the market attempts to choose its ultimate direction it begins to consolidate. These consolidating markets tend to be the most difficult for stops to navigate. It is quite rare for any market to move straight up or straight down. Along the way the market will pull back. Unfortunately, you never know whether the pullback is simply a market that is consolidating or there is a fundamental shift in the market's direction. Stops treat both situations the same, so when a stop is triggered you are forced out of the market, period. There is little you can do if the market was simply consolidating and it halts its move against you and begins to move in the direction of your original position. This is known as the whipsaw effect.

CONCLUSION

Since stops are an all-or-nothing proposition, they leave little room for the market's constant consolidation and retracement behavior. This has the effect of you potentially being right about the market, but being stuck on the sidelines because you were stopped out. A well-placed option can have the opposite effect. If you place an option where you would have placed your stop, you are able to hold on to a losing futures position slightly longer. Even if the delta of the option is different from the underlying futures contract, as you lose money on the futures position the option helps offset some if not all of your losses as it gains in value. This gives you the necessary breathing room to determine whether the market is consolidating or changing.

Finally, stops have difficulty navigating fundamental shifts in the market's supply and demand. When these fundamental shifts occur, the most benign result of using a stop is some slippage, as we discussed earlier. In the worst-case scenario you could find yourself in a lock-limit market unable to get out, with the potential of losing more money than you invested. Once a market is at the lock limit, all trading is halted until the price stabilizes. Markets can be lock-limit for days on end; all the while you have little recourse and you are racking up losses at a phenomenal rate.

When it comes to trading, there are no fix-alls, simply substitutions. An option in place of a stop loss order is just that, a substitution. By comparing stop loss orders and options side by side, options clearly come out the winner in each scenario. Over the years the difficulty of using stops alone has been recognized. There is a clear alternative to using stops alone to manage losses—options—but it requires that you look at trading the same way that money managers do. Money managers look at the interdependence of futures and options contracts and the built-in risk management relationship that they have with one another to diminish their losses. By taking this approach they are able to use finesse and control to protect themselves from fast-moving markets, consolidating markets, and fundamental shifts in supply and demand, and now you can, too.

CHAPTER 7

The Markets
on a Leash

R*andom House Unabridged Dictionary* defines a leash as "to
secure, control, or restrain . . ." or "a chain, strap, etc., for controlling or leading . . .; lead."

In Chapter 6 we explored using options in place of a stop loss order.
This strategy, while having the added expense of purchasing either an in-
the-money option or an out-of-the-money option, is the simplest way of
guaranteeing that your losses won't exceed the price you enter the market
at. Whether it is a hedge position or a synthetic futures position, it is the
only efficient way to protect your trading position.

It can be difficult to afford the protective option if your account is too
small, or if the volatility of the option is too high, making it very difficult
to pay a reasonable price. That's when you have to make the decision to
control the cost of the option and make the protection affordable enough to
protect yourself. A small but important technique that puts you in control
of your trading destiny is the simple ability to sell an option in conjunction
with your synthetic futures or hedge position. This is how you put your
trade on a leash.

The combination of being long the futures, purchasing an at-the-money
or out-of-the-money put option, and selling an out-of-the-money call is
called a *collar*. The mirror opposite can be done for a short position as
well. A collar is a limited-loss, limited-profit strategy that diminishes your
overall trading expenses, while still affording you the same protection that
a protective-option-only strategy gives you.

In this chapter we look at the long collar and short collar position.
The intent is to analyze how to use them, the benefits of using them, and
the drawbacks of using them as a risk management strategy. We then

113

explore how day traders can convert their spot and CFD positions into collar trades that may help them turn their trades into long-term protective position trades.

COLLAR

A collar is partly defined by Investopedia as "a protective options strategy." This is an oversimplification of a strategy that has the ability to lock in profits, reduce risk, and improve overall returns. The strategy itself can be implemented either at the inception of a trade, when you feel that you can estimate particular levels of support and resistance, or after a trade you have executed has moved in your direction for a while and you want to lock in profits.

With a little bit of trading savvy you can expand your hold on a trade almost indefinitely. By properly managing the trade through a collar you protect yourself from sudden drops in price while catching the profits when the market moves in your anticipated direction.

Collar at the Inception of a Trade

The collar requires three components: the initial trade, long or short; an out-of-the-money option that is purchased to lock in profits, either a call or a put; and an out-of-the-money option (which sits ahead of your initial trade) that you sell. For instance, if you have a long collar trade on the euro (see Figure 7.1), you purchase a put at support, go long the market, and sell a call at some point of resistance.

If we look at an example in a different time frame, we see a run up in the value of the euro. This time we see a peak, along with an opportunity to short the market. We purchase a call, short the market, and explore the two options to sell puts. The further out-of-the-money, the lower the premium we can collect. But we also give ourselves more breathing room by not capping off our profit potential too quickly. Figure 7.2 shows an illustration of a short collar trade.

Benefits and Drawbacks   Placing a collar on at the inception of a trade can make sense in some cases; there are some key benefits, as well as drawbacks, to keep in mind.

There are three key benefits to using a collar at the inception of a trade. First, you are able to calculate your potential profit right away, whether the contract is futures, spot, SSF, or CFD. This can be comforting when

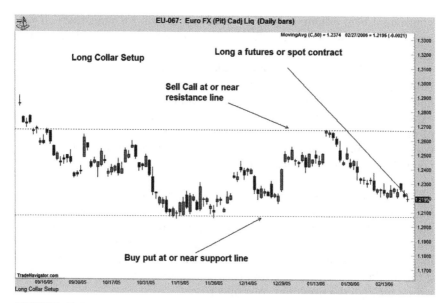

FIGURE 7.1 Euro FX
Source: TradeNavigator.com © 2007. All rights reserved.

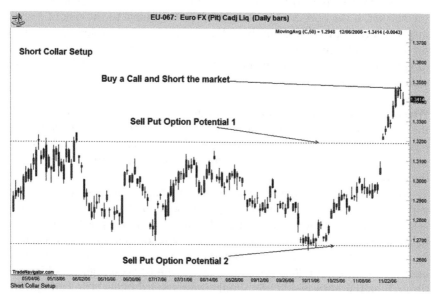

FIGURE 7.2 Euro FX Short Collar
Source: TradeNavigator.com © 2007. All rights reserved.

your intent is to adhere to a strict risk/reward ratio for your trade. If you intend to not risk more than $1 to gain $2 or $3, the potential maximum gain quickly becomes apparent.

Second, by initiating a collar trade at the beginning of a trade's execution, you are afforded some protection if the market moves against you quickly. You are essentially putting on a synthetic trade, which can be very expensive because you are purchasing an at-the-money option as a form of protection. The collar has a sold option component that allows you to collect some premium to offset the costs of the at-the-money option. While you will not cover the entire cost of your option purchase, you will be able to cover a part of your expense.

Finally, you have two distinct ways to profit. You can profit either from the trade with your primary short or long position or from your purchased option position and collect the premium. A standard trade would require you to be long or short and use a stop loss to protect you from the market moving against you. A synthetic trade will allow you to catch a market drop if the market moves against you, but a collar trade will pay you for being wrong through the premium you collect.

With all these fantastic benefits of using a collar immediately upon inception of a trade, there is one essential drawback. You make your money from picking the right market direction, not from the options. While the options are designed to protect you from various drops or pull backs in the market, if the core trade never develops, you have to the risk of losing money on the option you purchased as the time value erodes. Depending on how quickly this occurs, you could end up losing a significant amount of your principal while you wait for a trade to evolve. This is where understanding the option greeks becomes important.

When to Use a Long Collar at Inception   In Figure 7.1 we see that the euro has a well defined support line at the $1.2100 price level. In the past the euro failed to break through the $1.2680 area and created a point of resistance there. At the $1.2195 area we see an opportunity to go long the euro.

In establishing a collar position to take advantage of these key areas of support and resistance a trader can purchase a put option at $1.21. A call is sold at the resistance area of $1.27. To cap it off a long position is established at $1.2195. In Figure 7.3 we see the results of this euro collar trade.

The euro takes off and spends two months attempting to get back and break through the $1.2680 resistance level. The $1.2680 high gets blasted through as the euro heads on to make new record highs. The call option that we sold caps off profits at the $1.2680 level.

Each one-cent move in the futures contract is equal to $1,250. The long futures contract collects profits from $1.22 to $1.27; this is the equivalent

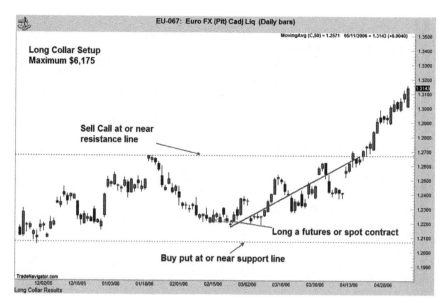

of a $6,250 profit, before option expenses. A long spot euro transaction would have made a $5,000 profit (one-cent move = $1,000).

In *Winning the Trading Game* we recommend that you never let your protective option decrease more than 50 percent of its face value. In this instance we exit the protective put when it loses $1,050, as seen in Table 7.1. This would make our long collar net us a total potential profit of $6,162.50.

When to Use a Short Collar at Inception In Figure 7.2 we took a similar euro chart, but this time we looked for a shorting opportunity. In this instance the euro has a spinning top candlestick pattern that tops out at $1.3500. A protective call can be purchased at the market's top

TABLE 7.1 Euro Long Collar Profits

	Long Futures	Buy Protective Put/Premium	Sell Call for Income/Premium Collected
Entry	$1.2195	$1.2100 (−$2100)	$1.2700 (+$900)
Exit	$1.2700	$1.2350 (+$1050)	$1.2700 (+$900)
Profit/Loss	+$6312.50	−$1,050 (50% loss)	+$900 (Don't Exit)

FIGURE 7.4 Euro Short Collar Option 1
Source: TradeNavigator.com © 2007. All rights reserved.

price of $1.35. A short can be placed at $1.3485 to catch any drop in price. Finally there are two places that an option can be sold. Option 1 finds strong support at the gap up area around $1.3200 and Option 2 finds support at the $1.27 area.

Figure 7.4 identifies the drop in the euro's price, filling the gap and actually breaking through it.

After the market drops in price the entire trade is able to accumulate a profit of $3,587.50 (see Table 7.2).

Figure 7.5 takes a longer view of the euro and attempts to place an option at deeper point of support. The strategy backfires and the market moves up aggressively, bouncing off the support we identified in Option 1.

While our futures position and call can be exited effectively, the fact that we sold an option so far out-of-the-money means that the paltry option

TABLE 7.2 Euro Short Collar Profits Option 1

	Short Futures	Buy Protective Call/Premium	Sell Put for Income/Premium Collected
Entry	$1.3485	$1.3500 (−$1,950)	$1.3200 (+$1,100)
Exit	$1.3208	$1.3335 (+$975)	$1.3200 (+$1,100)

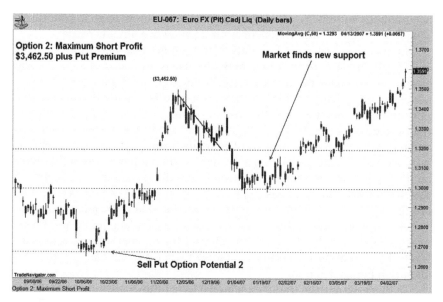

FIGURE 7.5 Euro Short Collar Option 2
Source: TradeNavigator.com © 2007. All rights reserved.

premium we collected barely offset the losses made by the protective call. Our net profit stalls out at $2,787.50. This is the danger of selling options too far out-of-the-money—the premium collected may barely make a dent in the cost of the option. Yet it still eats into the profits of the underlying profit-making position if it transitions from an out-of-the-money option into an in-the-money-option (see Table 7.3).

Collar to Lock In Profits

A slightly different approach of using a collar is similar to using an option as a stop or hedge. The trade is executed, either naked with a stop loss order or with an option as a hedge. The primary trade, long or short position,

TABLE 7.3 Euro Short Collar Profits Option 2

	Short Futures	Buy Protective Call/Premium	Sell Put for Income/Premium Collected
Entry	$1.3485	$1.3500 (−$1,950)	$1.2700 (+$300)
Exit	$1.3208	$1.3335 (+$975)	$1.2700 (+$300)
Profit/Loss	+$3,462.50	−$975 (50% loss)	+$300 (Don't Exit)

accumulates a profit. You feel that the market has more to go in your direction, but you don't want to risk everything you have already made.

In this case a trader has only a few choices at his disposal. If he uses a moving stop to lock in profits, the usual problems of slippage and attempting to chase the market arise. If he attempts to convert an option hedge into a moving option synthetic, then he is constantly fighting two phenomena simultaneously: the loss in option premium value for the initial protective option that is sold off while its intrinsic value is declining, and the high cost of constantly replacing the former options with declining intrinsic value with the purchase of new at-the-money options that have an increasing intrinsic value. Eventually the difference in value between the two option contracts has to be made up somewhere and they end up eroding most, if not all, of the profits accumulated in the primary position.

A happy medium is the collar. A collar can replace an option hedge or stop loss order that is no longer relevant for the market's current price levels. Figure 7.6 shows a prime example of when a collar can take over for an option hedge position.

In this instance the trader executed a long futures position by purchasing oil at $74.13 and underneath that, an option put is purchased at $72.50. This put is slightly out-of-the-money and costs $3,300. Depending on how you exited the option you could potentially lose only 50 percent, or $1,650 of the initial option.

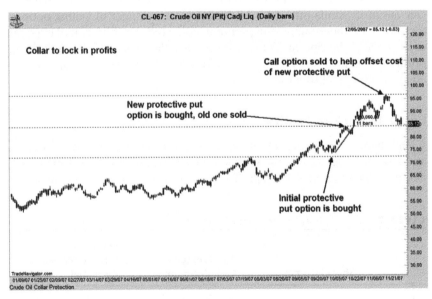

FIGURE 7.6 Crude Oil Collar Protection
Source: TradeNavigator.com © 2007. All rights reserved.

TABLE 7.4 Crude Oil Collar Protection

	Long Futures	Original Put Hedge Premium	Collar Protective Put Premium	Collar Sold Call Premium Collected
Entry	$74.13	$72.50 (−$3,300)	$84.50 (−$5,010)	$96.50 (+$1,710)
Exit	$96.50	$78.50 (+$1,650)	$96.50 (−$5,010)	$96.50 (+$1,710)
Profit/Loss	+$22,310	−$1,650(50% loss)	−$5,010 (Expire)	+$1,710 (Don't Exit)

The subsequent protective put that is bought as part of the collar is significantly more costly. In Table 7.4 we see that an at-the-money put costs $5,010 to purchase at a strike price of $84.50, which is where the market broke resistance. In the meantime, a call is sold at around the double top, hovering at the $96.50 area for $1,710. This collected premium of $1,710 is used to offset the losses of the first option hedge that was exited, giving a net difference in price between the option hedge that lost money and the premium collected of +$60.

See the dynamics of the final trade in Figure 7.7. The underlying futures have a gross profit of $22,310. The loss on the collar's put totals $4,950 (the premium of $5,010 minus the $60 left over from the sold call). This brings the collar trade to a grand total of $17,360 in profits.

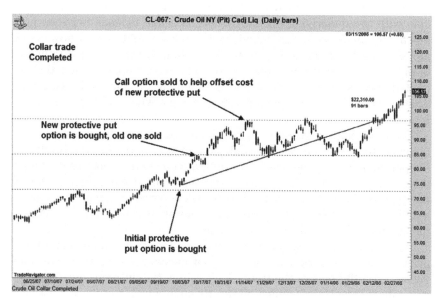

FIGURE 7.7 Completed Collar Trade
Source: TradeNavigator.com © 2007. All rights reserved.

Benefits and Drawbacks   By using a collar trade to lock in your profits, in this instance you protected a little over $10,000 in profits. On the other hand, you had to put up $5,000 in order to achieve this. Coupling this with an option hedge strategy may not be the best of all worlds because the option premium you collected is eroded by the value you lose in the option you purchased. The question to ask is whether the risk is worthwhile. Did you risk one to gain two? The answer is a resounding yes.

Because of the collar, by spending $5,000 on an option, you were able to double your profits from $10,000 to over $20,000. You were also able to make twice as much as the risk. Constantly being aware of your money management and what is at stake makes a collar like this worthwhile.

GENERAL COLLAR PITFALLS

Collar trades are not a panacea for all the world's trading ills. They have some serious flaws to be watched and monitored. You need to pay attention to the value of your options to determine whether they are too far out-of-the-money or too close. You also need to be concerned about expiration of the options to the underlying contract and whether you should be risking accumulated profits at all when making trading decisions.

The collar trade is heavily reliant on options and how well they coincide with the underlying position. There is a fine balance between how much premium can be collected on the option sold versus how much money must be spent on the protective option. If the collected premium is only a fraction of the value of the purchased option, then the unlimited risk associated with it and the capping of your underlying contracts profits must be weighed carefully against what you hope to gain in return.

In the scenarios presented in this chapter, each time an option was sold the collected premium was the equivalent of at least one-third the value of the potential loss on the protective option. You should consistently target this amount in your trading, while at the same time attempting to achieve a one-for-two risk ratio when it comes to risk and reward goals. This can be a difficult balancing act, but it must be consistently attempted to achieve the maximum benefit from using a collar.

Couple the price balancing act with the fact that options can expire prior to the underlying contract and that means there must be constant vigilance on the part of the trader in watching the different moving parts of a collar. Target profits must be strictly maintained, and there must be a willingness to hold on to the underlying contract until expiration to cover the costs of a potential sold in-the-money option occurring. For the retail trader who is intent on trading like the professionals, monitoring multiple bits of information simultaneously is a juggling act that is well worth the effort, as long as your principal is safe.

DAY TRADERS

There is nothing more important to a day trader than being flat the market at the end of the day. No matter the circumstances (win, lose, or draw), making sure that no capital is at risk of being exposed to overnight market gaps defines what day traders are all about. This attitude is both good and bad. The good is that it keeps traders focused on their activities, making sure they take no opportunity for granted as well as teaching them the discipline to exit losing trades quickly and efficiently. The bad is that many winning market decisions are cut off at the knees.

By ending your trading decisions during the day, large trends are being ignored. In spite of what random walk theorists propose, the market has a memory. What occurs today affects what will happen tomorrow. This effect is particularly felt when traders are involved in markets that deal with macro-economic influences, such as currencies and stock markets. Yet the two most commonly day traded or actively traded markets are currencies and stock indexes.

No one would argue that the Dow Jones has steadily increased in the past 20 years, nor would they argue that the euro has made a steady beeline up in value since its inception. Nevertheless, the insistence on day trading these markets negates the fact that there has been more value that has been achieved by buying and holding these particular markets for the long haul. This is in sharp contrast to attempting to scalp profits on the short and long side on a daily basis while simultaneously losing money because of predictive mistakes.

There is a reason why weathermen can predict the weather two months from now, but can't tell you precisely what it will be like on any given day. There are patterns that present themselves from a bird's-eye view that simply can't be seen when your face is pressed against the canvas. This is where collar trading comes in. Day and active traders can convert their winning trading decisions into something more than just a hit and run. They can use options to protect their downside risk as they go for a longer-term trending profit opportunity while having the market pay for their protection by collecting premiums.

At any given time a day trader or active trader can exit the primary trade, but there won't be a requirement that they do it. Worrying about losing everything in case the market gaps overnight against your position becomes a feeling of the past. Active traders can have an option in place to protect them and sell an option to collect a premium to offset the costs. A collar strategy, when compared to the actual amount of losses and commissions that can accumulate during day trading, is a small outlay of time and money in order to open up more profit-making opportunities. This can be an effective way for active traders to catch major trends in addition to the day-to-day fluctuations that they attempt to scalp.

Spot Forex Traders

Spot forex traders are some of the most volatile traders around. With leverage as high as 500 to 1 in some instances and penalties for holding positions overnight, spot forex traders are constantly in and out of the market. Trading under such extreme pressure is not for everyone. The majority of traders who are forced to operate like this actually end up making unnecessary mistakes and burning through their principal. Only by stepping back from the canvas of active trading can spot forex traders truly see the big picture.

Here we take two examples of the euro. The first example is in Figure 7.8. This is part of one day, 6/4/2008, of the euro's market activity using a 5-minute chart.

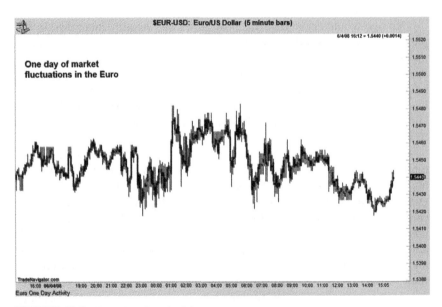

FIGURE 7.8 Euro One Day Activity
Source: TradeNavigator.com © 2007. All rights reserved.

Although the market moves with extreme highs and lows, no real discernible market direction jumps out at you. Large swings in bullish and bearish activity present various types of trading opportunities at different times. Yet this daily chart is like peeking through a keyhole. It doesn't present the fact that the euro has moved almost 80 cents since it began trading. It doesn't give you an idea of whether you are trading a trend or a counter-trend. Nor does it indicate, with any sort of reasonable expectation, the amount of momentum that the market will follow through with on the next day.

In Figure 7.9 we can clearly see that the market has had at least four definitive directions from 2/2008 to 5/2008, in sharp contrast to the erratic activity of the daily charts. In Chapter 5 we explored the option as a hedge in depth for the spot forex market and stock index trading. To make the option hedge for both of these commonly day traded markets even more effective, the strategy can easily be converted into a collar strategy to cover your option expenses. In today's sophisticated trading environment, every little advantage that you can get becomes increasingly important; this is that advantage for the active trader.

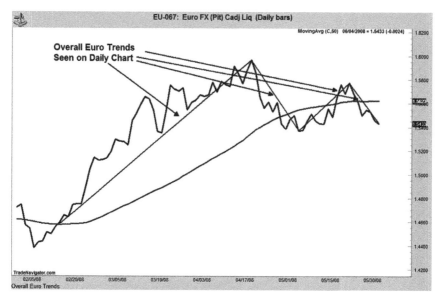

FIGURE 7.9 Euro Overall Activity
Source: TradeNavigator.com © 2007. All rights reserved.

CONCLUSION

The collar trade is not perfect. Like many of the strategies presented throughout the book, it has positives and negatives. Unlike many of the strategies in the book, it has a simple way of strengthening an opportunity while reducing your overall exposure. It can be applied in multiple situations with varying degrees of versatility. As a retail trader becomes more skilled in how the markets interact with one another, this particular strategy will become second nature.

CHAPTER 8

Replacing Traditional Options with Synthetic Options

O ption trading can be very liberating for individual traders. Options offer traders the opportunity to have unlimited profit potential with limited risk. No matter who you are, small trader or money manager, if you can limit your risk up front it becomes more comfortable to take the risk. Options have the ability to provide a high level of comfort. There is simply no misunderstanding what you are getting into when you purchase an option. If you invest $400 to purchase a call or a put, your risk is limited to the $400—no more than that, but possibly less if you sell the option early. This is not the case when it comes to all investment products.

Spot forex, stock, or futures trading cannot afford you the same protection that options can. A wrong decision in any one of these markets and your losses can mount up quickly. The usual stop losses or stop limits cannot protect you from slippage or gap ups or gap downs in price. Stop losses or stop limits cannot protect you from limit up days or limit down days. Nor can they protect you from fundamental changes in a market's supply and demand. In the end, no matter what money management goal you have in mind, when you trade spot forex, stocks, or futures you have to be willing to accept that one bad trade has the potential to wipe out your entire account, and in the case of futures and trading stocks on margin, your losses can actually exceed your account value.

However, while options can limit your risk to the premium paid, by no means are they perfect. They have two main problems: choosing the right strike price and managing volatility. Although the risk may be limited, success is predicated on the ability to pick the right strike price. The risk of an option is limited to what is invested, but in order to truly benefit from purchasing an option, a trader must be an expert at seeing the future. However it is done, a trader must pick the exact price that he believes the market will not only reach, but exceed, on a certain date. This is known as the strike price.

Choosing the right strike price is difficult, to say the least. A trader who is clever enough to choose the current market price is penalized. Buying an option at the current market price is known as buying at-the-money. Typically, at-the-money options are more expensive and have a tendency to be adversely affected by the second problem mentioned earlier, volatility. If the trader makes a decision to buy an out-of-the-money option, then the trade-off is paying a cheaper premium for a strike price that may likely never match up with the underlying asset's price.

Options are derivatives of an underlying asset. This means that they derive all of their value from another more important asset. By themselves they actually have no value and thus would not exist. This leads to a complex price relationship between the option's premium and the underlying asset's increase or decrease in value.

Various types of option styles exist, but for the purpose of this book we are strictly addressing American-style options. As a rule of thumb, American-style options grant the holder the right, but not the obligation, to buy or sell the underlying asset at any time. This simple fact increases or decreases the perceived demand for the underlying asset, which can affect the price of the option, regardless of what the strike price is or how close its price is to the underlying asset's price. This tenuous relationship has led to many traders, retail and professional alike, to simply not be comfortable with buying options. The difficulty of having to calculate the volatility, or theta, of the options (we discussed the greeks earlier, in Chapter 4), and then having to trade the volatility, independent of the actual price moves, can simply make option trading unappealing.

There is a third alternative, an alternative that couples the limited risk of options with the free-flowing opportunity of being in the actual underlying asset. This third alternative also has the unique ability to let a trader leg out of his position and profit from a market's move regardless of where it goes, up or down. This third alternative is known as the synthetic option. It successfully combines the best of all trading worlds.

SYNTHETIC OPTION VERSUS STANDARD OPTION

Synthetic options come in one of two flavors, synthetic calls or synthetic puts. They each are designed to simulate a standard call or put option without the drawbacks. A synthetic call is simple to initiate. A long position is first established in a spot forex market, futures market, or stock market; then an at-the-money put is purchased to protect the long position against any downside risk. A synthetic put requires that a short position be initiated first and an at-the-money call is purchased to protect the short position from any sudden moves to the long side. They are one of the most underused risk management tools available.

Throughout this book different ways to use options have and will be introduced. The two strategies of using options as a hard stop or using options as a hedge are distinct from the synthetic option because of one factor, the use of an at-the-money option. The at-the-money option is an essential component. While it may be more expensive to purchase an at-the-money option, it establishes the necessary maximum protection for the long or short position.

The Greeks and Synthetic Options

When trading a standard option, there is the constant stress of the greeks. In Chapter 4 we looked at delta, theta, and vega. The delta assesses how much the value of an option moves in relation to its underlying asset. No matter how successful the option, it will rarely move dollar for dollar with its underlying asset. This is not a problem for synthetic options. Since one side of the synthetic option is the actual asset, delta does not play a factor when the synthetic option moves into-the-money.

The greek value theta measures the time value left in a standard option. Since options have finite time until expiration, the more time you have until they expire the more valuable they can be, regardless of the strike price. As every day gets closer and closer to expiration, the time value erodes and the option decreases in value proportionate to the time it has left. With a synthetic option you can eliminate the time value completely. If one leg of the synthetic option is a share of stock, spot forex contract, or contract for difference (CFD), there are no time limits on when you have to exit or how many times you have to roll the contract over. Therefore, there is no built-in time value to actually lose in the position.

Finally, the third greek component, vega, was created to measure implied volatility. It measures how much an option's price will increase or decrease depending on an option's level of demand. Understanding and using vega is great when determining what strike price to purchase for an option. Volatility is everything when it comes to options trading. The lack of volatility in any particular option can be so detrimental as to make even a successful strike price be worthless because no one is interested in purchasing it.

Vega does not have an impact on synthetic options. There is no secondary market of volatility that has to be monitored or followed. If the market is moving up, your synthetic long position is gaining in value; if the market is moving down, your synthetic short position is gaining in value.

Delta, theta, and vega are just a few of the greeks that have an impact on option pricing. There are other greeks that are also followed religiously by traders who buy and sell options. None of these greek calculations directly apply to a synthetic option position. In fact, any attempt to follow the greeks for a synthetic option most likely is a waste of time.

Strike Price, Premium, and Synthetic Options

When you purchase an option, you must decide whether you are going to purchase an in-the-money, at-the-money, or out-of-the-money option. Depending on which option you purchase, you will pay either an expensive or a low-cost price for your premium. The price that is paid for the option premium plays a significant role in how successful an option can be in the long run.

The further out-of-the-money your option is, the less premium you pay. At the same time, the further out-of-the-money the option strike price is, the less likely it will be for the underlying asset to reach that price. If the underlying asset does move in the direction of the strike price, there is a missed profit opportunity that occurs due to the difference between where the underlying asset started from and when it reaches parity with the option's strike price. On top of that, even after the asset and the option strike price do reach the same value, the option does not become profitable until after the underlying asset exceeds the value of what was paid on the option premium. All of this activity takes time, which, as we learned through the greeks, options really don't have much of.

This what-if scenario then forces traders to assume that in order to be successful in options trading, the more money that is paid on the premium the better off they are. An expensive premium means that the option is either at-the-money or in-the-money, but this does not necessarily make it better than an out-of-the-money option. The moment an underlying asset begins to move against an in-the-money or at-the-money option, the value begins to decrease rapidly. Just like an out-of-the-money option, breakeven is the premium plus the strike price of the in-the-money or at-the-money option. This means that as a trader you already start your trade in the red when you purchase your option, and any move against you simply digs you a deeper hole.

For the most part, synthetic options do not have to deal with premium and strike prices in the same fashion as standard options. Since the underlying asset is the primary driving force behind all of the activity, the initiated position is at-the-money right from the start. There is no premium that is being eroded, nor is there any set strike price that needs to be hit before any money is made. In fact, the ideal scenario when putting together a synthetic option is to see the protective option's premium erode in value. That's when you know you have chosen the right side of the market.

However, when the premium erosion of the protective option does kick in, it can be a double-edged sword. Every dollar you lose in the protective option is subtracted directly from every dollar you make in the primary position. If the protective option is not monitored and acted upon immediately, the synthetic option has the potential to mirror a standard option. This means that your profits won't really kick in until the premium of the protective option is covered 100 percent. This could end up defeating your purpose for executing the synthetic option in the first place: control.

The Elegance of a Synthetic Option

A standard option has one risk management objective, to limit loss to the premium paid. That's it. It is not designed to follow the market's rhythm or flow. When you are wrong, your trade ends. For a synthetic option, things are not quite the same. Being wrong is just the beginning of something great.

Whenever a trade begins to move against a standard option or regular position, there are two things to consider. First, has there been a fundamental shift in supply and demand that is fueling this shift in the market's direction? Second, how long will this movement last against my position—is it a minor correction or a long-term shift?

For a standard option or regular position trader, if there has been a fundamental shift in supply and demand, then the position will most likely expire worthless (if it's an option) or accrue heavy losses (if it's a regular position). For an option trader, even a minor correction might as well be a long-term shift in supply and demand. With time against the option trader's position, every day that the trade passes through a correction phase is another day closer to losing everything.

By themselves, regular positions and options have a hard time with reacting to change. While all kind of crutches can be used to minimize the losses of a regular position or a trader can resign himself to losing his premium, there is another side to this story. Synthetic options take the best of both worlds by combining protection with instantaneous reaction.

A synthetic option combines the fast-paced movements of a regular position with the limited risk protection of an option, then adds in the ability to switch trading directions instantaneously. These three strengths are built right into the trading strategy.

If the market is having a minor correction, the protective option is there to collect value until the market turns back around. If there has been a fundamental shift in supply and demand, the losing position can be released and the protective option can easily pick up the slack without being perceived as chasing the market. These strengths are automatically recognized by the clearing firms; that is why they give synthetic option traders low margin rates on their futures positions.

Stop losses can't reverse your position at the drop of a dime. Limit orders can't. Even standard options fail in this respect. To trade successfully over the long run you will need to be able to have the prescience to change your market positions even before the market knows where it's going. By combining a futures contract or cash contract with an option to create a synthetic position, this is done for you automatically.

This strategy alone puts you in the advanced class as if you were hedger or trading professional. Trading with a synthetic reinforces your understanding of the interrelationship of the markets and how to hedge. This is a significant tool that places you ahead of the competition.

Synthetic Option Drawbacks

No matter how great the benefits are, when it comes to trading synthetic options there are still some drawbacks. The first drawback is the fact that it is capital intensive. The option must be purchased up front and the margin or cash for the position must be put in place. This means that you essentially have two trading positions at the same time.

Another drawback is the erosion of the protective option. Even though your profits are made by the primary position, the protective option is still subject to the same general problems of all options, time decay and volatility. Whatever money you spend on your protective option's premium has a direct effect on your overall profits. Therefore, it is important to maintain constant vigilance on the protective option to make sure you are getting the maximum value out of the trade. The general rule of thumb mentioned in *Winning the Trading Game* is not to allow a loss of greater than 50 percent of your premium. It can be even less than that if you are certain of the market's direction.

A third problem is the impact that the losing futures or cash position has on the overall trade. While losses mount $1 at a time, the maximum that the protective option can cover is approximately 80 cents of that (effects of delta), even if it is in-the-money. This is important to understand when attempting to determine how effective the protection can be. Therefore, the synthetic option cannot be considered a panacea for all trading ills.

A fourth problem is the timing of option expiration versus its same-month futures counterparts. When marrying the put to the futures or cash position, the option's expiration date is a key factor. If the option is purchased in the same month as the futures contract, then the option expires three weeks to a month prior to the futures contract. If it is not done properly, you could be left with either exiting your trade early or protecting your trade with a stop or limit order earlier than you expected.

The only alternative to purchasing an option in a near or front month is to purchase an option with a further-out expiration date. Yet this alternative has its own consequences. As we discussed earlier, an option has two values built in, intrinsic and time value. Therefore, an option purchased in a further-out month has more time value built into it. This makes it more expensive and more susceptible to changes in volatility.

Finally, a balance must be struck rather than having an all-or-nothing attitude when it comes to synthetic options that work against you. There is a school of thought, with this and all of the other risk management strategies, that when the primary position begins to move against you the entire trade should be scrapped. There is another school of thought that the trade can be legged out of, keeping the winning position and letting the bad position go.

If the trade is legged out of, then traditional forms of risk management, such as stops or stop limits, have to be put in place. Couple this with the loss of the special margin rates you may be getting from the clearing firm, and it may not be favorable to leg out. Legging out of a position also changes the dynamics of the trade. Where it may have been comfortable to put on a swing trade or a position trade with the synthetic option, if it is converted to a standard position the trading time frame will have to be changed.

How you tackle these drawbacks to synthetic options is a testament to your mettle as a trader. Whether it is the expense of the options, the erosion of the option value, the effects of delta, option expiration, or legging out the position to capture the profitable side of a market's move, it is the trader who will ultimately decide on how to best use a synthetic option for maximum benefit. Typically, during this discovery process, the opportunities of synthetic options will outweigh the drawbacks.

WHEN TO USE A SYNTHETIC OPTION

A synthetic option is both a subtle and a powerful tool. It is not meant to be taken lightly. It is simple to use and its nature lends it to be most useful to swing traders. If a market appears to have reached its absolute low or high, then a synthetic position can be put in place just in case the market doesn't follow through on its turnaround in a new direction. As the trade progresses, the synthetic position can be closed out at the end of the market's move.

Another place a synthetic option can be helpful is when the market is bumping against certain levels of resistance and support, with an eye to the potential that the market may break through. Traditionally, if the market did not break through resistance or support, a stop loss would be the only tool getting you out of the position. Instead, the protective option is there just in case the market fails its breakout. The synthetic option is truly a subtle way of attempting to outsmart the market while covering all your bases.

In the next few examples we will look at breakouts and support and resistance patterns, before and after, in order to get an idea of how best to use synthetic options.

Synthetic Calls

To reiterate, a synthetic call involves the simultaneous actions of going long a market and buying an at-the-money put in order to protect the position. We will first look at how a synthetic call can be applied to a breakout market in gold, and then we will find a point of support in the oil market and use a synthetic call to establish a trade.

Breakout Example   In Figure 8.1 we see that gold prices began an aggressive rally to the long side after failing to break through $850. The market is so strong that it rallies for five days in a row and breaks through the

FIGURE 8.1   Gold Before
Source: TradeNavigator.com © 2007. All rights reserved.

TABLE 8.1 Comparison of Choices

	Synthetic Call Option	Long Futures	Call Option
Premium	$1,830 (put)	$0	$2,030

50-day moving average (MA). Both of these signals are bullish. There is resistance at $950, and after that it is at $1,000. To not miss out any further on this aggressive move up, we initiate a synthetic call.

We purchase a put option as close to the money as possible at $930. The cost of the put is $1,830. The long gold futures contract is added to complete the synthetic call for a spread margin rate of $1,000 (spread and SPAN margin rates will vary from brokerage and futures commission merchant [FCM] rates), instead of $4,455. The total synthetic position requires a commitment of $2,830.

This is $1,625 less than an outright futures contract and is $800 more than an at-the-money standard call option (see Table 8.1).

The only way to make the long gold futures and call option work is to put stops to protect them in case this gold break turns out not to be sustainable. In Figure 8.2 we see this new rally stall and then collapse below the 50-day MA. It attempts to get above the 50-day MA, but the bulls simply cannot get their footing. The price eventually hits a low of $866, right around previous support.

FIGURE 8.2 Gold After
Source: TradeNavigator.com © 2007. All rights reserved.

The put option gains a profit from $930 to $866 for a total of $64. If the long futures contract is exited when the market crosses back below the 50-day MA around $910, the position nets a total of a $44 gain, which would net the synthetic call holder approximately $4,000, give or take a few hundred dollars based on delta changes.

This is a prime example of how a trader can attempt to catch the momentum of a breakout and actually get caught at or near the top. Nothing was done wrong technically, but the underlying fundamental supply and demand factors simply could not sustain the move. A standard long-oriented position (futures or call option) that simply followed the technical analysis would have simply lost money.

Bouncing Off of Support   In Figure 8.3 we take a look at the crude oil market as it finds support around $85 per barrel.

This is the third time that the crude oil market has come down to this price level. The prior two times the market bounced up and either broke through the 50-day MA or at least hit the 50-day MA. The Relative Strength Index (RSI) is showing that the market is oversold, and the price itself is sitting on the lower Bollinger band. These all point to the potential that it could be a turnaround to the long side.

Despite all of these technical analysis positives, three glaring negatives stick out like sore thumbs. First, the market is having a down day; therefore, any long move is preemptive of the market's actual move. Second,

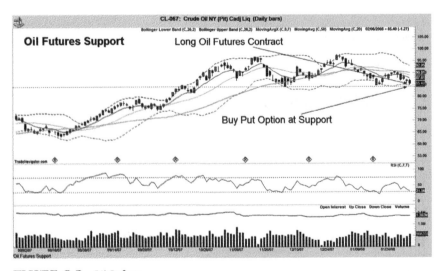

FIGURE 8.3   Oil Before
Source: TradeNavigator.com © 2007. All rights reserved.

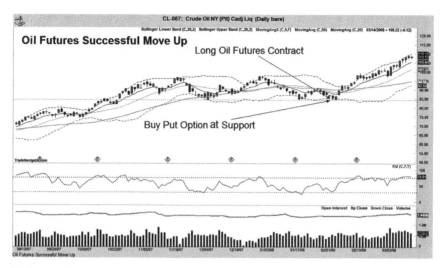

FIGURE 8.4 Oil After
Source: TradeNavigator.com © 2007. All rights reserved.

neither the 9-day nor the 20-day MA is showing any signs of turning around. Third, the 50-day MA, while fairly tight, is at least five bars away as indicated by the last time the market failed to break the 50-day MA.

By taking advantage of the indicators early, a synthetic call makes the most sense just in case the market drops like a stone.

In Figure 8.4 our early assessment is rewarded. The market turns around and in three days breaks through the 50-day MA and doesn't look back. It makes a beeline from $85 per barrel to $110 per barrel. This time the synthetic call costs us money. Whereas in the gold example the protective put became an asset when the market collapsed, the put we used for the oil synthetic option turned into a liability immediately.

In Table 8.2 we can see that the capital that was committed to the synthetic call came out to about $7,700; while less than the actual futures margin of $9,788, it is more expensive than a call option by $3,310.

This is an example of the greeks rearing their ugly heads. Since the market was moving downward when the original synthetic call was

TABLE 8.2 Comparison of Choices

	Synthetic Call	Long Futures	Call Option
Premium	$5,200 (put)	$0	$4,390
Margin	$2,500	$9,788	$0

initiated, the put option turned out to be more expensive than the call option. By the time the market moves up to the 50-day MA at $90 per barrel the put option should have dropped in value by $5,000 (every $1 move is equal to $1,000). The delta, intrinsic value, and time value will each play a role in how much and how fast the put will lose value. Nevertheless, it is important to note how quickly an at-the-money option can lose value once the market begins to move in the direction of the primary trade.

Had a call or an outright futures contract been purchased at the time, none of the standard option problems could have become an issue. Nor would the profits from the primary position been eroded by the losses of the put. This is the trade-off for operating with a synthetic position. It is there for the just-in-case scenario. The loss on the option is a cost of doing business. That is why set rules of when and why you will get out of the losing side of your synthetic option become paramount to your long-term success.

Synthetic Puts

Synthetic puts face the same challenges that synthetic calls face. In this instance a synthetic put is comprised of buying a call and shorting the market. When the market moves in the direction that the trader wants, the protective call option will be afflicted by loss. When the market moves in the direction that the trader doesn't want, the protective option will gain. This is the nature of the synthetic option. Exiting the losing trade quickly will test the prowess of any trader.

Failure to Break Out   In Figure 8.5 we take a different approach. The primary trade is a spot euro transaction. We use a futures call option to protect against any sudden moves to the upside. The futures options, as of this writing, are more liquid than the spot euro options and ultimately more reliable.

The top half of the figure is the spot euro contract. The market has penetrated the 50-day MA, confirming weakness.

In Figure 8.6 the euro currency finds support at $1.34 and begins to turn around. Eventually it hits the 50-day MA on the way up. This is definitely the cue to exit the spot euro position. A small loss is accumulated while the market moves sideways. The call option gains value from $1.36 to $1.40, netting 4 cents on the option position and bringing in approximately $5,000 in profits.

This example is simply meant to show you that the synthetic call can be implemented in any format. Even if there are no benefits to be gained on a decreased margin rate, it does not mean that a protective option cannot pick up the slack if the market moves against your primary position.

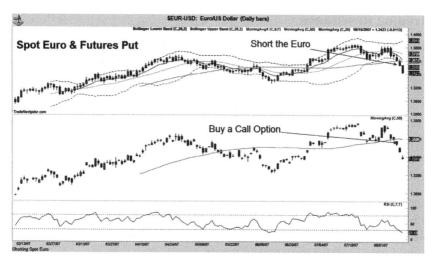

FIGURE 8.5 Euro Before
Source: TradeNavigator.com © 2007. All rights reserved.

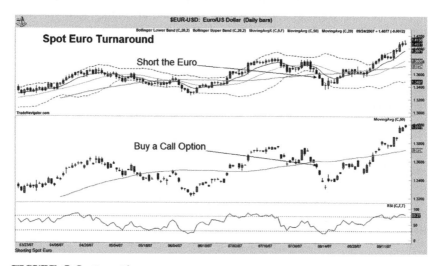

FIGURE 8.6 Euro After
Source: TradeNavigator.com © 2007. All rights reserved.

Trading Resistance

The S&P 500 in Figure 8.7 is coming off of a triple top. The RSI is turning down, indicating a collapse from the market being overbought. The 50-day MA is fast approaching the price. Everything is indicating a possible breakthrough to the short side.

This market can be attacked either as a full-size contract or as an Emini contract. However it is tackled, the mechanics are the same. A call option is purchased at 1570 and the market is shorted at 1572. A two-point gap dictated by the option pricing puts you as close to an at-the-money option as you can possibly get.

With this market our profit target is obvious: the point of support at 1526. This would give the trade 46 points in profit on the short position. For a full-size contract, that translates into a profit of $11,500, minus whatever we could potentially lose on the call position. An Emini S&P 500 contract would net $2,300 for the same 46 points.

The spread margin for a full-size contract can be as low as a few thousand dollars compared to a full margin of $22,500. In order to get the maximum profit, it may be worthwhile to trade the full-size contract as a synthetic call and tap into the spread margin rates instead of the Emini S&P 500. The ability to implement this type of strategy is 100 percent dependent on how flexible your brokerage will be. It would also mean that you may not be able to unmarry the option and the contract, even if the option is

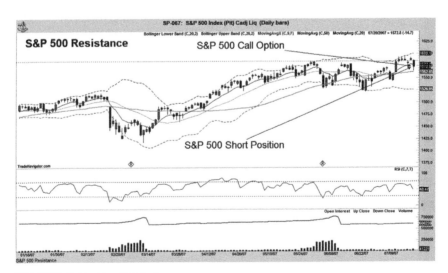

FIGURE 8.7 S&P 500 Before
Source: TradeNavigator.com © 2007. All rights reserved.

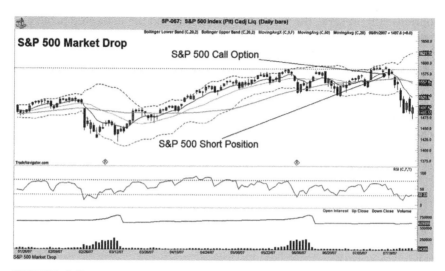

FIGURE 8.8 S&P 500 After
Source: TradeNavigator.com © 2007. All rights reserved.

losing money, without getting slapped with a margin call to hold on to the position.

In Figure 8.8 the S&P 500 not only hits the first target of 1526, it drops even further to a low of 1475. This is a perfect example of the type of windfall that can occur when the rules of a trading system are adhered to. The complete drop from 1572 to 1475 represents almost a doubling in the profit opportunity.

CONCLUSION

There are benefits to using synthetic options for both swing and position traders. There is the flexibility of the trade, the superiority over volatility, and the elimination of the strike price. Synthetic options simply have a way of outshining their traditional option counterparts, particularly when there are clear signs that the market is about to break out, either into a rally or into a collapse.

Synthetic options have overcome the limitations of time decay and intrinsic value as well. They leave the nasty greek calculations that pertain to these elements in the dust. The synthetic option has the power to liberate and protect your trading both at the same time. This is an unprecedented leap in the world of risk management. The trade is protected from downside risk, margins are cheaper for the futures traders, and the synthetic options still preserve the limited loss function and the unlimited profit potential of standard options.

No matter what the drawbacks to synthetic options are, they have the ability to even the playing field between retail and professional traders in one fell swoop. How a trader handles this newfound footing is entirely dependent on what his midterm and long-term goals are. The more realistic his expectations are in understanding what profit and loss truly mean, the easier it will be for him to adapt his style of trading to the hedged trading that synthetic options represent.

CHAPTER 9

Everything in
Its Season

I f it can be said that one concept in this book has most influenced every seasoned trader's idea of what risk management can be like, that concept would be spread trading. The idea of seasonal spread trading has been around since the inception of the commodities exchanges in the United States. Based on the dual impact of storage and planting, seasonal spread trading has greatly influenced the way all types of traders, retail and commercial, interact with various commodities. The concept is very well promoted, and had I not discovered the concepts behind seasonal spread trading this book would not have been written.

There is a dark side to seasonal trading. Companies run radio advertisements and late night infomercials touting seasonal trading opportunities, without the spread component. These advertisements hyping up seasonal opportunities are intended to create a sense of urgency.

As harvest season approaches, you will see ads focusing on droughts or floods that could affect corn crop yields. As summer approaches, there will be ads that are intended to make us believe that American summer drive-time behavior is a new phenomenon, although it is well known that gasoline prices historically have increased during summer months. Commercials also promote natural gas prices when winter storms hit the northeastern United States. Other naturally occurring trading phenomena are promoted but rarely understood. While all of these occurrences are based on historical, well-known facts, the actual seasonal opportunities rarely materialize the way they are promoted.

Seasonal trading has gotten such a bad rap that licensed NFA brokers are legally required to tell their clients that seasonal trades cannot be relied

143

upon when making decisions. The clever statement used is "Past results are not indicative of future returns." Therefore, if you decide to take advantage of a seasonal trade, caveat emptor, buyer beware! Many traders, both hedgers and speculators, have attempted to take advantage of any seasonal trade or common market discrepancy by using spread trading. This simple strategy requires the willingness to do two things—have a market bias and be willing to both buy and sell contracts of a particular commodity in different months.

Spread trading is designed to simulate hedging, which forces clearing firms to offer deep margin discounts to spread traders. Clearing firms do this because the act of selling in one month and buying in another month is assumed to be a protective trading activity—in other words, that one contract will protect the other from loss. By their very nature spread trades are considered to be low-risk, high-profit transactions. Despite all the positives, though, they are still flawed. It is always possible that a spread will narrow when you want it to widen and widen when you want it to narrow. In either instance you will find that not one but both trades are losing money simultaneously.

In this chapter we first explore the long and the short spreads. Next we look at various spread opportunities. While seasonal trades are great opportunities to put spreads on, you can take advantage of other spread opportunities that are based on what counts most: current market conditions. A retail trader who takes advantage of these additional spread opportunities moves out of the realm of fundamental guesswork into the realm of financial arbitrage.

SPREAD OPPORTUNITIES

Spread opportunities can take multiple forms. Whether based on substitute goods, differing time frames, or predictable supply and demand chains, spread trading opportunities exist everywhere in some form or fashion. Detailing all of them is a subject for another book. Therefore, I have narrowed down the spread opportunities to a few that are easily recognizable and easily researchable and I provide some basic information that will take you far in your spread trading, seasonal or otherwise.

First, there are two ways to trade the spread, long the spread or short the spread. If you are long the spread the front month is expected to move up greater in price than the further out month of the market that you may be trading. If you are short the spread you expect the front month to fall greater in price than the further out month of the market that you are trading.

Second, spreads operate in pairs and the difference in the price of a pair over time is what is being calculated. As the spread pair increases or decreases in value the joint value of their movement determines their success. For those new to spread trading it can be shocking when a trade appears to be successful until the difference between the two spread components is calculated and you discover that the actual difference between the two contracts has decreased—which means you are losing money on a long spread, or increased, which means you are losing money on a short spread.

Finally, spread trades are affected by supply and demand. Since a spread trade involves the same type of commodity with contracts spread out over differing time frames, it is necessary to understand the life cycle of the commodity that you are spread trading. If it's grains, you have to understand the planting and harvest seasons; if it's natural gas you have to know how natural gas is used both in the winter and the summer; or if it's a currency then you need to know the policies of the central bank that influences that currency.

Differing supply and demand needs at different times of the year can have different effects on the contracts being held in the spread. One side of a spread can end up moving quicker than another. These same contracts, if you are spreading the futures contracts, can end up not converging with their underlying asset counterparts. Shortages in crops can also impact further-out months in a spread pair in unexpected ways. So while non-pair traded contracts only have the influence of one set of supply and demand factors a spread pair has to take into account the influences on each contract and how those influences relate to one another.

With these three factors in mind four different types of spread opportunities are explored in this chapter. Professional traders have a tendency to incorporate any one, if not all four, of these spread opportunities into their trading programs. What makes these great is that they are 100 percent accessible to everyday retail traders. No special software is needed, no fancy mathematical algorithms, no neural networks. Good old-fashioned price feeds are all you need to get started using these spread opportunities.

These four different types of spread opportunities— the old crop/new crop spread, the interest rate yield curve, futures price backwardation, and price convergence of cash and futures—are all accessible. While I have focused on only one type of commodity or exchange for each spread opportunity, keep in mind that all of the ideas are applicable to commodities with a similar profile to that of any one of these opportunities. What also makes these contracts exciting is that each one of these spread opportunities can be quickly spotted on a chart and then be acted upon quickly.

To get the most out of any one of these different types of spread trades a solid understanding behind their underlying principles is important. Knowing the "why" of what is happening is just as important as knowing the "what to do" when these scenarios arise. All of these spread trading opportunities have been around for quite some time. It's a good idea to research past examples regarding these four types of spreads on the Internet or in various books. In fact the Chicago Board of Trade (CBOT) has great tutorials on their web site regarding spread trading grains and the yield curve. You also have to be willing to demo trade or paper trade these spread trades before committing capital. If you have robust charting software, these spreads can be back-tested for their effectiveness. However, your approach to these different spread trading opportunities will entirely depend on your risk/reward levels and your trading plan. If their risk/reward levels don't match up with your goals, move on to another set of risk management tools.

Old Crop/New Crop Spread

The old crop/new crop spread is one of the most well-known spread trades around. It takes advantage of the difference between the diminishing crop that has been sitting in storage all year long and the upcoming new harvest projection. This old crop/new spread affects all of the grains to some degree or another, as well as any product that must be planted and harvested. The most common old crop/new crop commodities are soybeans, corn, and wheat. These are all grains that can be kept in storage for long periods. As the year progresses, supplies crisscross the world fulfilling cereal, material, and feed needs. This dwindling of "old" supplies intersects with the new year's harvest, creating spread trading opportunities.

A surplus of grains leading into the new year can depress the price of both the current stocks and the upcoming harvests.

A dwindling supply of grains drives the prices up on the current grain stores and increases the value of the new harvest grains. Throughout the year the USDA releases reports on crop plantings and storage levels. The information that they release directly affects how the old crop/new crop spread is bought and sold.

One of the most popular grain spread trades is the old crop/new crop spread for soybeans. The majority of the United States' soybeans are planted between May and June. These same crops are harvested approximately six months later between October and November. This cycle leads to a sales cycle that runs year round, beginning in September, right before the new harvest, and ending in August, right after the new plantings.

South America is on a slightly different old crop/new crop spread. Their planting season operates between April and May, with their harvest occurring in September-October months. In fact, their cycle is different enough that the Chicago Board of Trade (CBOT) created a futures contract focused solely for the soybeans grown in Brazil.

Depending on which soybean cycle you wish to trade, the United States' July/November or May/November old crop/new crop spread trade or South America's April/September or May/November, the spread trade is based on the fundamental activity of the underlying commodities as well as the technical signals in the charts that can indicate whether or not the front month should be sold or bought.

The old crop/new crop is also called an *intracommodity* or *intermarket* spread. Since we are operating with the same commodity but in different months it is a lot easier to track, compared to the substitute good spread known as an *intercommodity* spread. In later chapters we look at a few intercommodity spreads based on specific commodities and their byproducts. The important concept to remember when it comes to the old crop/new crop spread is that the sum is more important than the parts.

Since the typical soybean intracommodity trade is long the spread, we are looking for the July contract to increase in value faster than the November contract. Therefore on a July/November spread we are looking for the prices to increase in value in relation to one another, a narrowing of the spread. Let's say that the difference between July/November is equal to plus 20 cents. This means that the July contract is 20 cents greater than the November contract. As long as the difference between the July and November contracts is plus 20 cents or more, the long spread is intact. This is known as a 20 cent premium.

The success of the old crop/new crop spread, a seasonal trade, depends on one of three occurrences: The July contract's price must continue moving up while the November contract stays the same, or the July contract's price can move up while the November contract's price moves down, or the July contract's price can move up while the November contract's price moves down simultaneously. With so many possibilities it is no wonder that this old crop/new crop interrelationship can have a significant impact on position traders who attempt to roll over an existing position trade.

If for any reason the July contract's value dips below the November contract's value, it is known as a discount. The onset of a discount type of spread scenario can be the beginning of a widening of the spread. For traders who are long the spread this can be disastrous. As the spread widens, the July contract drops in value and the November contract increases in value. A long spread trader begins to lose money on both sides of the spread trade. This is the chief danger of any type of spread trading, but with the old crop/new crop spread trade it can quickly become apparent that the spread is not working. Any failure to jump ship immediately from a long spread or to convert a spread position from a long spread to a short spread can quickly lead to insurmountable losses.

Interest Rate Yield Curve

The interest rate yield curve is a staple of all investing, quite similar to the old crop/new crop spread in the grains. The concept is simple to trade. The interest rate yields for bond and note products, with the equivalent rating but different maturity dates, should be at different levels. The rule of thumb is that the longer the money is lent out the more interest should be paid; this is commonly referred to as the "normal yield curve." This normal yield curve is designed to ensure that the 30 year U.S. Treasury Bond has a greater yield than the 5- and 10-year Treasury Notes because there is more risk associated with the length of time.

The interest rate yield curve has a direct impact on how mortgage rates are set, bank lending practices, and credit cards. The interest rate yield curve also has a predictive component. A normal yield curve is indicative of a solid economy and positive growth. Any change in the yield curve away from normal can portend a significant adjustment in the economy.

The Federal Reserve's policies for the U.S. economy and the U.S. government's desire for either a weak or strong currency also play a significant role in what interest yields are being offered to the public. In the blink of an eye interest rates can move from a normal yield to an inverted yield; this is when near-term notes command higher interest rates than long-term bonds. The inverted yield can indicate whether a country's economy is faced with the potential of a recession.

A flat market occurs when short-term interest rates and long-term interest rates match up in value. A flat market can be worse than a normal or inverted yield solely because of the level of uncertainty that it represents. Either interest rates can cooperate and become normal or there may be a sudden drop in value with long-term interest rates forcing an inverted market on the public.

In order to effectively trade the yield curve most traders have one of two choices. They can actually purchase and sell the associated short-term notes and long-term bonds or they can trade in the futures markets. If the yield curve is traded in the futures market then the issues associated with leveraged trading will also have an impact on how a retail trader approaches this spread opportunity.

Backwardation

Of all of the different types of spread trading this is the most straightforward. When it comes to the pricing of futures contracts the futures price is expected to be greater than the underlying asset. Earlier futures contracts are also less expensive than later futures contracts. This is known as contango. This is a normal byproduct of the carrying charges associated with futures contracts. The longer a commodity or futures contract is held the more expensive it becomes.

When supply tightens or demand increases significantly the spot price or the earlier futures contracts increase in value compared to further-out futures contracts. This price change overrides the normal carrying charges and puts the market into a state known as backwardation. There are two spread opportunities that can be initiated when backwardation occurs.

Both opportunities can be executed but there is an issue of timing involved. The window of opportunity is small. If you miss when a market moves from backwardation to contango and back again, it will be more difficult to take advantage of these opportunities.

The first spread opportunity requires that you catch a market moving into backwardation immediately. Your charting software should be programmed to alert you automatically when the front month increases value above further out months. Once the alert kicks in you can take advantage of the narrowing of the gap by going long the front month and selling the further out month; sound familiar—old crop/new crop spread—anyone?

The second spread opportunity involves a market going back to contango from backwardation. Once the front month begins to decrease in value, moving from a backwardation market to a regular contango market, there is an opportunity to short the front month and buy the further out month; a widening of the spread.

Unlike the old crop/new crop spread, backwardation is not limited to the grains. It can occur at any time in any market. Therefore, it is necessary to scour most, if not all of the tradable markets, in order to catch either their transition from contango to backwardation or from backwardation to contango. This is one of the simplest exploitable spreads around, but the drawback is that it is labor intensive.

The basic rules of spread trading still apply, though. Make sure that the difference between the front month in a backwardation is at a premium if you are long the spread, and at a discount if you are short the spread. Plus your profits still derive themselves from a difference in the contract prices.

Price Convergence with Cash and Futures

Futures contracts have a set expiration date, on which the price of the futures contract is meant to converge with the underlying asset or cash position's price. This convergence of the cash price and the futures price is known as the narrowing of the basis.

For those entities that use futures contracts to hedge their cash position this narrowing of the basis is essential. If a farmer grows soybeans he hopes that the cash price will continue upward while the short futures contract is simply a hedge, a protective position designed to lose money. A soybean processor that wants to protect himself from prices moving upward will buy a futures soybean contract, while still hoping that prices will drop. If the price moves up they will gain it back in the futures market; if the price gets weaker they are ready to lose money in the long futures position so that they can make cheaper purchases in the cash market. Both types of hedgers really have nothing to lose as the futures price gets closer to the cash value.

For retail traders this experience can be duplicated by playing the convergence of the spot currency market with the futures currency markets. For example, by following the 50-day MA you can determine the currency market's trend or counter-trend. Once the trend is determined the spot market can operate as the primary position and the futures can operate as the hedge, with the goal of holding on to the position until they reach the same price.

There is a drawback to playing a convergence spread, though. In 2008 the Commodity Futures Trading Commission's Agricultural Committee had an emergency meeting regarding the convergence of grain futures and their cash counterparts. Apparently, for several years the effects of carrying charges and speculation were so severe that even at expiration the futures grain prices were not matching up with the cash prices. This blatant discrepancy effectively ruined the cash grain market's ability to instill confidence in the commodity exchange mechanism of price discovery.

This problem, while currently concentrated in the grain markets, may portend the future of all commodities exchanges around the world. A significant number of money managers have been putting investors into futures contracts because of global inflation in the value of raw materials. This is a new phenomenon. Add to this new phenomenon the fact that a number of new exchanges are starting up mirror commodity contracts in order to siphon off liquidity from major exchanges around the world and you have a recipe for price discovery disaster occurring.

The number of hedgers out there is finite. All of the exchanges compete with each other for a limited number of hedgers looking to protect themselves, while speculators flood contracts with cash as they look for new opportunities to profit from worldwide demands. There is little doubt that the convergence spread between futures and the cash market days are numbered.

CONCLUSION

Spread trading is not perfect. On one hand, you have the opportunity to profit. On the other, you could end up with one successful side that doesn't really cover the losing side, or with two losing sides. Spread trades are also difficult to unwind. While your margin is inexpensive when the spread trade is on, if you try to unwind the spread you are immediately hit with new margin requirements. Finally, many of the traditional seasonal spreads are simply too well known to be as effective as they may have been years ago. Still, with all of these imperfections spread trading makes for a more than decent risk management strategy.

When done right spread trading allows a trader to take advantage of arbitrage opportunities. Those are the small discrepancies in price that speculators thrive on financially. Spread trading can reduce the most expensive markets to reasonable margins. Plus, spread trading transcends exchanges or trading vehicles. The spot price can be spread with the futures price. Different futures months can be spread against each other and options can be spread in any number of ways. Spread trading is simply one of the most versatile ways to trade for a trader of any skill level. The majority of the problems with spread trades can be resolved quite easily. As long as a spread trade is either backed up by another risk management strategy or there are stop limits in place to protect a spread trade from going terribly wrong there is no reason to fear this exciting risk management technique.

CHAPTER 10

Gunning for Premiums with Covered Options

M any of the risk management strategies that have been explored throughout the book have involved some form of option. Whether it be a strangle strategy, a synthetic futures, or an option as a stop purchasing, options have played an integral role in helping to manage the risk associated with a core futures or spot position. Depending on the market and type of option this can mean thousands of dollars tied up in option premiums, with the realistic expectation that part or all of the premium could be lost. This chapter is designed to help you change gears. For once the option premium can actually come to you.

The premium generated from option selling is real money that can add to any trader's bottom line. The difficulty comes in being able to decide which option to sell and how to sell it in the same protected way that you use for any of the other risk management strategies in the book. As we have learned time and time again, options are inherently different from futures and spot transactions. Successfully navigating those differences can help any trader generate a consistent cash flow from option premiums.

It was difficult to make the decision to include a chapter on option selling in a book primarily focused on futures, spot, and cash markets. Yet, in the end no book that is designed to manage risk can truly discriminate against one of the most touted limited risk trading strategies around, selling options. Major Commodity Trading Advisors (CTAs) have made a name for themselves by solely selling options. Their strategies range from selling options that are about to expire to devising option strategies that exploit volatility or the lack thereof in stock indexes. Yet some flaws and misinformation accompany option selling. Many of these flaws can be overcome with the proper approach, but unfortunately the misinformation has to be attacked head-on.

PROBLEMS WITH SELLING OPTIONS

Option selling should be a straightforward endeavor. See an option you want to sell, sell it, wait until expiration, and collect the premium. You would think that it was as easy as pie, but for some reason it isn't. There are margin requirements along with inherent flaws in the structure of options that make the prospect of selling them difficult. Couple these problems with the claims that 70 percent to 80 percent of options are worthless when they expire and it's no wonder that the average trader who ventures into selling options quickly finds himself in over his head.

Margin Requirements

While selling options should be a simple, if not easy, proposition, somehow selling options does not live up to the hype. In fact, while promoters tout the benefits of selling options and the easy money to be had, the truth is a lot less glamorous. Selling options is actually considered just as risky, if not more so, than buying options.

Technically the structure of an option does not favor option sellers. Once an option is sold it exposes the seller to unlimited risk. At the same time it only offers the option seller the meager profit that the premium has to offer. This unlimited exposure has led clearing firms in the futures market to require that option sellers have enough capital to protect themselves in case the market moves against them. Amounts may vary from clearing firm to clearing firm, but as a standard rule they will require the same margin amount as if you had initiated a futures contract.

For example, if you sold an option on a full-size S&P 500 contract, you would be able to collect $5,000 in premiums, but you would be required to put up $22,000 in margin for the privilege. So, even though it is assumed that selling options is superior to buying them, the simple fact that they can be so cost prohibitive leads traders to avoid them.

What about the collected premium?

The $5,000 in premium is treated like any futures or options position. Options are traded marked to market. If the volatility is on your side they will increase in value, if the volatility is against you they will decrease in value. The only time that the premium is actually considered yours by the clearing firms is when the option has expired and the trader is no longer exposed to unlimited risk. Until then the premium is not counted as part of your overall count value.

Poor Returns

The requirement that traders put up margin when they sell options also leads to what can be perceived as poor returns in comparison to the risk involved. If a trader has to expose $22,000 in margin in order to make $5,000, knowing full well that he could lose the entire $22,000 and possibly more if he's wrong, then it most likely is not the best possible bet to take. Add to this the fact that, depending on when the option expires, the trader's capital can be tied up for months at a time, which can make option selling a discouraging endeavor for small traders.

If you are a small trader and you only have a $5,000 account your opportunities to sell options decrease even more. You would be lucky if you could comfortably sell an option worth $500, or 10 percent of your account value. This $500 income would not change the average retail trader's life. For an account of this size there may only be four or five successful opportunities every year. If you are lucky and have no losses you could net $2,000 to $2,500 annually.

This definitely does not coincide with the one for two rule discussed in previous chapters. In fact, it's inverted risk—risk two to gain one. In addition, the possible annual returns look dismal, ranging from 40 to 50 percent, which is not what the average trader signs up for. This negative feeling toward such returns may not be warranted, though. A return of 40 to 50 percent a year exceeds the historical returns of the S&P 500, while at the same time beating out any bond, junk or otherwise. Even if the option selling strategy works out twice a year, producing $1,000 in premium based on this scenario, a 20 percent return would still exceed the stock market's past returns.

It goes without saying that CTAs that trade an option selling strategy benefit from a different financial scale than does the average retail trader. Small profits for a CTA accumulated over time turn out to be great gains. For a larger entity, 20 percent on $50 million yields a $10 million return. This kind of profit would put a CTA among some the top traders in the world.

The unglamorous nature of option selling leads retail traders to misunderstand the performance. There is no comparison between collecting option premiums and aggressively catching moves in the market. One is a passive action and the other is proactive. Therefore, selling options should not be put in the same category as buying options or obtaining a cash or spot position.

Percentage of Options that Expire Worthless

The perpetual myth is that 80 to 90 percent of options expire worthless. If this is the case, selling options should be like shooting fish in a barrel. Yet something is amiss. Not every trader, professional or retail, sells options. In fact, option selling is considered a specialized field that only a few select traders focus on. This simple fact gives a true glimpse into the nature of selling options, their difficulty, and the reality of the number of contracts that do actually expire worthless. In Chapter 14 we take a more advanced approach to selling options and further break down the option expiration myth.

COVERED OPTION TRADING

Selling options has problems—margin requirements, poor returns, and expiration issues—yet this can still be an effective way to generate income and increase returns when done correctly. All of the problems are tied to selling options by themselves, or naked. When an option is sold naked there is no counter side to limit the unlimited risk that it has. The secret, like every other risk management strategy in this book, is to couple the selling of an option with another strategy designed, intentionally or unintentionally, to protect the trader from any erratic moves. This is known as *covered option* trading.

Without question selling options can have a positive affect on a trader's account. It is a simple income-producing trading strategy that can power-boost any trader's returns. To make it a successful enterprise, a trader is required to do two things—control his profit expectations and increase the vigilance over his trading. Then it becomes a simple endeavor to implement the strategies in this chapter.

Traditionally a covered option is the combination of an option and a futures or cash position. The option is sold against the futures or cash position to generate income. Yet there are many different ways to cover an option. Options can be staggered with multiple strike prices or they can be tied to other risk management strategies such as Collars or Synthetic Options. However selling covered options is approached, it diminishes if not eliminates many of the problems that selling naked options can have.

Selling Options against Futures or Cash Position

The simplest approach to implementing a covered option position involves the combination of a cash position with an option. The crux of the idea is that when a stock's shares flatten out or get weaker in price call options can be sold to generate income.

If the stock's price goes down the trader gains the premium, which diminishes his losses in the shares. If the price goes up the stock trader has one of two choices—buy back the option at a higher premium or give up any gains in his shares above and beyond the option strike price. The same scenario can be played out for the futures, forex, or CFD markets.

Initiating a Covered Position   Few decisions have to be made when it comes to trading covered positions in the stock market. Those people who buy stocks are automatically long-side specialists who therefore understand that they will only be selling calls. Also since there is no leverage on the stock itself it is simpler to purchase one stock option for every 100 shares of stock owned. Finally, since the option is sold as a secondary position to the actual stock shares the option strike price is not given much thought.

The ease with which covered option positions can be implemented in the stock market gives us a contrast to the difficulty that can be associated with the futures and forex markets. When it comes to putting on covered option positions in the futures market, unlike stocks, there are too many choices. Since longs and shorts are treated equally in the futures market covered positions can be implemented with puts or calls. Delta also has a larger impact on the option selling decision. The less the delta is, the more likely multiple options at the same strike price will be sold in order to match the movement of the underlying asset.

Finally, in a covered position the sold option may actually be the primary position with the futures or spot contract acting as the protective position. This makes the option strike price more important based on how much premium can be collected.

The spot forex market has one flaw that the futures market doesn't have—lack of a true option market. Spot forex options tend to be customized contracts between the traders and the deal makers. This makes for liquidity issues and can limit the strike prices that deal makers are willing to work with. In the end, since there is no centralized exchange in the spot forex market, it is difficult for spot options to be both fairly priced and liquid enough to be realistically used in a covered option scenario. This does not mean, though, that you can't cross trade with forex futures options to create the exact same trades.

In this section we look at two different ways to initiate a covered option position. One is an aggressive way to put on a covered position. This action, when all of the indicators are pointing one way and a covered option is intentionally initiated in the opposite direction, is known as fading the market. The second way to initiate a covered option is when a position has already gained a profit and is stalling out. In fact, if done properly it can actually give the winning position a way to weather temporary pullbacks or retracements.

Rules for Working with Covered Options   To make covered options work a strict approach must be taken. First, make sure you are a trend or counter-trend trader, long side or short side specialist. This specialization is paramount to having a consistent approach when selling options. In the stock market you are forced to be a trend specialist, but in futures or spot forex you can be either a trend or a counter-trend specialist. Choosing a side helps dictate how comfortable you will be with your option selling decisions and how you will react to the market's moves.

Second, the delta can play an important role in the number of options you will want to sell. If the option's delta is moving at one third of the underlying contract's actual price it makes sense to sell three options, not one, in order to gain the full benefit of protective option. This can backfire if the delta and volatility gets closer to the value of the underlying asset while at the same time prices are moving against you.

Third, you must make a decision regarding what type of option will be sold. While three types of options are available—out-of-the-money, in-the-money (ITM), and at-the-money (ATM)—only two, ITM and ATM, are of importance to futures and forex option sellers. Stock traders want to hold on to their stock position, but futures and forex are happy to collect as much premium as possible while totally disregarding the underlying position. This can best be accomplished with an ITM option, but if the trader has a conservative streak then selling an ATM option may be a better bet.

Finally, there is an issue of timing. There are no rules set in stone requiring that a sold option must be held until expiration. If a profit is evident, then the option can be bought back ahead of time. This requires the option seller to have a set goal on his profit targets and to stay in control of the maximum loss on his underlying futures or forex position.

Examples of Fading the Market   The following are two examples of a market setup that is perfect for selling an option. The prices are sitting around the 50-day MA and to the naked eye the market could go either up or down. Based on the technical analysis it can clearly be seen that the market will be going long or short. Then the covered option is put in place to fade the actual direction of where the market is predicted to go.

Fading the market means that if the market signals suggest that the market will move up in value, long, you initiate a covered put position to collect the premium. If the market signals suggest that the market will drop in value, short, you initiate a covered call position to collect the premium.

This allows the trader to put on in-the-money trades and collect a significant premium in the process.

Long Market, Covered Put Position Crude oil's price in Figure 10.1 is $85.40 and there is support sitting at $84.25. That means there is at least $1.15 difference before the market may stop moving downward and decide to turn around. With that in mind you can sit on the sidelines before initiating a covered put trade. You are looking to put the odds in your favor. If the market breaks through support then you can initiate a covered call strategy.

In Figure 10.2 the market hits the $84.25 support line and bounces back around, stopping beneath the 50-day MA. As we know from *Winning the Trading Game*, the 50-day MA plays a significant role in determining a market's direction. If it can successfully break through the 50-day MA, a new long market will be initiated; if it hits the 50-day MA and collapses, it will continue its bearish trend aggressively.

With all of the momentum on the bullish side, this is the perfect setup to put on a covered put. You want to make sure you collect the premium with few or no problems. So as it gets close to the 50-day MA it makes sense to sell a put, with the hope it will break through the 50-day MA and start

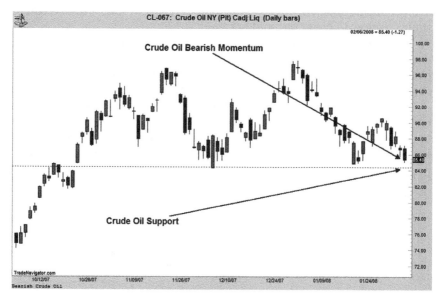

FIGURE 10.1 Bearish Crude Oil
Source: TradeNavigator.com © 2007. All rights reserved.

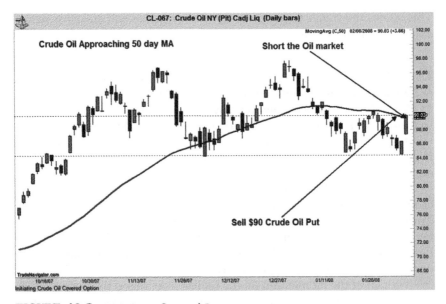

FIGURE 10.2 Initiating a Covered Put
Source: TradeNavigator.com © 2007. All rights reserved.

a new bullish trend. Just in case the market drops in value you execute a short position, to cover the sold put.

In Table 10.1 several strike prices are compared to the premiums that can be collected. Since the market in Figure 10.2 has an overall bearish bias it makes sense that the put options with a higher strike price are more expensive than the premiums that are closer to the money.

In Figure 10.3 the price breaks above the 50-day MA and stays above it for 2 or 3 days. This is a significant clue to whether this is a false breakout or there has been a fundamental shift in the supply and demand of the commodity. It also signals you to exit your short position and stop eroding the premium you have collected.

TABLE 10.1 Oil Put Option Premiums

Strike Price	Premium	Dollar Amount
90.50	5.20	$5,200
90.00	4.39	$4,390
89.50	4.09	$4,090

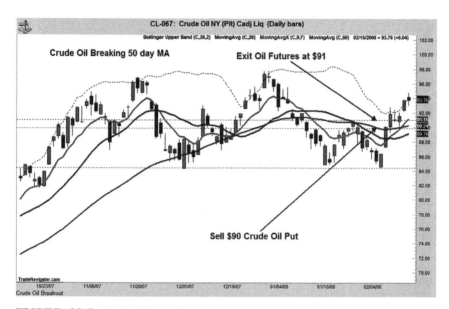

FIGURE 10.3 Crude Oil Breakout
Source: TradeNavigator.com © 2007. All rights reserved.

In this instance you enter your short position at $90 and exit your short position at $91.15 for a total loss of $1,115. This is subtracted directly from the premium you collected depending on the strike price you sold.

There are a few things to keep in mind when you unwind your position. First, once you get out of the protective short you will need to put a stop on the sold call in order avoid losing the premium you have already made. Second, you will immediately lose the special margin rate you were receiving; therefore you will need to have enough margin in the account to maintain the position. Finally, you need to be sure that you are willing to exit the trade without carrying it all the way until expiration. At some point you will be risking too much premium compared to what you will earn if you hold the position until expiration, so keep the rule of risking one to gain two in mind.

Short Market, Covered Long Position   In the covered long position we take a look at the corn market. In Figure 10.4 we can see that the corn market has built up a lot of bullish momentum. It has filled at $4.60 and is heading straight for the resistance at $4.90. Again, we are looking for a setup to occur. If corn breaks $4.90 it can get as high as $5.20.

In Figure 10.5 we see the corn market slow down and reverse at the $4.90 price. At the time the corn $4.90 options are worth $1,400. If you sell

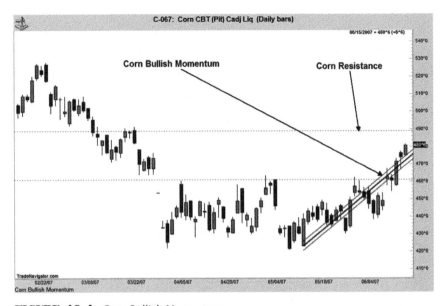

FIGURE 10.4 Corn Bullish Momentum
Source: TradeNavigator.com © 2007. All rights reserved.

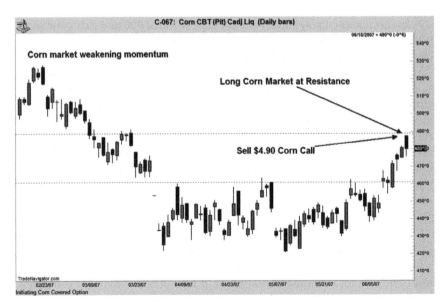

FIGURE 10.5 Initiating Corn Covered Option
Source: TradeNavigator.com © 2007. All rights reserved.

TABLE 10.2 Corn Call Option Premiums

Strike Price	Premium	Dollar Amount
495	23	$1,150
490	28	$1,400
485	30	$1,500

a call option at that price a premium of $1,400 can be collected. A long position is put into play to cover the position in case the market breaks through $4.90. This is a preemptive move. Unlike the previous example, the market has proven itself for several down days. The only reason it is worthwhile to take a chance on it is because of gravity. Markets have a tendency to fall faster than they can move up. So as a rule I have a tendency to be more adventurous when taking signals for the short side as opposed to the long side (see Table 10.2).

In Figure 10.6 everything is against corn. The price is collapsing off the upper Bollinger band, RSI is overbought, and the price gaps down the next day. The long position cannot be exited fast enough. In fact, slippage would most likely end up giving back half of your collected premium. But that's okay—you have the protected position to ensure you don't expose

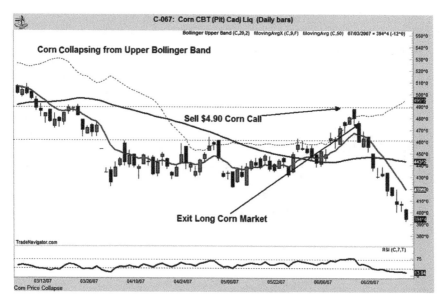

FIGURE 10.6 Corn Price Collapse
Source: TradeNavigator.com © 2007. All rights reserved.

yourself to unlimited losses. If the market had shot up your position would have been naked. This is the trade-off of having a protective position.

Enhancing the Profits of a Winning Position   Another type of covered option position can come after holding onto a successful position for some time. If a position trade has been placed on and has become successful, for instance if a long spot forex has racked up decent returns, but suddenly stalls out, there is an opportunity to sell a call option to generate income from the successful position. As soon as the market returns to the direction of the winning trade the sold call is immediately offset, hopefully with a small profit or at least at break-even. This strategy works just as easily for traders who are in a successful short trade.

In Figure 10.7 a trader has entered the S&P 500 on a 50-day MA crossover. As the market moves up for a significant gain the S&P 500 slows its move upward at 1560 and the market begins to move sideways. This is a definite bearish signal after such a long move upward.

There is an opportunity to sell a call at these heights and generate a significant income. An at-the-money full-size option can easily command thousands in premium. Therefore you can have the best of both worlds; you can protect your trade from any temporary pullback with money collected

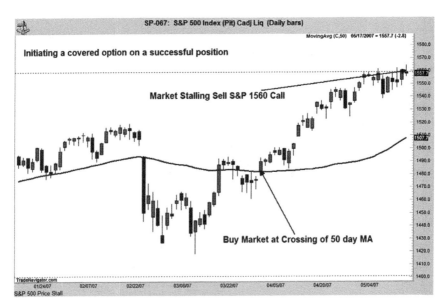

FIGURE 10.7   S&P 500 Price Stall
Source: TradeNavigator.com © 2007. All rights reserved.

from the premium. You will also reduce your margin requirements since the position is a covered option sale.

In Figure 10.8 we see the S&P 500 drop in value and come back to the 50-day MA. At that time the long position and the sold call should be exited. Profits should be set aside and a reassessment of the trade should be made to determine what the new direction could be.

Two Advanced Covered Option Strategies

In Chapter 7 and Chapter 8 we looked at two different strategies that involved options, collars, and synthetic options. In each instance we used a protective option to protect the cash, futures, or stock position. The protective option was put in place to protect against any sudden drops or jumps, but with a little more imagination an option can be sold on either type of position to generate income to add to the overall profit of the position.

Selling an Option against a Synthetic Option   This strategy is slightly advanced because there are three moving parts, but it is another way to initiate a covered option position, and thus it's important to expose you to the idea. As we learned in Chapter 8, a synthetic option is the combination of an at-the-money option and a futures, spot, or cash market.

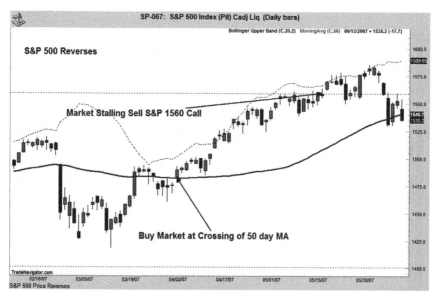

FIGURE 10.8 S&P 500 Price Reverses
Source: TradeNavigator.com © 2007. All rights reserved.

Whether you go long or short, the protective option is purchased to protect against any risk of loss.

There is no set rule that the position the option is covering has to solely be the futures, spot, or cash position. In fact another option can be added to the mix. An option can be sold out-of-the-money, a few points away from the synthetic's protective option. If the position is working in favor of the underlying asset, then the extra premium is added to your overall profits. If the position fails, the protective option covers any price move that may occur in the sold option. You give up the profits from any market move against your position, but at the same time you have a way to capitalize on your protective option or at the very least have a way to pay for part or all of it.

Let's take a market example from Chapter 8.

In Figure 10.9 we see the market rally through the 50-day MA. A put was purchased at $930. The option cost $1,830. It would take little effort to sell a put at $925 or at $935, if you're aggressive. A sold option at either strike price will produce enough premium to either match or cover the cost of the purchased option.

Selling an Option against a Collar In Chapter 7 we attacked the collar trade. By now you may have figured out that the very nature of a collar is based on the covered option concept and the synthetic option combined. Even though the sold option is a far out-of-the-money option, once the

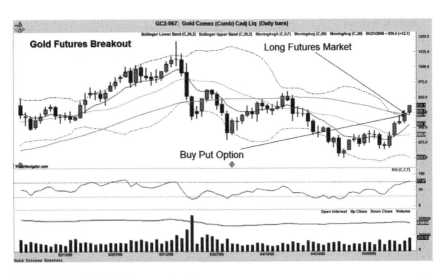

FIGURE 10.9 Gold Futures Breakout
Source: TradeNavigator.com © 2007. All rights reserved.

underlying asset breaks through the strike price it immediately turns into a covered position.

But the fact that a synthetic option is the core component of a collar means that an option can be sold out of the money against the purchased option to produce a little extra income as well.

CONCLUSION

Selling options can be a complex proposition. Myths, like the belief that 80 to 90 percent of options expire worthless, do more harm than good when making an informed decision to sell options. Add to that the impact that margin rules have on the ability to sell options, plus the effects that volatility has on choosing the right option to sell, and it's easy to see that in the wrong hands option selling can be disastrous.

Selling options requires a healthy dose of respect and discipline. Once it is accepted that the option has the potential for unlimited losses, the proper measures can be taken to minimize or eliminate that loss. Proper measures can mean selling an option against a futures or spot position, tying a sold option to the tail of a synthetic option, or being aggressive with a straddle or strangle position. As long as a trader is willing to step out of the box when it comes to selling options, its liabilities can become assets over time.

As with all of the strategies presented in this book, the goal is to put you in control of how you interact with the market. Whether that means combining various tools so the odds are in your favor or avoiding this strategy altogether, then so be it. Whatever will make you ultimately feel comfortable with selling options is exactly how you should employ them in your trading. This strategy is solely a means to an end—increased profits coupled with diminished risk. If you fail to see an opportunity, don't force it. Just let it flow.

CHAPTER 11

Outflanking
the Market

I n Chapter 9 spread trading was explained in detail for futures contracts and the cash market. In this chapter spread trading is being explored once again, but from an option perspective. There are many different types of option spreads, from iron condors to horizontal spreads to vertical spreads, along with a myriad of other exotically named spreads. Many of these are outside the scope of this book, either because they are too exotic or because they cannot be easily tied back into a futures or cash position. In no way does that mean that they are inferior, and in fact you can benefit from learning how they work.

For the purposes of this book, the most effective option spread for our dual goals of minimizing losses and maximizing profits is a very specific ratio spread. The overall definition of the ratio spread requires that an unequal number of long and short positions be held. There can be a multitude of ways to execute this strategy. In one scenario a ratio spread can, if done properly, limit the overall risk of a trader through simultaneously diminishing losses and practically setting up a free trading opportunity. In another scenario of the ratio spread, things can be exactly the opposite. This type of ratio spread can expose a trader to unlimited losses if the market moves aggressively. In fact, being on the wrong side of this type of ratio spread can ruin all but the most astute trader's account.

Distinguishing between these ratio spreads is just the tip of the iceberg when it comes to trading the ratio spreads. There is the matter of being able to select the proper ratio based on the underlying asset's market direction, and there is the question of whether the ratio between longs and shorts should relate to price or delta or both. Regardless of how the ratio spread is implemented, it is a simple way for a trader to participate in various market moves without having to risk too much of his own capital, which can be important if you are trading with tight capital constraints.

FRONTSPREADS AND BACKSPREADS

Since a ratio spread is simply the act of holding an unequal number of long and short positions, two different permutations of this scenario can occur. Either you can buy one call or put and sell two calls or puts (known as a frontspread) or you can sell one call or put and buy two calls or puts (known as a backspread).

Frontspreads

Let's look at the frontspread first. The frontspread is typically considered the default ratio spread. It simply requires that an option be purchased at a set price, preferably out-of-the-money, and two options be sold at a slightly higher strike price. The goal is to profit from the difference between the option strike prices. The trade is designed as a way to exploit a decrease in option volatility. It is assumed that with less volatility the options are less likely to move, and the premiums, along with the call's profit gains between strike prices, are assured.

The downside of the frontspread is self-evident, though. As highlighted earlier, there is an inherent flaw when it comes to selling options. When an option is sold the trader is subject to the potential of unlimited losses. This means that when a frontspread ratio spread is initiated the trader is at an automatic disadvantage. If the underlying asset takes off in price and the option volatility increases, then the sold options will gain in value quickly. While there is one purchased option covering the increase in value of one sold option, the second option is uncovered and thus exposes the trader to unlimited loss potential.

For example, a trader may purchase a gold put for $950 and then sell two gold puts at $940. There is an apparent belief that there is a window of trading opportunity between $950 to $940, or $1,000 in profits. The two sold options, particularly at this close strike price range, produce enough premium to pay for most if not all of the bought gold put.

The primary drawback would be if the price of gold drops past $940, then the unlimited risk of one of the sold options kicks in. The secondary drawback is if the price actually moves in the opposite direction. In this example if gold moves from $950 to $960 the purchased option begins to lose value. At that time the hope is that premium collected from selling $940 puts will cover the losses and help the trade to break even.

For a more advanced trader who has a thorough understanding of option volatility and has the ability to juggle the risk of multiple positions, this type of ratio spread may be just the ticket. For those traders who are a little more conservative with both their capital and their time, a second type of ratio spread exists: the backspread.

Backspreads

The backspread is so powerful that it has the ability, depending on the market's volatility, to give you 360-degree protection from risk. At the outset the backspread ratio spread is designed to manage the risk. Instead of buying the at-the-money call and paying a significant premium, the backspread requires that you sell the more expensive option and use that premium to purchase two slightly out-of-the-money options. Instead of dreading any market move, the backspread thrives on the volatility.

If the market moves aggressively in the direction of the backspread, bullish or bearish, the purchased options create the opportunity for unlimited gains. While the frontspread is exposed to unlimited risk by the one uncovered option, this setup is inverted in the backspread. The original sold call is covered by one of the purchased options. The second option is where all of the profits accumulate. This is liberating.

Add the fact that the backspread trade protects itself from accumulating losses by setting up a break-even scenario between the sold option and the two bought options, and the backspread ratio spread beats out the frontspread any day. The worst loss that can occur is the premium paid for the bought options, and most of that can be made up by the premium collected by the sold option.

For example, if the technical analysis is pointing to the oil market moving up in price, but the high cost of the margin (as of this writing $10,000 per contract) drives you away, a backspread ratio spread has the ability to get you in. You sell a call option at a strike price of $145 per barrel and collect a premium of $6,000. You then purchase two out-of-the-money options with a strike price of $150 per barrel for a total of $7,000 in premium. Your net expense is $1,000, plus the clearing firm runs the SPAN risk management software program and reduces or eliminates any margin requirement for the sold option.

If the market moves in the direction of the purchased call options at $150 per barrel, then the risk between $145 per barrel and $150 per barrel equals $5,000. At the same time the options are increasing in value because of increased volatility as the underlying asset moves closer to the strike price. Once the underlying asset breaks through the $150 strike price, the premium increases rapidly.

If the market were to hit $160 per barrel, then gross proceeds would be $20,000. However, $10,000 would have to be subtracted to cover the increase in the premium of the sold $145 call. An additional $5,000 would have to be subtracted as well, the difference between the two strike prices. This leaves a net profit of $5,000, give or take a few dollars due to slippage. This is not a bad return for a $1,000 investment, 1 for 5.

What happens if the market moves against the position? Let's say it falls from $145 per barrel to $135 per barrel. The collected premium of $6,000 begins to erode in value at the same time that the options you bought at $150 decrease in value. Even if both of the options lose their entire premium, the net expense to execute the trade is $1,000. This is in sharp contrast to the futures oil margin of $10,000—practically a tenfold increase in the leverage without the tenfold increase in risk.

In a one-for-one comparison, the frontspread has just as many variables as a backspread, but its unlimited risk makes the frontspread an inferior trade to the backspread. Yet they both are trades that suffer from the one-trick pony syndrome. While selling a call is a way to have a bearish bias in the market or selling a put is a way to have a bullish bias in the market, they are both passive ways to be involved in a trade. This in effect can cut your returns in half if the market dictates that you have to reverse your position quickly.

TRADING BACKSPREADS

The core benefit of trading a backspread ratio spread is the ability to use the market's money to trade. There are few times when the market actually works on your behalf to help you succeed, but this is one of those times. Throughout the book we have looked at the favoritism given to hedge traders and commercial traders for daisy-chaining multiple positions together; there is no better place where this is exemplified than in the backspread ratio spread. Selling an option and buying two options provides a sincere opportunity to trade practically for free. It is therefore important to discern how many options should be bought, whether price or delta should be the guide, and when a call or a put should be sold to establish the beginnings of a backspread trade.

Price versus Delta

Thus far we have talked about the ratio spread as if there is a specific number of options sold versus options bought, in this case two. The reality is that for every option sold you can determine the number of options purchased in any fashion. Some have strictly adhered to the price difference between the bought and sold options, whereas others have used delta as a guide to optimizing how many contracts to initiate.

Price If price is used as the litmus test of what options to buy and sell, then the premium collected should represent no less than 50 percent of the total value of the options purchased. This goes back to our one-for-two money management trading rule. If the price of the sold option is less than 50 percent of the value of the bought options, then the question that has to be asked is, "Can I use a less exposing risk management tool to achieve the same results?" The answer is most likely yes. Regardless of whether the sold option is being covered by a bought option, the less capital you commit to the trade, the more profitable the trade will be for you in the long run. Ideally you would like the sold option to cover the cost of both of the bought options, but this can be a difficult task.

There are trade-offs when attempting to make a backspread ratio spread entirely free; they involve the strike price. The closer an option strike price is to the underlying asset price, the more expensive that option's premium is. When the goal is to collect premiums, at-the-money or in-the-money options are great. Unfortunately, the inverse is also true: The closer you buy options to the underlying asset's fair market value, the more you will spend.

So when it comes to trading the ratio spread, the further out that the strike price is for the bought options, the more likely you will be able to use the premium collected to pay for most or all of them. Yet at the same time the further out that the bought option strike price is from the sold option, the greater the loss difference before the positive effects of the bought options can kick in.

In our oil example earlier, we sold an option at $145 and bought two options with a strike price of $150. The difference between $145 and $150, $5, equates to a built-in loss between the prices of $5,000. If the strike price for the purchased options were to be stretched out to $155 per barrel, the loss gap would extend from $5,000 to $10,000. This would mean that more patience would be required on the part of the trader, more volatility would be necessary on the part of the option, and the opportunity costs would simply have a disastrous effect on any trader who was right about the market's direction but had used two strike prices that were simply too far out to take advantage of a move.

Therefore, when an option's premium is used to determine the buying of a covered position, it is essential that the difference in strike prices plays a role in the decision-making process for a ratio spread.

Delta Delta is a little trickier than choosing a strike price or collecting and comparing premiums. Delta measures how closely an option's change in price mirrors the change in its underlying asset. If the delta is .8, that means that it moves 80 cents for every one-dollar move in the underlying asset. This also means that your ratio of sold options to bought options can have multiple permutations. You could buy two options with a delta of .4 or you could buy four options with a delta of .2. This is known as a delta-neutral strategy.

This significantly changes the trader's dependence on the strike price. If the delta of the underlying sold option is flat or slightly increasing in value while the bought options are rapidly increasing, then the trade is succeeding.

For instance, if the sold option has a delta of .6 and the purchased options have a delta of .3, then any change in delta value of the bought option enhances the ratio trade. Let's say the market moves in the same direction as the purchased options, the sold call moves deeper into the money, and the delta shifts from .6 to .8. At the same time, the purchased options shift from a delta of .3 to .6 each. This is a very bullish sign. Where once before there was a one-to-one ratio regardless of the number of options, now the ratio has moved in favor of the bought options, making it .8 to 1.2 (a 2:3 ratio), and climbing.

In this breakdown we are looking purely at price in relation to the underlying asset. In this way we can assess whether we can exit a trade with a profit, regardless of whether it has actually reached the underlying strike price. Of course there is no hard-and-fast rule when it comes to using the delta. This is simply a tool to help you play with the ratio spread and adds another dimension to help you succeed in your trading.

Bullish Backspread

The bullish backspread is also known as a call ratio backspread. This is the strategy that is used if a trader wants to catch the long momentum of a market. The call ratio backspread consists of two components: the sale of calls and the purchase of a greater number of calls at a higher strike price. This strategy has the exact same profile as a standard call option: limited downside risk and unlimited profit potential. If this strategy is established at a credit, the trader stands to make a small gain if the price of the underlying asset decreases dramatically.

Let's take a look at how a call ratio backspread would be executed in the corn market (see Figure 11.1).

The September corn futures price is $5.74 per bushel after dropping from a high of $6.20 per bushel. The price is sitting on the 50-day MA with one of two scenarios presenting itself. Either the market will bounce off

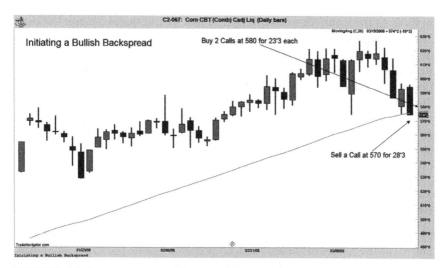

FIGURE 11.1 Initiating a Bullish Backspread
Source: TradeNavigator.com © 2007. All rights reserved.

the 50-day MA and resume its up trend or it will break through the 50-day MA and make a fundamental shift in becoming a bearish market.

With the bias being on the upside for as long as it has been for this chart, two months, putting on a bullish backspread is not unreasonable. Based on Table 11.1, a bullish backspread could work based on our 50 percent or greater criterion.

The 570 call commands a premium of 28'2 and the 580 call commands a premium of 22'2. If you are willing to be 30 cents out-of-the-money, you can get a 605 call for 14'6. This would definitely be a two-for-one scenario, but in the process you would be exposing yourself to a loss of $1,500 (30 cents times $50/cent) before you could make any money.

By selling the 570 call and purchasing two 580 calls, the maximum amount of loss you are exposing yourself to between the two strike prices

TABLE 11.1 Corn Option Prices

	Call	Put
570	28'2	21
580	22'2	26
590	19'4	32'2
600	16'2	39
605	14'6	42'4

is $500. At the same time the 570 option has an additional 5 cents left over after paying for its covered option. This means that the second call option effectively cost just 18'3, making the cost of the 580 premium less than that of a 590 option, 19'4. There is a $500 difference between the two strike prices, which you get to collect if the market moves in your direction.

As shown in Figure 11.2, the price of corn drops briefly below the 50-day MA before turning around and resuming its upward trend. Each of the bought calls grosses $1,800 in profits for a total of $3,600. The net proceeds to the trader come out to around $1,300.

Bearish Backspread

On the opposite side the bullish backspread is the bearish backspread, also known as the put ratio backspread. Everything is done the exact same way as in a bullish backspread, but instead options are bought and sold to take advantage of the drop in prices.

Let's rewind the corn contract to a time before it dropped down toward the 50-day MA.

In Figure 11.3 the price has stalled out at around 620. Significant horizontal resistance has developed around this price. This is definitely an indicator that the market has the potential to pull back at least to the

FIGURE 11.2 Completion of a Bullish Backspread
Source: TradeNavigator.com © 2007. All rights reserved.

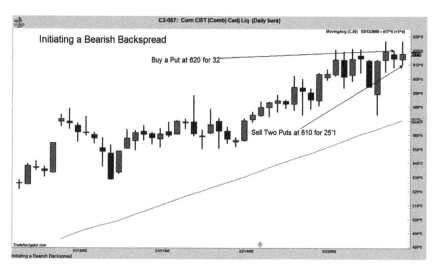

FIGURE 11.3 Initiating a Bearish Backspread
Source: TradeNavigator.com © 2007. All rights reserved.

50-day MA. A drop from 620 to 570 is a potential gross profit of $2,500 (50 cents × $50/cent).

In Table 11.2 the premium received from a 620 put is 32 cents. By selling one 620 put and buying two 610 puts, the effective cost of the profit-making put is just 18'1, almost the same price as the 590 put, which is 20 cents away or $1,000.

In Figure 11.4 the price of corn drops, and it grosses the trader $2,775 for each sold put because it gaps below the 50-day MA. The net profit for the trader is $2,275. In order to arrive at the figure, we have to take the $2,775 and subtract $500, which is the difference between the 620 and 610 strike prices.

TABLE 11.2 Corn Option Prices

	Call	Put
620	26'1	32
610	28'1	25'1
600	32'2	21'4
590	38	17'1
580	43'2	15'2

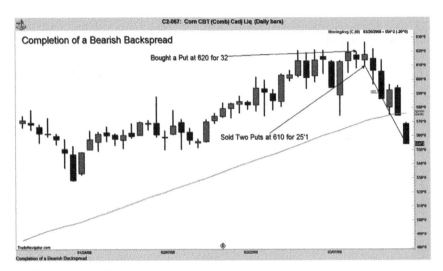

FIGURE 11.4 The Price of Corn Drops

Weaknesses of the Bullish and Bearish Backspreads

The bullish and bearish backspreads are highly effective strategies if you have both the time and the capital. Yet there are some key weaknesses that can't be overlooked. First is the cost of the bought options versus the premium collected. If you hope to not be caught off guard by a huge difference in the strike prices, you will be paying top dollar for the close-to-the-money options. As we have seen, this can play a significant role in how much of a discount can truly be applied to the bought options from the sale of an option. The premium can be used to acquire more options the further out-of-the-money their strike prices are, but that also means more missed profit opportunity.

A second problem is the one-sided emphasis on the market's direction. When you are bullish or bearish, that is your market bias. In our examples the market behaved, but what if it doesn't? Then the premium you paid for the second option is fully at risk. Another risk management strategy would need to be implemented to protect the option that is meant to make you a profit.

Finally, if the market moves but not significantly enough to gain a profit, the option seller is still on the hook to give back the premium, plus any gains due to the purchaser. So while our idealized scenarios showed the market dropping or moving up significantly, what would happen if it moved only halfway or a quarter of the way? Those near successes would be as bad as a complete failure in some instances.

CONCLUSION

Ratio spreads are an exciting way to get the market to pay for part if not all of your trading activity, but they come with some significant pitfalls and risks. Whether you trade frontspreads or backspreads, there are no surefire ways to guarantee that you won't be exposed to losing something. The question that needs to be answered is, "Is the risk worth it?" That can only be determined by the level of faith you have in your technical and fundamental analysis. How well you pick market direction and set profit targets will directly impact whether ratio spread trading can work for you.

PART III

Advanced Strategies

I n this section we look at six advanced risk management strategies. While some basic strategies were mentioned briefly in *Winning the Trading Game*, these strategies are altogether brand-new. We explore synthetic futures, selling straddles, selling strangles, intercommodity spread, naked option selling, and bull/bear call spreads. These strategies, while having some risk management components associated with them, also provide more exposure to the unlimited risk aspect of selling options.

I discuss these strategies because they have the potential to minimize costs and maximize profits. These strategies are broken down by definition, potential application, the risk and rewards associated with them, and when (and when not) to use them.

This section lays the groundwork for you to be able to add a higher level of sophistication to your trading. You will be able to think beyond the trade that you may have just executed and see the bigger picture of the market's movements. Knowing how to use these advanced strategies will lead to a better understanding of the market and give you the know-how to react appropriately to the market when it does the unexpected. This skill is just as valuable as knowing how to get into a trade in the first place.

We explore the concept of synthetic futures and the simultaneous buying and selling of options, and we discover whether a synthetic future is superior to a pure futures position. Then we tackle the elusive sell side straddle and sell side strangle. This section also contains information on how to create any one of the most common intercommodity spreads (grains, metals, energy). We also analyze how to sell a naked option with the help of the greeks. Finally the bull call spread and the bear put spread are introduced. Traders learn how to match the premium gains with the strike price differences in order to optimize the benefits of the bull call–bear put spread.

Much information is covered in few pages. As you progress in your understanding of the various ways that the markets interconnect, it becomes easier to take chances. Eventually you will be able to fluidly combine basic and advanced strategies based on the demands of the market, with little separation between the two approaches.

CHAPTER 12

Exposing Yourself to Loss

P reviously we focused on risk management—investing and trading with few if any chances being taken with your principal. This chapter and the next take a different approach. Now that you have a thorough understanding of how to minimize risk, these more advanced techniques can show how to optimize profits. You can expand your versatility by mixing these strategies, which expose you to loss, with the risk limiting strategies found in earlier chapters.

We explore three advanced strategies: synthetic futures, intercommodity spreads, and bull call–bear put spreads. Each strategy revolves around the interrelationship of two or more different markets or two different contracts all combined together to help maximize returns. Once these strategies are applied in a trading environment they can diminish margin expenses, give traders access to market relationships that they didn't know existed, and put a trader in control of how he interacts with the market.

SYNTHETIC FUTURES, LONG-SHORT

Throughout this book I have liberally included information on trading futures and forex. In fact I have even paired futures contracts with options to create synthetic option positions. As we learned earlier, a synthetic position combines various types of derivatives to simulate the risk associated with a pure position. A trader would use a simulated contract for various reasons. Sometimes it is not easy to obtain a pure position (price, liquidity, and regulations can play a role). Other times a pure position can prevent a trader from maximizing all the different types of profit available to him (as is the case with options). Finally, a pure position can simply be too expensive in relationship to a synthetic position.

Putting on a synthetic futures position can solve the problems that can be associated with having a pure futures, spot, or cash position. A synthetic futures position is the combination of buying an option and selling a second option at the same strike price, but in the opposite directions. This option combination gives you unlimited access to profits and loss simultaneously. It's worth having because the sold option has the potential of paying for most, if not all, of the premium of the bought option. The combined sold and bought premium can end up being a fraction of the cost of an outright futures contract or of purchasing a cash position.

An exchange market you trade a pure position on can have just one of the problems discussed previously or the complete trifecta. The stock market is a prime example of an exchange market that is affected by all the problems that traders have to contend with. This is in sharp contrast to the fact that the stock market is very versatile. There are at least three active derivative markets available to stock investors. At any given time a trader can buy or sell options, futures, and/or contracts for difference (CFDs). While there are varying levels of availability, each derivative has its own associated risk as well as margin and premium price figures.

Often the most economical stock derivatives to trade are the CFDs. They tend to have the greatest liquidity and can have some of the best trading margins, depending on the publicly listed corporation you trade shares in. Unfortunately, as of this writing, it is illegal for U.S. traders to trade directly in CFDs; they're only allowed to trade stock options and stock futures. This is an example of how the first problem—regulatory issues—can stop traders from participating in the best possible market.

The closest trading alternative to CFDs is single stock futures contracts, created by the Commodity Futures Modernization Act of 2000 and designed to be a compromise for both the SEC and the CFTC. Instead, single stock futures have become the laughingstock of the investment world. While good in theory, they lack the same mainstream support that CFDs have gained around the world. This demonstrates the second problem, the inability to maximize opportunities. The weakness of single stock futures leaves stock options as the only realistic derivative left to trade.

To get a better understanding of the stock derivatives, let's break down the numbers. The regulatory compromises that established single stock futures require that there be a uniform margin of 20 percent of a stock's face value. Depending on the shares that are traded, putting up 20 percent of the face value can quickly get expensive. Each single stock futures contract is based on 100 shares. Before a contract can even be established a trader must have the required 20 percent margin available to him. If the underlying 100 shares are valued at $5,000 then a trader is required to put up $1,000 in margins to obtain one single stock future contract.

A consistent margin rate may actually be the only advantage that single stock futures have over their CFD counterparts. On the other hand, CFDs can have margins that range from as little as 10 percent to as much as 50 percent of a stock's face value. This wide range in margin requirement is solely dependent on the underlying liquidity of the stocks that the CFD is based on. Therefore, a trader would have to put up a margin that could vary anywhere in price from $500 to $1,750.

Stock option premiums tend to come out the clear winners whether they're the fixed margin rates of single stock futures or the variable margins of CFDs. Stock option premiums are quoted in 100 share increments. Depending on the strike price of a stock option the premium could be just a few hundred dollars or less. This can play a significant role when deciding if stock options should be used to create a synthetic futures contract or not.

While the focus has been on the stock market, the same scenario can also play out on expensive futures contracts such as natural gas, the full size S&P 500 contract, or the big contract silver. Each of these markets have margins that are so expensive that it simply makes sense to find the right combination of options to convert into a synthetic futures position. What would cost possibly thousands of dollars can be reduced to a few thousand dollars at most. This is a significant modification, particularly when the margin for natural gas, as of this writing, is almost $10,000, a full size S&P 500 contract has a margin requirement at over $22,000, and the 5000 oz silver margin is $10,000.

When compared side by side with each other a synthetic futures contract will be less expensive, on the face of it. Depending on how your brokerage or your FCM handles the matter there may be additional margin requirements. This will come down to your relationship with them. In the examples below we dissect what a long and a short synthetic futures contract actually looks like and compare it to futures counterpart.

Synthetic Futures Long Position

The components required to establish a long synthetic futures contract are the purchase of a call option and the sale of a put option of the exact same price. That call gives you access to unlimited profit potential, but the sold put opens you up to unlimited loss on the downside. This strategy works best when you buy and sell both options at-the-money; you can collect the maximum amount of premium. Let's look at the S&P 500 as an example.

A full-sized S&P 500 futures contract has a margin requirement of $22,500. Earlier we discussed straddles. At that time, we looked at the

FIGURE 12.1 Synthetic Long Futures
Source: TradeNavigator.com © 2007. All rights reserved.

straddle option prices as a financial commitment to profiting from the market's moving in one direction or another. What if we had decided to create a synthetic futures contract instead (see Figure 12.1 and Table 12.1)?

These two scenarios are a huge difference in price. The first margin requirement of $22,500 doesn't compare to the net margin requirement of $725. This is like night and day. This is a huge difference in price, $21,775 to be exact. But the trade can't be left naked. It has to treated and protected just like a naked position. Either you can use an option as a hard stop or you can create a collar on the position.

Based on this example for $3,000 to $4,000, a slightly out-of-the-money protective put can be purchased at 1345. This would make the maximum loss of the sold put limited to 5 points. This protective measure also has the potential to encourage your FCM or brokerage to minimize their restrictions on your selling options.

TABLE 12.1 Synthetic Long Futures Position

	Strike Price	Premium
Buy call	1350	−16.70 (−$4,175)
Sell put	1350	+13.80 (+$3,450)
		−2.90 (−$725)

So for a total of $4,725 you are trading the value of a full-sized S&P 500 contract, with risk management protection—the same margin price that an Emini S&P contract would cost without any risk management in place.

This contract is still a futures contract, though, so you do end up picking a side, long or short. If the market doesn't move in that direction, you will lose value in your premium. Therefore you must watch the values of the various premiums, and if the market is moving against your position, simply exit the position entirely.

Synthetic Futures Short Position

A short synthetic futures position is simply a mirror of a long synthetic futures position. An at-the-money put is purchased and an at-the-money call is sold. This opens the door for unlimited profits if the market drops in value, but it also allows for unlimited loss if the market moves towards the upside. The actions to protect the synthetic short position are the same as a normal short position. Purchase a call to protect you from upside risk or use a collar. Any other form of risk management can be used, but may also be too complicated to keep track of.

The Brent light sweet crude oil contract is another great commodity to use a synthetic position with. The Brent light sweet crude oil futures contract margin is $12,488 (see Figure 12.2 and Table 12.2).

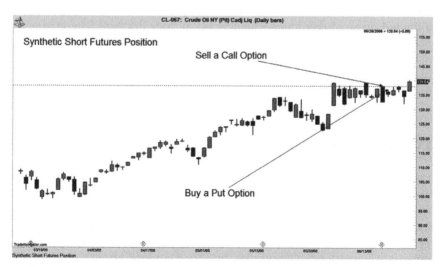

FIGURE 12.2 Synthetic Short Futures
Source: TradeNavigator.com © 2007. All rights reserved.

TABLE 12.2 Synthetic Short Futures Position

	Strike Price	Premium
Buy put	138.00	−2.43 (−$2,430)
Sell call	138.50	+1.50 (+$1,500)
		−.93 (−$930)

There is no comparison in value for your investment. The actual contract is valued at $12,488 and the synthetic is only $930. Another $2,000 (estimate based on the example prices) spent on a protective option position would still only set a speculator back by $2,930. The mini crude oil contract has a margin of $6,244. The amount of capital committed is half of the mini contract and you are still gaining value in your position at the full contract rate.

PRIMARY DRAWBACKS

The key problem with the synthetic futures position is its potential for unlimited loss whenever you sell an option. Another drawback is how your brokerage firm will treat you when you decide to execute an order of this type, whether they are flexible and allow the SPAN risk management software to handle the risk analysis or if they fly by the seat of their pants in determining the actual risk associated with this strategy. Finally, you have a limited array of risk management tools at your disposal. The goal is to not only make sure that you are protected from unlimited risk, but to also decrease your overall risk profile. This can only be done with some sort of protective option position. A stop loss or a stop limit will not cut it, and most likely will backfire by forcing you to maintain futures margin rates.

INTERCOMMODITY SPREAD

From the outset of this book I have been working on you to think like a professional as well as a hedger. With that in mind there is no way I could leave out one of the essential concepts of commodities trading, intercommodity spread trading. This is a big word for the simple concept that there is more than one use for a single commodity, such as corn. When you sit down at the dinner table you may be eating a piece of corn on the cob, while drinking a soda (which has corn syrup), eating a nice piece of chicken fried steak (which was probably fried with corn oil), all while watching an exclusive special on TV on ethanol (mainly corn) as the next big alternative fuel source.

Many commodities have multiple uses and purposes in our everyday lives. Corporations are constantly attempting to figure out more ways to slice, dice, and shred their way through a commodity to make sure every last piece is economically viable. They then go to the commodities market to minimize their risk by splitting up the various risk associated with each of their commercial products.

Nowhere is this seen more readily than in the commodity markets of soybean and oil. Each commodity has its own contract and so do their more popular derivative markets. In soybeans this is known as the crush spread and in the oil market this is known as the crack spread, named after the sound oil makes when it's being refined.

Crush Spread: Soybean, Soybean Meal, Soybean Oil

When soybeans are processed, two by-products are produced, soybean meal and soybean oil. A soybean grower is always attempting to determine the value of the two products in relationship to its raw commodity, and protect himself from any changes in either. The by-product purchasers are in the same boat. Therefore, when soybean prices are high a buyer will buy soybean to protect himself while simultaneously shorting soybean meal and soybean oil just in case prices drop. The sellers/growers, on the other hand, want to protect themselves from any sudden drops in price so they will short the soybean market and will go long the soybean meal and soybean oil markets to make sure they don't miss out on any jumps in price. The difference between the spread becomes their net profit, known as the gross processing margin.

The November/December crush spread is the most common to trade. It was developed to protect the new crop. Growers attempting to protect themselves from the traditional cheap prices at harvest tend to exploit this spread to their best advantage. Regardless of what factors affect soybeans every day, traders can participate in the crush spread just as easily as the pros.

The spread trades themselves can give you access to very cheap margins, known as spread margins, which can be 10 times cheaper than standard margins. In order to trade a standard soybean contract you would have to put up over $5,000 in margin; the listed spread margin is just $500. This is a big difference. The reason spread margins can be so low is because of the perceived risk management, of being both long and short in the same commodity complex. By now you are probably beginning to see a pattern.

To trade the crush spread is quite simple. The Chicago Board of Trade (CBOT) has determined that 60 pounds of soybean is the equivalent of 11 pounds of soybean oil and 48 pounds of soybean meal. There are two choices: either you can use a trading ratio of 1 soybean contract to 1 soybean meal and 1 soybean oil contract or, if you are going for absolute accuracy you can trade 10 soybean contracts to 11 soybean meal contracts and 9 soybean oil contracts. The latter ratio will approximate 50,000 bushels for each contract. The CBOT calls this the package trade (see Figure 12.3).

In fact, the CBOT established a crush options contract in 2006. Due to high demand and popularity of the intercommodity soybean crush trade, they wanted to allow the corporations (that is, the pros) to protect their crush position conveniently. In doing so, they have allowed everyday buyers and sellers to have one tool, without having to muck about with ratios and conversions, to track the crush spread and to treat it like any other option trade.

In keeping with the focus of the option being primarily for the professionals, buying a call means you are long the by-products and short the soybeans and buying a put means you are short the by-products but long the soybeans.

The primary drawback of any spread, as we discussed earlier, is that you can be wishboned in your trade. Therefore stops and stop limits are necessary to protect yourself from your position going south on you.

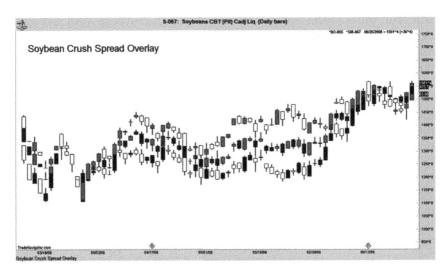

FIGURE 12.3 Soybean Crush Spread Overlay
Source: TradeNavigator.com © 2007. All rights reserved.

Crack Spread: Crude Oil, Heating Oil, Gasoline

Another popular intercommodity spread is the crack spread (see Figure 12.4). This spread shows the interrelationship between heating oil, gasoline, and crude oil. In identical fashion to the soybean crush spread, oil refiners attempt to hedge their risk from crude oil prices and its refined products. The most popular ratio is the 3:2:1 ratio: three crude oil futures contracts to two unleaded gasoline futures contracts to one heating oil futures contract.

The oil is bought in the front month and its by-products are sold in the following month or vice versa. In 1994 the New York Mercantile Exchange (NYMEX) made the crack spread convenient for all traders by considering this spread as one purchase, similar to the CBOT option. With oil shortages being predicted for decades to come this is a simple and inexpensive way for speculators to trade oil futures with a margin value that doesn't exceed $10,000.

Gold-Silver Ratio Spread

Finally, there is the gold-silver ratio spread. This spread has long been used to determine how expensive or inexpensive gold is at any given time. The theory follows that if it takes more ounces of silver to purchase gold than it did previously, then gold is considered expensive. If it takes less silver to purchase gold, again regardless of the price, then gold is inexpensive.

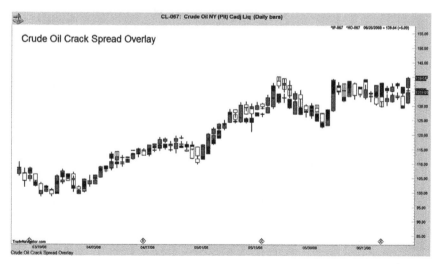

FIGURE 12.4 Crude Oil Crack Spread Overlay
Source: TradeNavigator.com © 2007. All rights reserved.

By playing around with this relationship, a trader can buy or sell gold and silver in the hope that they can profit from sudden increases or drops in value of both these precious metals.

Silver bugs believe that the prices of silver and gold should naturally revert to their historic interrelated monetary ratio of 16:1. As the prices wrestle for position there is a belief either that now is a good time to short gold and buy silver or that silver can increase in value to bring the ratio back in alignment. Whatever the case there is a constant hope that the prices will revert back to the mean to recreate this historic relationship. With this hope in place, whenever gold is stronger than silver there is a short gold, buy silver bias.

Whether you believe in trading the gold/silver ratio spread or not, others do. As a result, it is important to understand the psychology of those around you so you can better recognize opportunities in the precious metal sector for yourself.

In Figure 12.5 we see gold on the top and silver on the bottom; this chart follows these two commodities from January 2008 until July 2008. As you can see, the two precious metals move in tandem pretty closely. Nevertheless, it looks like the swings in the silver market are a little more aggressive. On July 9, 2008, silver was at $18.175 and gold was at $929.60. According to those numbers the ratio of silver to gold was 51:1. In order for the traditional ratio of 16:1 to come into effect, silver would have to triple

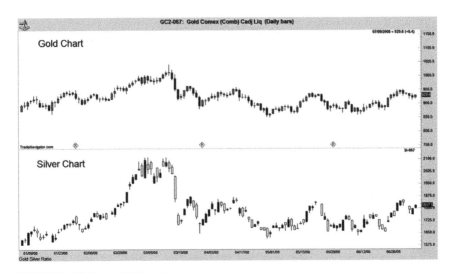

FIGURE 12.5 Gold Silver Ratio
Source: TradeNavigator.com © 2007. All rights reserved.

in price to $54 an ounce or gold would have to drop to $290 an ounce. You would have to be the judge of what most likely would happen.

PRIMARY DRAWBACKS

Spread trading can be tricky. While you are given cheaper margins because the trades, on the surface, appear lower risk, don't let down your guard. These trades are meant to be treated with the same respect as any naked position out there. Using options as a stop loss or putting stops in place to protect yourself is required. There are no shortcuts when using spread trading.

THE BULL CALL SPREAD AND BEAR PUT SPREAD

The third advanced technique that can be employed is the bull call spread and bear put spread. These are mirror images of each other. They are a sophisticated way of combining an at-the-money option and an out-of-the-money option. This type of strategy is a way to get the market to pay for part of your trading. By collecting a premium you are able to reduce the overall expense of an at-the-money option while giving yourself the opportunity to profit from the market's move.

Bull Call Spread

A bull call spread is the simultaneous purchase of an at-the-money option and the sale of an out-of-the-money option. The difference in value between the two different strike prices is what creates the profit opportunity for the trader. What makes this strategy attractive is the fact that you are able to purchase an at-the-money option at a discount. For expensive or highly volatile markets such as the S&P 500, euro, or crude oil, this is the easiest way to get into their options. If you have an account of $15,000 or less you can find that when you purchase an at-the-money option, one-third to two-thirds of your capital can be tied up for an extended period of time. The bull call spread gives your capital much needed relief.

In return for this reprieve you have to give up the main trading advantage that options have—unlimited profit potential. Your trading activity is locked between the difference in the two strike prices. This cap in your profits, while unpleasant, if done right, can add enough to the bottom line so that this technique will no longer be necessary.

Call premium paid	$1.2500 (−$2,975)
Call premium collected	$1.2700 (+$900)
Difference	$1.2700 (−$2,075)

In the bull call spread example there is an overall bullish bias for the euro market, so a bull call spread is used. By selling a $1.27 call, $900 in premiums are collected. An at-the-money call option is purchased for $2,975. This leaves a net cost of $2,075.

Bull Call Spread At-the-Money   One of three scenarios can play out. First, the trade is successful and the difference between $1.25 and $1.27 is collected as a profit. That would make a total profit of approximately $2,500. If the market stays at the $1.27 level and doesn't break through you will be able to keep your profits, plus the premium you collected, for a grand total of $3,400.

The second scenario would force the price past the $1.27 strike price. Any money above and beyond $1.27 will be forfeited along with the $900 in collected premium. That would leave you with $2,500 in profits, but you would have to hold on to the position until expiration.

The third possible scenario is that the market tanks below the $1.25 level. You have one of two choices: You can hold on until all of your premium is eroded, which would give you an official loss, or you can exit once the accumulated losses are equal to the amount of the premium that you have collected. This would let you exit your trade at almost breakeven.

If you fiddle around with closer strike prices you will be able to collect more premium on the sold option, but at the expense of your profit potential between the two strike prices. This requires a balancing act between profit goals and risk management that needs to be calculated before the trade is ever executed (see Figure 12.6).

Bear Put Spread

A bear put spread is the mirror opposite of the bull call spread. In the bear put spread a put option is purchased at-the-money and an out-of–the-money put option is sold. The premium collected offsets the costs of the bought put, and the difference between the two strike prices is your profit.

This strategy is designed to catch any move in the market's value to the downside. All the same potential scenarios exist for the bear put spread: The market price can drop, but not break past the sold option's strike price;

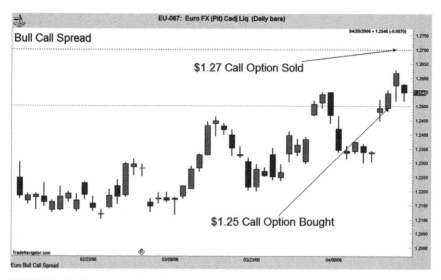

FIGURE 12.6 Euro Bull Call Spread
Source: TradeNavigator.com © 2007. All rights reserved.

the market price can drop and break through the sold call's strike price; or the market can move up and break through the bought option's strike price.

Each example is a different opportunity to interact with the market, but in a limited fashion. The bear put spread limits you from having unlimited profit opportunities, but it can strengthen your understanding of the market's rhythms. In Figure 12.7 we look at the corn market and see how a bear put spread would have looked like had we executed this kind of trade.

PRIMARY DRAWBACKS

When investing in real estate, location is everything. When trading the bull call spread and the bear put spread, premium is everything. If the collected premium is too little to justify the cap in profits, don't do it. If the collected premium is a lot, maybe your two strike prices are too close in value and you are capping your profits too tightly.

It also must be kept in mind that these trades can lose money. There is *no* risk management associated with these trades. In a volatile market that is moving against you, you can end up losing your entire premium if you are not prepared for any sudden drop in value. This adds another level

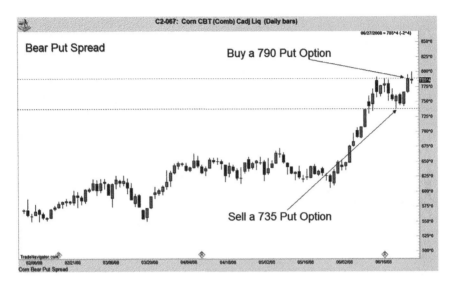

FIGURE 12.7 Corn Bear Put Spread
Source: TradeNavigator.com © 2007. All rights reserved.

of vigilance to your trading or more complexity if you use any of the risk management tools mentioned earlier.

CONCLUSION

This group of advanced strategies can be exciting to use as long as you understand the exposure to loss. The synthetic futures expose you to unlimited loss, the intercommodity spreads expose you to being wishboned and losing on two sides of a trade simultaneously, and the bull call spread and the bear put spread expose you to losing most if not all of your option's premium. What makes any of these strategies worthwhile is that they reduce your costs and give you the ability to trade in markets that otherwise may be out of your accounts trading range.

Trade these strategies with the intent of including other risk management tools to fully optimize them. This will have the immediate effect of power-boosting your account and helping you find trading opportunities that you may otherwise overlook or ignore.

CHAPTER 13

Advanced Option Selling Strategies

All that glitters is not gold.
—William Shakespeare, *The Merchant of Venice*

The epigraph chosen for this chapter is intentionally misquoted. The original sentence from the play is "All that glisters is not gold." Over the years we have given the original a modernized turn of phrase. While there are only subtle differences between *glitters* and *glisters*, they are significant enough to warrant two separate words. That is the case with the subject of this chapter.

The majority of the book has focused on pairing up your buy and sell strategies. Whether you were purchasing options to protect your futures positions or putting on spread positions with two or more futures positions, you were constantly covering one risk with another. In this chapter we shift gears. Prevailing knowledge says that "90 percent of options expire worthless"; but if that is the case, why would anyone ever buy options? Just as the Shakespearean quote "All that glisters is not gold" has changed over time, so has a real understanding of what it means that 90 percent of options expire worthless.

In this chapter we return to charts used in Chapter 4 to review how to sell a strangle and a straddle, as well as how to put on a naked short position. Yet before we can delve deeply into the strategies, a popular myth about options must be busted. The myth that "90 percent of options expire worthless" leads to a fallacy of logic that can create problems for the savvy trader attempting to make money selling options.

With any statement there is an inverse logic that can be used to test the accuracy or truthfulness of the statement itself. So if 90 percent of options expire worthless, that means that if you only sell options you will have a 90 percent success rate. Anyone who has ever attempted to test this theory has soon found himself or herself at a disadvantage. The presumed 90 percent success rate rarely, if ever, materializes.

In life there are few absolutes, and possibly even fewer near absolutes. The idea that "90 percent of options expire worthless" simply doesn't ring true, but somehow it has stuck. Although options do have a high expiration rate, there is a reason for that high rate that is best understood before attempting any of the income-generating ideas in this chapter.

DO 90 PERCENT OF OPTIONS EXPIRE WORTHLESS?

A lie told often enough becomes the truth.

—Vladimir Lenin

All over the Internet the option rhetoric is the same: 90 percent of options expire worthless. Others will claim that the figure is not as high as 90 percent, but possibly 70 to 80 percent. Where do any of these figures come from? Let's look at the language of the research to see if there is a discrepancy between this statement and the statements of some the research studies that have been done regarding options.

The Chicago Board Options Exchange (CBOE) has been maintaining data on options since 1973. The CBOE's researchers discovered a largely overlooked fact: that not all options are held until expiration. This is monumentally important when attempting to determine where figures such as 90 percent actually come from. The CBOE broke down option outcomes into a simple formula: 10/60/30. Ten percent of all options are exercised (converted to the underlying asset); approximately 60 percent of the options are closed (offset) before expiration; and the remaining 30 percent are held until expiration.

It is very likely that all of the remaining 30 percent of options actually expire worthless; the CBOE's formula does not mean that 90 percent of all options expire worthless. In a study done by the Chicago Mercantile Exchange (CME), ranging from 1997 to 1999, the researchers decided to come to a definitive conclusion on the exact percentage of options that expire worthless. In their research they concluded that 76.5 percent of the options that were held until expiration expired worthless.

This is significant. If only 30 percent of options are held until expiration, and of those that are held until expiration 76.5 percent expire worthless, then the statement that "90 percent of options expire worthless" is not only false, but a bold-faced lie—a lie that has been perpetuated over and over until it has become a marketing fact. The idea of "options held until expiration" and "options expiring" have been merged into one monolithic idea that is simply comparing apples to oranges.

The fact that only 30 percent of options reach expiration does not mean that the remaining 70 percent of options are successful. We know that 10 percent of all options are converted into the underlying asset; this is a sign that 10 percent of all options are guaranteed to be successful. We also know that about 60 percent of options are offset before they ever reach expiration. Some of those are profitable and some are not profitable, but none of them have ever reached expiration. So where does the 90 percent figure come from?

It likely derives from the fact that only 10 percent of options are converted into their underlying asset. That means 90 percent of options aren't converted into the underlying futures contract or stock. So undoubtedly the assumption is that if 90 percent of options aren't converted then they must expire worthless. This is a false assumption that is simply not supported by the numbers. Even in the small percentage of options that do expire, 30 percent, some of these expire with a cash value (13.5 percent, according to the CME).

So while we know that the percentage of options that expire worthless is not 90 percent, there is reason to believe that a majority of options do lose money. With 50 to 60 percent of contracts being offset before expiration and the majority of options that reach expiration expiring worthless, the odds are in favor of 50 to 60 percent of options to be losing trades. While 50 to 60 percent is less than the touted 90 percent figure, selling options is still a promising opportunity.

Becoming an Option Seller

It is exciting to hear that "90 percent of options expire worthless." It gives you the feeling of being an insider and the hope of finding a magic bullet with which to win the so-called trading game. Only once you attempt it do the numbers not add up to the hype. It is easy to be down on yourself and assume that somehow you are doing something wrong. This is not the case; it is just the classic example of being overpromised and underdelivered on that promise.

There are some empowering realities in knowing the truth about options that will make your option sales easier. First, the fact that the majority of options are not held until expiration releases you from holding on to the hope that the option that you sold, that is now losing you money, is worth holding on to until the absolute end. This reinforces the concept of cutting your losses as quickly as possible.

Second, you can feel confident, as a seller, that if you make money on the contract you can sell it into the marketplace (offset) along with the majority of traders with little or no worry that you have somehow missed out on profits. You are doing nothing different from what other option traders are doing.

Finally, you are releasing yourself from making a financial commitment that you cannot afford to make. When you sell options, you are limiting your profit to the premiums that you collect and exposing yourself to unlimited risk. If you believe that 90 percent of options expire worthless, it becomes easier to take risks and chances that you would otherwise avoid, because you believe the odds are in your favor.

How differently will a trader operate if he knows that when he sells an option he possibly has a 60 percent chance of the trade going in his direction, and only half of those will make it to expiration? One hopes he will operate with the caution and respect that selling options requires, and will sell options with his eyes wide open.

The following option selling techniques—selling straddles, strangles, and naked options—all have the opportunity to be profitable, in much the same way that purchasing options is successful. Selling options requires the same vigilance and common sense as purchasing options if you hope to make your trading plan successful. The ability to stick with your money management techniques and your trading goals will help you make sure that selling options is worthwhile.

WHAT TO EXPECT WHEN SELLING OPTIONS

In Chapter 4, where we began this journey, we introduced the concepts of straddles and strangles. At that time we looked at the straddle and strangle as opportunities to take advantage of sideways markets and news announcements, and to hedge your bets against wild fluctuations in the market's movements. One of the key drawbacks to both the straddle and the strangle is the possibility that the market will do nothing. If that occurs, you have the opportunity to lose part or all of your option premium, on both your put and your call, if you are not careful.

Options and futures trading is a zero-sum game; as we have discussed before, the premium you pay doesn't simply evaporate into thin air. Someone on the other side of your buying transaction has collected that premium. There is a trade-off, though. While the option buyers have an opportunity to make as much money as possible, the option sellers are restricted to the premium they receive, while being exposed to unlimited risk.

With added exposure to unlimited risk, the question is, "Why would anyone sell options?" As we have seen, the old adage "90 percent of options expire worthless" is not true, but the reality still favors that at least 60 percent of options most likely lose money. Couple the fact that more options lose money than make money with the advanced knowledge of what type of return on your money you will receive when you sell options, and selling options becomes a more comfortable alternative to the unknown.

Selling options cannot occur in a vacuum, though. You can't sell an option and forget about it. You must use stops, stop limits, and preferably protective buy options to back up your option sales. However you protect yourself from your option sales, it is simply important to do it. The reality still is that 40 percent of options are likely profitable. If you are caught on the wrong side of your option sale it can be disastrous. One misstep can wipe out all of your accumulated profits.

Margins and Option Selling

In futures and commodities trading it is not easy to sell options. While long and short futures contracts are treated the same, options are not treated with the same deference. When you purchase an option, your entire capital commitment is limited to the cost of the option premium. If the option premium is $500, then you are required to put up $500. Option selling is different.

Selling options exposes the seller to unlimited risk. This risk, while the responsibility is on the seller, is shared by the brokerage and the clearing firm. If the market moves excessively against the seller and for some reason he cannot pay, the loss first falls on the shoulders of the brokerage to pay for the loss, and it is extended to the clearing firm to cover any difference.

Similar to how protective the stock market is against shorting shares, selling options can be difficult to accomplish. While the stock market monitors shorting shares by restricting the number of shares available for borrowing, selling options has no such mechanism. Instead, clearing firms and brokerages force option sellers to make a capital commitment to their trade. This typically comes in the form of putting up the equivalent margin that would be needed to take an actual futures position.

For example, if you decide to sell an option worth $500 on corn and the margin is $1,350, you will receive a credit in your account for the premium, but you will also be required to have at least $1,350 in your account in order to initiate the option sale.

Another quirk of options is the fact that you will not be able to collect 100 percent of the premium until the option has expired. Only at that time will you have the profits transferred to your account free and clear.

This can be frustrating for those who want to accumulate the premium to initiate new trades, as we saw earlier when we discussed ratio spreads.

If you succeed in holding on to your sold option until expiration, the odds are in your favor (76.5 percent according to the CME) that you will collect your full premium. Alternatively, you can offset your successful sold option at any time by purchasing the corresponding option back. This same concept applies to selling calls.

For example, if you sell a put at a particular strike price, you must purchase a put at that exact same strike price in order to offset it. If you sold the put at $500 and you purchase the same put back at $200, your net profit will be $300. Your account will be adjusted accordingly, and you will lose $200 in premium from your account.

There are numerous reasons why you would offset your option position ahead of expiration; perhaps you achieve your target profit, you are worried that the market may shift suddenly based on some news event, or it is part of a broader strategy. Whatever the reason, do not hold on to a losing position until expiration in hopes that the trade will turn around all of a sudden.

STRANGLES, STRADDLES, OR NAKED OPTIONS

Strangles, straddles, and naked options—which type of trade is best? Naked options have a tendency to fall into the same category as simply buying options. If you have a bearish market bias, you sell calls; if you have a bullish market bias, then sell puts. While having a market bias is essential to anyone's long-term success, trading that market bias can be dangerous, particularly when you have all or nothing riding on one premium. This is what selling naked options means.

If the trade fails, we know that selling options exposes you to unlimited risk. The worst-case scenario for a naked option seller is for the underlying asset to become lock limit against the option. The underlying asset cannot be exited, so the option's volatility increases exponentially. The potential to lose thousands to gain a few hundred quickly becomes not worth it.

While there are ways to salvage or at least minimize the impact of a market moving against a naked option seller, it is best to have the proper option selling strategy set in place at the outset. This can best be accomplished by selling options only in sideways markets and using a sell straddle or sell strangle to let the market dictate what direction it wishes to go. This eliminates the need to have a market bias, while at the same time expanding your trading opportunities.

Naked option selling can be profitable. By monitoring the theta (decline of option time value) and the vega (measure of increase and decrease of option based on volatility), along with the expiration date, you can attempt to go through the option candidates and cherry-pick the ones most likely to sell. However, if you overoptimize your decision-making progress, you may find that there is not enough intrinsic value to make selling the option worthwhile.

When executing straddles and strangles, the same type of market bias as in selling naked options evolves from the market's movement, not from any type of arbitrary decision-making process. Selling two options can be expensive, but it is a solid way to be able to participate in some of the most profitable options around. Theta and vega are also important, but there is no need to be 100 percent dependent on these two values in order to determine what options to select. They become secondary monitoring tools to reinforce a decision that the market has already made.

In the following examples we analyze straddles, strangles, and naked options in order to determine the best opportunity. From there we will learn exactly how to pick profitable opportunities.

SELL STRADDLE

A sell straddle is also known as a short straddle. This is a strategy that is designed to take advantage of the market's volatility. The object is to sell a put and a call, both at-the-money options. At-the-money options have the highest built-in premium because of their high level of volatility. This volatility works in the option sellers' favor because they collect the maximum amount of money possible, knowing for a fact that when the volatility decreases they have an opportunity to profit from both the put and the call simultaneously.

The primary drawback of a straddle is the fact that the market rarely stays at the exact same price. So it is important to pay attention to the value of the underlying asset in relation to the options that were sold.

Short Straddle Examples

In Figure 13.1 we have a view of the gold chart on February 26, 2008. The underlying contract expires in April, and the option has one more month before expiration on March 28, 2008. The market is flat in anticipation of the upcoming February 27, 2008, Federal Open Market Committee (FOMC) interest rate announcement.

We have an opportunity to sell a 940 call for $1,830 and a put for $1,950. When selling options, we have to take into consideration the breakeven

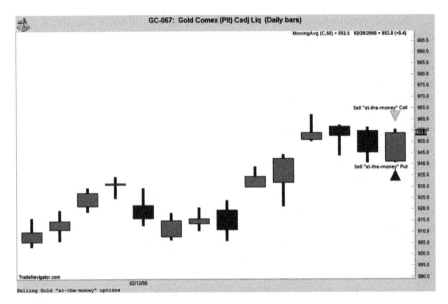

FIGURE 13.1 Short Straddle
Source: TradeNavigator.com © 2007. All rights reserved.

point of the option buyer. Options purchases don't break even on their purchase until the underlying price of the option exceeds the cost of the premium paid.

Breakeven for the person who buys the call occurs when the underlying price of gold reaches $958.30—total of premium paid ($18.30) plus the strike price (940). The person who buys the put won't break even until the price reaches $920.50—premium paid ($19.50) minus the strike price (940). (See Table 13.1.)

As an option seller you are collecting nearly as much premium as possible. An optimal at-the-money option delta is approximately 50 percent, the 940 call's delta is at 48.3 percent, and the 940 put's delta is at 51.4 percent. This means that you have to be willing to cut your losses on the losing

TABLE 13.1 Short Straddle Premiums

	Gold 940 Call	Gold 940 Put
Margin	$5,400	$5,400
Premium	$1,830	$1,950
Delta	.483	.514
Return on investment	34%	36%

option position as quickly as possible in order to retain as high a return on investment (ROI) as possible.

If you have to exit either option, the projected ROIs of 34 percent and 36 percent are cut in half. Once you have to pick the call position to keep, then your 34 percent ROI on $5,400 becomes a 17 percent return based on $10,400, minus whatever loss you may incur on your put position. The inverse is equally true. Once you decide to keep the put position, your 36 percent ROI turns into an 18 percent ROI.

The only factor working in the option seller's favor is the decreasing time value. Every day the contract gets closer to expiration it loses more of its value, as long as the underlying asset fails to move significantly toward either breakeven point. In Figure 13.2 we see the market's big spike over the next 30 days.

On February 26, 2008, we see the underlying gold market begin to take off. In one day it moves $13. This is an obvious cue to exit the gold market call option. The obvious winner in this pair, for the option seller, is the put option. By letting go of the call option as close to breakeven as possible, the option seller can keep the put option premium of $1,950, minus the call expenses.

With a delta of almost 50 percent, that means every $1 move was equal to 50 cents. If you exit after the $13 move, the potential hit would be $6.50

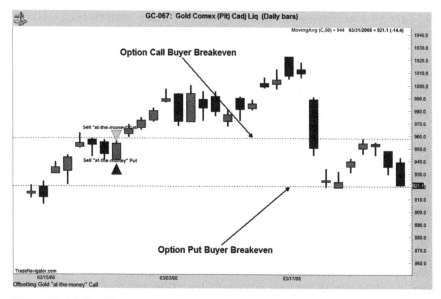

FIGURE 13.2 Offsetting Gold Call Option
Source: TradeNavigator.com © 2007. All rights reserved.

or $650. This puts your total profits at $1,300, approximately a 12 percent return on $10,800 in 30 days.

While the return is a little way away from the hoped-for 18 percent, and a third of the value had you simply sold a naked option, it is still significantly better than the stock market's historical return of 12 percent *a year*. This is the reason option sellers are willing to endure the potential for unlimited risk. The ability to not only calculate your potential returns in advance, but also hold on to your money in your account the entire time is a significant comfort for a certain type of investor.

As we look at Figure 13.2 we see the roller-coaster ride that the market can take. It actually moves up rather quickly, only to die down and reverse itself as the option gets closer to expiration. Had we held on to the call we offset early on in the move we, would have profited from both positions.

That is the beauty of having 20/20 hindsight. With money management rules and profit goals in place we couldn't hold on to the call we sold. We could only follow what the rhythm of the market was at that time. For this reason alone the statistical option model of 10/60/30 is most likely true.

Had we held on to both the call and put until expiration, we would have fallen into the 30 percent category, with the majority of those expiring worthless. Unfortunately, the reality of the short-term situation didn't allow us to hold on with the threat of unlimited risk hanging over our heads. So instead we fell into the 60 percent category (with the call option) of those who offset their options contract before the expiration date and into the 30 percent category (with the put option) of those options that are held until expiration.

Short Straddle Wrap-Up

There are a great number of benefits in putting on a short straddle; you can take advantage of volatility, you're able to gain the maximum premium possible, and you can collect your return on your investment ahead of time. The risks and rewards have to be weighed out, though. Selling options exposes you to unlimited risk, and even though they don't move in tandem with the underlying asset, if you are not careful you will quickly erode whatever little returns you expected.

Unlike the unlimited profit potential of purchasing options, selling options limits your profit to the initial premium, and any unexpected movements or volatility in the markets can jeopardize your opportunity to keep this profit. The primary saving grace of selling options is the simple fact that the majority of options do lose value. This and this alone makes it worthwhile to incorporate shorting straddles into your trading plan from time to time.

SELL STRANGLE

The New York Mercantile Exchange (NYMEX) has an excellent glossary on its web site regarding options. NYMEX defines a short strangle as similar to a short straddle, but the short call and the short put have different strike prices. This definition is just as good as any other definition. Some of the nuances of shorting or selling a strangle are lost in the definition, though.

On average, while selling options does expose traders to risk, that risk is diminished when an out-of-the-money option is sold. Whenever you sell an option you are faced with the potential of unlimited risk, and this risk is only mitigated by the fact that the further out-of-the-money an option is, the less likely for the underlying asset to hit its strike price.

There are a few drawbacks to putting on a short strangle. One of the main drawbacks is the amount of premium collected. While you are putting up a significant margin to protect against the unlimited risk you are exposed to, the premium that you receive may bring in only a small ROI.

Another drawback is that in order to be profitable, short strangles need to thrive in a low-volatility marketplace. The less volatile the market is, the better it can be for the option seller. The lack of volatility is great on the one hand because it increases the likelihood that the options will expire worthless. On the other hand, a low-volatility option market means that you cannot sell options and command a high premium. It becomes a serious measure of risk versus reward before deciding to put on a short strangle.

Short Strangle Examples

These examples are meant to highlight what a potential short strangle position can look like. The examples have been plucked from Chapter 4. At that time we were purchasing a strangle, whereas in these examples we are taking a second look at the charts from the perspective of the seller. By mastering the short strangle you can apply another approach to your trading repertoire.

In the examples that follow we look at two different markets, the gold market and the S&P 500 commodities market. Each market has its own rhythms and behavior, but they still follow the same rules when it comes to using the strangle as a trading technique.

In the first example (see Figure 13.3 and Table 13.2) we take another look at the gold market. There is a simple setup. We sell a 960 call and an 890 put. With only the limited information provided by the charts and the options, we can make an informed decision about a few fundamental factors.

FIGURE 13.3 Gold Short Strangle
Source: TradeNavigator.com © 2007. All rights reserved.

For the call position we know the following: First, we have found a decent resistance level at 960; the gold market has bumped against this high for three days without breaking through. Second, if the market does break through the 960 level, we will lose only $31.50 for every $1 move. Third, the market would have to hit and break through $968 before the option buyer would begin to profit.

For the put position we know that the market is currently $70 away from our $890 strike price. We also know that not only will the market need to drop to $890, but it will have to hit $885 before it begins to move in-the-money. In the meantime, for every $1 that the gold market moves up, our $890 put loses $18 in value. This means that if the market moves up $30 ($960 + $30 = $990), the option that we sold will be virtually worthless

TABLE 13.2 Short Strangle Premiums

	Gold 960 Call	Gold 890 Put
Margin	$5,400	$5,400
Premium	$820	$530
Delta	.315	.188
Return on investment	15%	9.8%

and we could offset our gold 890 put and still gain the majority of premium without waiting for expiration.

In Figure 13.4 we see gold break through $960, moving into new territory. On February 27, 2008, gold moves $4, eventually closing at $965.90. This is less than $3 away from the option buyer's breakeven of $968. This move requires that we offset the 960 call that we sold. In order to accomplish this we would have placed a stop order at $960, with the hope that we would not lose more than $100 on this side of the trade.

With a $100 loss on the sold call, that effectively leaves us a profit of only $430 on our sold 890 put option. On March 5, 2008, gold closes above $990, reaching as high as $999.90 that day. This move signaled gold touching just below an important psychological number of $1,000 per ounce. This move also triggers the $30 target we needed in order to offset our 890 put to obtain the maximum premium.

In Table 13.3 we see that the total gain on the gold short strangle is $420 over the course of five days. On a $10,800 investment this produces nearly a 4 percent return. On the face of it that is not a very impressive return. If you extrapolate it to a monthly return figure, though, you would have a monthly return of 24 percent, since six sets of five days equals 30 days or one month. If you extrapolate it out to an annual return, you are looking at a simple, noncompounded, return of 288 percent!

FIGURE 13.4 Offsetting Gold Short Strangle
Source: TradeNavigator.com © 2007. All rights reserved.

TABLE 13.3 Offsetting Gold Short Strangle

	Gold 960 Call	Gold 890 Put	Total Gold Option Values
Initial premium	$820	$530	$1,350
Offset	−$920	−$ 10	$ 930
Profit/loss	−$100	$520	$ 420

These numbers are hypothetical, but are indicative of why selling options is considered an attractive alternative to purchasing options. You can easily calculate your annual rate of return on a case-by-case basis and determine whether the risk of the trade is worth taking. So even though $420 is not a phenomenal return on the face of it, it can be a significant income boost to anyone's portfolio. Who would turn down an effective annual rate of return of 288 percent?

In Figure 13.5 we put on the exact same type of strangle on the S&P 500. We sell an S&P 500 1400 strike price call for $1,250 in premium along with an S&P 500 1325 put and collect $2,250.

In Figure 13.5 we see that the S&P 500 closes at 1310, 15 points beneath our put strike price of 1325, on March 6, 2008. This is the first signal to offset our short put immediately. The fact that the delta for our put is

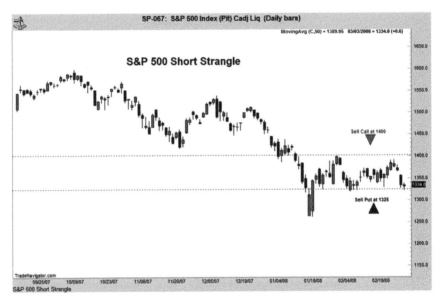

FIGURE 13.5 S&P 500 Short Strangle
Source: TradeNavigator.com © 2007. All rights reserved.

FIGURE 13.6 Offset S&P 500 Short Strangle
Source: TradeNavigator.com © 2007. All rights reserved.

.367 means that our option's value increases by one-third of the underlying asset, in this case only about 5 points. As the option stays in-the-money, the delta increases and if we are not careful we will continue to bleed money. We get off easy with an approximate $250 loss (5 points × $50).

In Figure 13.6 we see that in order to offset the S&P 500 1400 call in this environment the price of the underlying futures contract has to drop a little over 50 points. Every point drop is the equivalent of $50, but since the delta rate of change is a little under one-half, we would need a total of a 50-point drop to reach the total value of the premium, $25 (one-half point movement) × 50 points = $1,250. Our ideal exit to offset our call position would be 1275 (1325 − 50 points) (see Tables 13.4 and 13.5).

TABLE 13.4 Short Strangle Premiums

	S&P 500 1400 Call	S&P 500 1325 Put
Margin	$22,500	$22,500
Premium	$1,250	$2,250
Delta	.483	.367
Return on investment	6%	10%

TABLE 13.5 Offsetting Short Strangle

	S&P 500 1400 Call	S&P 500 1325 Put	Total S&P 500 Option Values
Initial premium	$1,250	$2,250	$3,500
Offset	−$ 50	−$2,500	−$2,550
Profit/loss	$1,200	−$ 250	$ 950

Two days after closing below 1325, the S&P 500 market hits 1277, two points above our target goal. We can still offset the call we sold by purchasing an inexpensive S&P 500 1400 call at $50. In Table 13.5 we see that the entire strangle brings in $950 after only eight days of being in the trade. We risked a total of $45,000 to earn $950; this is a return of 2 percent on our money. If you could make 2 percent every eight days, you would make 7 percent per month, or an annual return of 84 percent.

Although you are not breaking the bank, an annual rate of return of 84 percent exceeds both the stock market's and the bond market's annual historic returns. This is a prime example of how a small 2 percent return can play a significant role in changing your investing success.

Short Strangle Wrap-Up

Strangles are a less profitable alternative to straddles, but they clearly have a leg up when it comes to risk. There is little doubt that if you sell the right option you will have the opportunity to collect the premium with little or no hassle. The only thing standing in your way is simply the challenge of picking the right option to sell. The short strangle strategy allows you to hedge your bets. At the same time, a short strangle gives you enough breathing room between different strike prices to get you out of the trade altogether if, for some reason, it proves too difficult to hold on to.

Short strangles are also perfect for markets that just can't break out of their sideways momentum. If the market is stuck between a significant support and resistance point, there is an opportunity to profit from both the put and the call. This type of double-dipping with option premiums can't be accomplished in a straddle. This is what makes selling a strangle a lot more desirable to selling a straddle in the long run.

NAKED OPTION SELLING

For the record, I do not recommend naked option selling. Of all of the techniques, I consider naked options to be the most risky. This is the only advanced strategy that I have discussed in the book that is not automatically paired up with a spot, futures, or other option position to protect you from the risk. The key reason that it is even mentioned in this chapter is because shorting straddles and strangles can't be honestly discussed without at least acknowledging their origin.

Naked option selling has two handicaps: misinformation and leverage. The first handicap, misinformation, was discussed at the outset of this chapter. The fictional number of 90 percent of options expiring worthless was rightly dispelled, but it also reduces the level of confidence that can be had in believing in its overall success, particularly when only 30 percent of options actually make it to their expiration dates.

The second handicap is leverage. When initiating a futures contract, doing a spot forex transaction, or purchasing an option, it can be comforting to know that the leverage is on your side. The amount of money you can earn on your positions is vastly superior, in terms of percentage, to the actual amount you have put up. In gold trading a $1 move is equal to $100. It only takes a $54 move to match the necessary futures margin, $5,400. This leverage works against naked option sellers.

If an option seller sells an at-the-money option and collects $1,800, it only takes an $18 move into-the-money, at $100 per $1 move, to eliminate his entire collected premium. If an out-of-the-money option is sold for $800, then it simply takes an $8 move into-the-money against the seller before he gives up all of his profits. Although there is more leeway between the strike price and the cash price when it comes to an out-of-the-money option, it still doesn't take much to eliminate the collected premium.

There are two primary benefits of selling naked options. First, your margin reserves are 50 percent of what it would take when putting on short straddles and strangle positions. A second key benefit is that you know ahead of time what your potential return on investment can be. In Table 13.6 we see that a gold 940 call has the potential to return 34 percent, and in Table 13.7 we see that a gold 960 call has the potential to return 15 percent.

As you sell options further and further out-of-the-money, your overall return diminishes, but the likelihood of you getting that return increases.

TABLE 13.6 Example 1: At-the-Money Option Premium

	Gold 940 Call
Margin	$5,400
Premium	$1,830
Delta	.483
Return on investment	34%

TABLE 13.7 Example 2: Out-of-the-Money Option Premium

	Gold 960 Call
Margin	$5,400
Premium	$820
Delta	.315
Return on investment	15%

This is a constant trade-off when it comes to selling naked options. How far can you sell your option contract out-of-the-money before the amount of capital you tie up doesn't justify the unlimited risk you are exposed to and the limited returns you are capable of earning?

This is not an easy question to answer. It becomes a personal choice of whether you wish to earn 15 percent or 5 percent. Your technical analysis tools or market opinion will determine how you expect to interact with the market and where you expect it to go. The more aggressive may sell only at-the-money options, and the less aggressive will sell out-of-the-money options. However you approach selling options, do not take it lightly.

There are two other ways to sell naked options, in-the-money and based on theta, that have not been discussed at length. First, selling an in-the-money option requires a level of understanding of the greeks that is outside the scope of this book. And even if you understand the greeks, there is still no guarantee of success. This would make selling an in-the-money option akin to a suicide mission, no matter how much premium could be collected. Second, using time decay or theta to make your selling decision may not always be prudent. Just like out-of-the-money options, the closer you get to expiration, the less premium you will be able to collect. So make theta a component of your decision-making process but not the sole reason for selling; otherwise you may be disappointed at the results.

Naked Option Wrap-Up

Tackling a naked option is much like tackling a regular futures contract. There is so much exposure to risk that the rewards may not be there. If you sell an at-the-money option you can collect a significant premium, compared to shorting a straddle or a strangle. Selling only one option diminishes your capital commitment to the brokerage firm as well. Nevertheless, with the increased premium comes increased exposure to risk. The exposure to unlimited risk compared to the premium that can be collected makes the sale of an at-the-money option less attractive.

Selling out-of-the-money options can be slightly more attractive. While unlimited risk still looms over the seller's head, time decay and decreased volatility work in favor of the option seller. The key trade-off between selling an at-the-money option versus an out-of-the-money option is the amount of collected premium. Where an at-the-money option premium has a potential return as high as 30 percent or more, an out-of-the-money option may bring in as little as 5 to 7 percent. If the market suddenly moves against an out-of-the-money option seller, the limited rewards—5 to 7 percent returns—simply don't justify the exposure to unlimited risk.

If a trader chooses to be a naked option seller, the risk and reward must constantly be weighed. Once the rewards are significantly diminished by the potential risk, a reassessment must be done on how to approach that risk. This may mean either avoiding selling options altogether or making sure you take advantage of the daisy-chain relationship of the spot, options, and futures markets combined for maximum opportunity.

CONCLUSION

Whether you are selling straddles, strangles, or naked options, you are exposing yourself to a significant amount of risk. Much of this risk can be offset by buying options to counter the risk, but once that is done, we move into more exotic trading of synthetic futures and synthetic futures collars, techniques we discussed earlier in the book. Purchasing an additional option as protection forces you to use the premium you collected inefficiently, practically eliminating the entire reason you sold the option in the first place.

The smart way to manage your option selling risk is to simply use a stop. Since options do not move at the same speed as the underlying asset, you have an opportunity to exit with a little less sticker shock, as opposed to dealing with slippage in the futures market and the volatile forex market.

Also keep in mind that these techniques have been shoved into the advanced section, deep in the back of the book, for a reason. This is a style of trading that should not be taken lightly and quite literally is not meant for everyone. Paper trading and demo trading the ideas in this chapter should not need to be emphasized, but I will point out one more time that selling options involves unlimited risk, and when it comes to trading in futures and commodities you can not only lose your entire investment, but you can also lose much more.

Sell options with both caution and common sense, and you will find yourself tapping into small, but consistent, profit opportunities for the rest of your life. Many successful Commodity Trading Advisors have successfully created practices solely around selling options or establishing straddles and strangles. The trick to being successful at selling options comes from your ability to temper your profit goals. If you are willing to turn your back on the potential of unlimited risk in favor of taking small bite-size chunks from the market, your entire market outlook evolves.

CHAPTER 14

Retreat, Recovery, Opportunity

Coming together is a beginning. Keeping together is progress. Working together is success.

—Henry Ford

T his book has been an unparalleled journey into how professional traders approach the market and deal with the risk of loss. The information throughout these chapters has been broken down into basic and advanced strategies to highlight the differences between concepts that are solely designed to manage risk and ideas designed to also generate income. By themselves the basic and advanced concepts presented here are not inherently more difficult from one another. Nor are the basic and advanced strategies really required to be operated on their own.

As you have probably learned, in reading through the various chapters, it takes only small changes to convert one strategy into another. If you were to add an out-of-the-money option to a futures or spot position, you could create a hedge. To make another change only requires that you turn an out-of-the-money option into an at-the-money option and tie it to a futures or spot position to make a synthetic put or call option. It simply requires the willingness to sell an option and purchase an option with the same contract month to create a synthetic futures. If you sell one option and purchase two options slightly out-of-the-money, then all of a sudden you have a type of ratio spread.

Subtle changes and modifications to a position can make it morph into an entirely different trade altogether. By being open to combining the basic strategies in this book along with the advanced strategies that you learned, you have the ability to manipulate the markets, even if you are losing.

217

In the face of a losing trade, the majority of retail traders either freeze up or head for the hills. Those who do exit their losing positions do so with their emotions. It is important to know that whether it is the same moment that they exit their losing trade or days later, the simple fact that they can take the loss at all is a testament to their trading maturity. It is a far better solution than freezing up in the face of adversity.

Professional traders do not look at taking a loss the same way as retail traders do. Often professional traders think in terms of how to manipulate the losing trade into an opportunity to profit. Whether they convert a trade into another form, such as an option hedge into a synthetic option, or they unwind an advanced trade, such as a collar into a ratio spread, they are looking for a way to put the odds of success back in their favor. With that being said, for the majority of retail traders simply closing out a losing trade is most likely the intelligent way to approach loss. Don't stop doing that.

Taking a loss gives you a chance to take a break from the market and come back to it with fresh eyes. You can review your technical analysis as well as determine whether there has been a fundamental shift in the supply and demand of the currencies or futures you are currently trading. When you have only a finite amount of capital available to you, closing out your losing trades is simply the most prudent thing to do, nine times out of ten.

The decision to combine strategies or morph one strategy into another strategy should occur only that tenth time—that one time when you know for a fact that your technical analysis signals have pegged the market's reversal or your original assessment is simply experiencing a setback. You can see the shift in the market and you can tell that it only requires that you make one or two changes to your approach in order to be successful over the long run.

That is what this chapter is about. We will look at five different scenarios and ask ourselves up to three questions: Should we hold on to the trade, should we walk away from the trade, or should we convert the trade? For each one of our choices we will look at our risk and reward profile to determine what makes the most sense for our goals.

The examples in this chapter are designed to show you that no matter what the situation is, you can manipulate any one of these strategies to give yourself the best opportunity for success, even if that means exiting the trade altogether.

Analyze the charts and see how the various trades can flow from one scenario to the next. Eventually you will see the lines of opportunity and be able to manipulate the various strategies accordingly. There are no hard-and-fast rules to trading with risk management strategies; as long as you keep your mind flexible to the market's behavior, you will be able convert from one strategy to the next with ease.

MANIPULATING THE STRATEGIES

In the following five examples, charts that were presented in various chapters throughout the book will be reintroduced. In each example we look at how an initial trade can be modified into another trade, either through necessity or because of a change of circumstance. The ability to fluidly react to the market is an essential skill for long-term success.

There are many reasons why you may want to interact with the market differently than you set out to do. Professional traders use a myriad of techniques in order to effect that change. The following are just a few ways to manipulate and modify trades from their original intent.

Example 1: Collar Trade into Bull Call Spread

In Chapter 7 we took an extensive look at long and short collar trading. A collar is a position that caps off your losses with an option that you purchase, and the cost of the option is partially offset by an out-of-the-money option that you sell. The potential to profit is capped between the strike price of the protective option and the sold out-of-the-money option.

Figure 14.1 is a classic example of a collar setup in the euro.

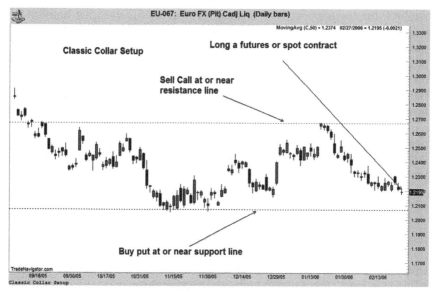

FIGURE 14.1 Classic Collar Setup
Source: TradeNavigator.com © 2007. All rights reserved.

In this example the euro has a well-defined support line at the $1.2100 price level. Looking at the same chart, we can see that the euro moved up to $1.2680 and collapsed soon after gapping up in price. Collapsing after the gap shows the development of a decent point of resistance. If the euro does begin to move up again, then it has to look forward to facing resistance at the $1.2680 level once again. This is the perfect place for the market to pull back if it fails to develop enough momentum to break through.

At the same time, this market has been generally unpredictable. A lot of downward pressure has developed over the course of just 14 days. Fourteen days after the market hit the $1.2680 price it has collapsed back down to the $1.2100 price level, eventually creating a candlestick formation at $1.2195 called a doji. A doji pattern is considered a straightforward reversal signal. Since it has formed at $1.2195 area, we are given a buy signal to act on.

The doji could just represent a small turnaround signal, indicating the beginning of a retracement, not necessarily a shift in the overall buying pressure of the euro itself. With this understanding, it's only logical that a collar be put on.

To successfully put on the collar for this chart, we have to take three distinct actions. We have to purchase a put option at or near the money. With the price of the euro futures at $1.2195, we have an opportunity to buy an option at $1.2200, $1.2150, or $1.2100. For this example we look for the support line that can protect us for the least amount of expense. We choose a strike price of $1.21. While the doji pattern suggests that the market can move up, our goal is to insure ourselves against any downward pressure that the euro may suddenly experience. Based on the technical analysis, the euro has the ability to drop suddenly in the same aggressive fashion as it did when it failed to break $1.2700 the first time.

A combination of the doji pattern, support near $1.22, and resistance near $1.27 gives us a potential setup for a decent collar trade. There is no guarantee that the doji pattern will signal a market reversal that has enough momentum to break through the most recent high of 14 days ago. With two what-if scenarios possible, a collar trade can allow a trader to get the best of both worlds.

Figure 14.2 shows the conclusion of the euro's move and the impact that it has on the established collar trade.

The doji was a good signal and the euro does move upward. It spends a total of two months attempting to get back and break through the $1.2680 resistance level. The $1.2680 high gets blasted through as the euro heads on to make new record highs at the time. So while the doji was right about the market's upward movement, the resistance level can't hold and affects

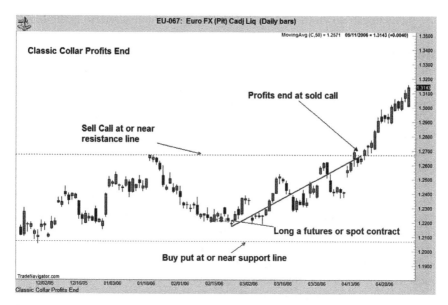

FIGURE 14.2 Classic Collar Profit Ends
Source: TradeNavigator.com © 2007. All rights reserved.

the ultimate fate of our collar trade negatively. By putting on a collar, we are forced into a tough set of decisions that literally make us pay for our mistake.

The call option that we sold caps off our profits at the $1.2680 level. That means that we entirely miss out on the 4 cent move from $1.27 to $1.31. With each 1 cent move equal to $1,250, this is a total opportunity cost of $5,000. While one of the cardinal rules of trading dictates that we shouldn't fixate on missed moneymaking opportunities, in this case it can't help but be noticed that a good amount of potential profits has been left on the table.

The actual profits that were made from the trade are significant, though. In this case if you had a long futures contract it would have collected profits from $1.22 to $1.27; this would equal $6,250 in profit before option expenses. If a long spot euro transaction had been put on, the move would have yielded a profit of $5,000 (a $100,000 contract represents that every 1 cent move or 100-pip move equals $1,000).

In the face of leaving an additional $5,000 ($1.27 to $1.31) in potential futures contract profits on the table, a collar trade leaves a trader few choices on how to react to the market. The collar trade can be held until it reaches expiration, it can be exited immediately, or it can be converted into another type of trade entirely.

Let's break down the choices to determine which scenario is the best.

Hold It   In Chapter 4 the "hold it" option of the collar was explored. Table 14.1 shows that, by holding the option until expiration, you are able to collect your futures profits of $6,312.50. The protective put expires worthless, so you lose $2,100. This brings your profits down to $4,212.50. The call that you sold doesn't break even until $1.2772. In this scenario we will assume that the option expires before it can reach breakeven for the buyer. This leaves you a profit on the sold option of $900 for a net profit of $5,112.50.

Risk   This trade exposes the trader to two significant risks. First, by holding on to a collar until expiration, a trader is exposed to multiple ups and downs in the market, without the guarantee that the underlying futures contract will actually reach the resistance level where the call option was sold. The call option's premium may not be enough to make up for the lack of momentum of the underlying futures contract and the amount of premium that was paid to put on the protective put.

The second risk is the potential that the sold option does move past the breakeven point and is exercised by the option buyer. The $900 in premium that was originally collected is removed from the balance sheet, and the maximum profit that can be achieved on the entire trade is $4,212.50.

With the uncertainty of the outcome of holding on to the collar trade until expiration looming over a trader, along with the missed profit opportunity, there are few viable alternatives. The trader can either walk away from the collar trade by selling it off or use a bull call spread to modify and extend the life of the trade.

Walk Away   Taking the same chart, this is what would happen if a trader decided not to hold on to the collar until expiration. On the chart the euro gives the trader an opportunity to get out of the trade before the options contracts reach expiration. In this instance the euro futures contract is

TABLE 14.1   Euro Classic Collar Hold

	Long Futures	Buy Protective Put/Premium	Sell Call for Income/ Premium Collected
Entry	$1.2195	$1.2100 ($2100)	$1.2700 ($900)
Exit	$1.2700	$1.2700 ($2100)	$1.2700 ($900)
Profit/loss	+$6312.50	−$2100 (Don't exit)	+$900 (Don't exit)

exited as soon as it hits $1.27. At 1.27 the futures contract is profitable, making a total of $6,312.50.

The protective put is exited as well. While the protective put has no real intrinsic value, there is a little time value left, so there is an opportunity to collect $475 by selling the put back into the marketplace. This leaves the trader with a total loss on the put of $1,625. The trader also decides to buy the call option back. Even though the call is not fully in-the-money, it has increased in value. This forces the trader to buy back the call at its current at-the-market value of $2,675. This leaves a net loss on the call of $1,775 (see Table 14.2).

This brings the net profits on the trade down to $2,912.50; this is a far cry from the profits that would have accumulated had the trader simply decided to go long the futures contract ($6,312.50), and $1,300 less than holding the collar trade until expiration ($4,212.50).

Risk By just collecting $2,912.50, profits are diminished compared to the other potential trading scenarios, but it may make the most sense because of how the market is behaving at the time. What should dictate your trading decisions is your market bias. In this case the decision was to go long the futures market. By making the decision to go long, the trader must stay focused on how the long position behaves or doesn't behave. This is how profits are made, by paying attention to what is affecting the futures position.

If the futures position begins to weaken in value but doesn't drop far, how does that affect your profit potential? If the market finally hits your target goal, does it really make sense to continue to hold the protective option contracts unnecessarily?

There are two potential scenarios:

The first scenario involves the trade hitting the price target of $1.27 and pulling back, never to come back to $1.27 again. This has the potential of ending up to be a giant goose egg for a trader if he is not careful.

TABLE 14.2 Euro Classic Collar Liquidation

	Long Futures	**Buy Protective Put/Premium**	**Sell Call for Income/ Premium Collected**
Entry	$1.2195	$1.2100 (−$2,100)	$1.2700 (+$900)
Exit	$1.2700	$1.2700 (+$475)	$1.2700 (−$2,675)
Profit/loss	+$6,312.50	−$1,625	−$1,775

So even if the futures contract is profitable, the overall position is weak. Let's suppose the market pulls back and stays around $1.2445. This has the potential to produce a futures profit of $3,156.25. Let's take it one step further and let the market end at that price as the options expire. You would lose $2,100 on the protective put you bought. Subtract your futures profits from your put option losses, and you are left with $1,056.25 in profits.

Add to that the collected premium of $900 from the call you sold, and you end up with $1,956.25. That's a $1,000 difference from just exiting once your profit target of $1.27 is hit. If the futures market were to drop any lower than 50 percent of the total value, it quickly becomes apparent that the amount you are risking isn't worth the reward.

If this scenario were to occur independently, never actually reaching the $1.27 target price, that would be is okay; but if the market were to hit $1.27 and you didn't take advantage of it, then you would have created an unnecessary opportunity cost.

The second potential scenario would require the trader to leg out of the position. When legging out the position, the goal is to exit each of the individual components of the trade independently as it becomes profitable. By legging out of a trading position, the trader is exposed to a lot of unnecessary risk. In fact, if the market moves against any leg of the position there would be significantly more trouble involved compared to the potential profit collected.

For instance, if a trader decides to collect the profits from the long futures position ($6,312.50), but decides to stay in the options, there are two situations that could come from doing this. The first one could be a loser, but the second one could be profitable. Unfortunately, there is no way to predict which one will occur with 100 percent certainty.

First, as long as the futures market stays at the $1.27 area it can actually break through $1.27 and drive the sold call up in value. Without a futures contract protecting the sold call, the call is exposed to unlimited risk. A few cents of movement above $1.27 could wipe out all of the profits that the long futures position has accumulated and then some. This makes the premium that was collected for selling the call a liability as opposed to being an asset.

If the euro breaks through the $1.27 price level, the put option that was bought for thousands of dollars will definitely expire worthless. This will compound the position's overall losses. The money from the sold call will evaporate as prices increase in value, and you will lose the premium you paid on the option. This is completely counter to the original intent of the collar.

The second scenario that could evolve, the only one that could potentially work in favor of legging out of this position, is for the market to collapse in value by breaking the support level of $1.22. This would increase the value of the put option, and allow the sold call to expire worthless so you can collect the premium.

The likelihood that the second scenario will occur is small. The fact that the futures position was exited with a profit means the momentum of the market is on the long side. A trader will be forced to wait and hope for the market to move in the short direction. In the meantime there will be a constant fear of losing the premium that was paid and being nakedly exposed to the unlimited risk of a sold call option.

Neither scenario is a healthy way to trade. Walking away from the trade makes for the best option in this instance. Yet, there is a third opportunity available. There is an opportunity to convert the trade from a collar trade into something else, a bull call spread.

Convert   A bull call spread is the purchase of an at-the-money option and the sale of an out-of-the-money option. You profit from the difference between the two strike prices. The fact that you have to spend money to purchase an option creates a debit in your account, which gives this type of transaction its second name, bull call debit spread.

Figure 14.3 takes an entirely different snapshot of the euro in another time frame.

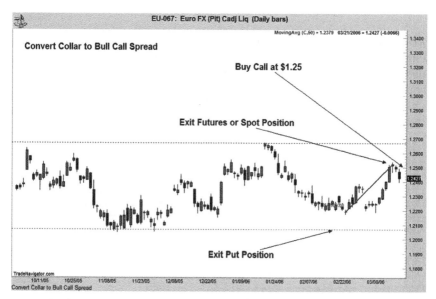

FIGURE 14.3   Convert Collar to Bull Call Spread
Source: TradeNavigator.com © 2007. All rights reserved.

This time we see that the euro has rallied up to $1.25 after gapping down. With no foreknowledge of where the euro's price will eventually end up, we see an out from our collar trade. On March 13, 2008, the candlestick pattern "hanging man" forms on the euro chart. After the most recent market collapse, this does not bode well for the euro. In fact, this a clear signal that the market can reverse.

Seeing an overall bullish bias for the euro market, yet at the same time not wanting to see the futures contract's profits erode for our collar trade, we unwind the trade and replace it with a default bull call spread.

In Table 14.3, the long futures contract is exited and $3,812.50 in profits are collected. The protective put is exited with only a $600 loss. If the $900 in collected premiums is added, then there is a total net profit of $4,112.50. That gives a trader enough capital to purchase an at-the-money option at the exact same exit price of the futures contract; or the market can be allowed to pull back as low as it can go before reentering the euro with a call.

In Figure 14.4 we see the euro take off and not only hit the $1.27 target, but exceed it, getting up to $1.29. Had we stayed in the futures position, we would have made $2,225, but at the same time we would have risked a pullback to $1.23 before we could have achieved that.

As always, hindsight is 20/20, so while we were trading we had no idea if the market would rebound, and there were few clues that would have alerted us to this potential outcome. Therefore, the risks involved with taking such a bold move have to be assessed.

Risk There is no guarantee that the $1,912.50 in profits made from the purchase of the 1.25 option would have occurred. In fact, there were two scenarios that had the potential to happen from this conversion to a bull call spread.

The first scenario is to purchase the at-the-money option for $2,975. In doing that there is exposure to the risk that the market will pull back

TABLE 14.3 Euro Classic Collar Convert to Bull Credit Spread At-the-Money

	Long Futures	Replace Future with Call	Put Premium	Sell Call for Income/ Premium Collected
Entry	$1.2195	$1.2500 (−$2,975)	$1.2100 (−$2,100)	$1.2700 ($900)
Exit	$1.2500	$1.2700 (+$4,887)	$1.2500 (+$1,500)	$1.2700 ($900)
Profit/loss	+$3,812.50	+$1,912	−$600	+$900

If an at-the-money option is executed, then a total of $1,912 in profits will be added to the original $4,112.50 profit, giving a grand total of $6,024.50.

FIGURE 14.4 Market Move

(like it did) and erode all of the paid premium. While there is the ability to exit the option to diminish losses and repurchase an option with a lower strike price, it would be better to exit the market altogether instead of chasing the market.

Since no one knows if the market will rebound, the smart thing to do is to not risk more than the premium collected from the sold option; in this instance that would be $900.

The second scenario is what did evolve for this trade; the market pulled back, and then rebounded. The trader held on to the option, and the opportunity to potentially earn $1,912 came about. This was just a $300 difference from staying in the futures contract and collecting $2,225. The trader didn't have to commit any margin capital to the keep the trade going, nor did he have to give up all of the profits originally accumulated in the futures contract in hopes that the market would rebound.

Comparison of Different Potential Returns   In the table that follows we see the ideal situations: Had we held the trade, we would have had the potential to make over $5,000. Had we simply walked away from the trade by exiting everything at the first sign of a pullback, there was the potential to walk away with a little under $3,000. Finally, if the trade was converted into a bull call spread and the market continued to move up, there was the potential to pick up a little over $6,000.

Hold it	$5,112.50
Walk away	$2,912
Bull call spread	$6,024.12

The questions that a trader has to ask are:

"Is an extra thousand dollars worth the risk of converting the trade from a collar into a bull call spread?"

"Would I have been better off simply holding on to the collar?"

"What if the market had gone the other way—could I live with my decisions?"

The reason why these strategies exist is to help diminish risk. The market will dictate your trading behavior. It is difficult to say what is exactly right or what is exactly wrong when it comes to trading, solely because we work with imperfect knowledge.

The information we see on the screen is our best indicator of what is happening. Even after you have the right tools for success, there is no guarantee that you will always be successful. Keep that in mind as you attempt to trade these and any other strategies in your arsenal.

Example 2: Collar Trade into Ratio Backspread

In Figure 14.5 a put collar position is placed on corn futures. Using the indicators discussed in *Winning the Trading Game*, we wait for the candlestick indicator "spinning top" to show up. Based on the candlestick formation, we enter the market by going short and protect ourselves with a $5.10 call while simultaneously selling a $4.30 put to cover part of the call option's at-the-money premium costs.

There are three potential scenarios for this collar position: We can hold it until expiration, we can walk away from the trade once our target price has been hit, or we can convert it. In the preceding example we converted the collar trade into a bull call spread. In this example we will convert the collar into a ratio spread, also known as a call backspread.

A standard definition of a ratio spread can be found on Investopedia as "an options strategy in which an investor simultaneously holds an unequal number of long and short positions. A commonly used ratio is two short options for every option purchased." Therefore, depending on whom you

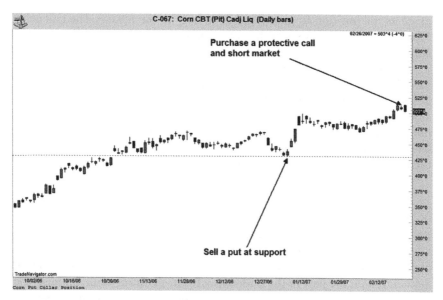

FIGURE 14.5 Corn Put Collar Position
Source: TradeNavigator.com © 2007. All rights reserved.

talk to, by purchasing more options than you sell you are essentially in what is known as a call backspread or a ratio backspread.

The key difference is that a standard ratio spread exposes you to unlimited risk, because you have an extra short position, whereas a ratio backspread exposes you to unlimited profit potential, because you have an extra long position. Regardless of the technicality of the name, selling one option and buying two options is less risky than buying one option and selling two options. Therefore, you always want to do the former, not the latter, if your goal is to manage your risk.

Hold It In the example found in Table 14.4, all of the indicators are pointing toward shorting the corn market. Placing a protective call at $5.10

TABLE 14.4 Corn Classic Collar Hold

	Short Futures	Buy Protective Call/Premium	Sell Put for Income/ Premium Collected
Entry	$5.10	$5.10 (−$1,000)	$4.30 (+$250)
Exit	$4.30	$4.30 (−$1,000)	$4.30 (−$250)

protects the position from any sudden moves to the upside. The call costs $1,000. To offset the costs of the call option, a put can be sold at a point of support, $4.30. The sold put brings in $250 of premium.

Simply holding on to the trade until it reaches expiration results in a $1,000 deduction from the profits. The call option expires worthless, leaving $3,000 in profits. The sold put has to reach $4.25 before it can be considered profitable (determined by subtracting the strike price from the premium collected), and even if it gets that low, the short futures position can end up covering your losses. A simple profit of $3,000 can be achieved if the trade is held on to with little fanfare.

Risk The risk for this collar is no different from the risk associated with the first example. Holding on to a collar until expiration exposes the position to multiple ups and downs in price as the market fluctuates. This occurs without the guarantee that the underlying futures position will actually ever reach the resistance level where the put was sold. Any lack of momentum on the part of the underlying futures contract will diminish the impact of the sold put. By itself the sold option cannot produce a significant source of revenue to cover the call that was bought, nor will it make up for the futures contract's disappointing results. This leaves the trader with a maximum opportunity to gain $3,000 while at the same time leaving the trader open to making a lot less.

Walk Away If the market is moving in the right direction but there is no desire to hold on to the trade until expiration, then the trade can be liquidated early. When we look at Table 14.5 we can see that the market has hit the $4.30 level, but it simply cannot break through the $4.10 level. Tremendous support has built up in the $4.30 to $4.10 range with the potential for the market to turn around and go up at any given time.

With the threat of that occurring, it may be best to exit the trade without waiting until expiration.

TABLE 14.5 Corn Classic Collar Liquidation

	Short Futures	Buy Protective Call/Premium	Sell Put for Income/ Premium Collected
Entry	$5.10	$5.10 (−$1,000)	$4.30 (+$250)
Exit	$4.30	$4.30 (+$150)	$4.30 (−$700)
Profit/loss	+$4,000	−$850	−$450

Risk Exiting the trade before expiration entails two additional costs associated with the trade, both of which will drag down the profits. First, by exiting the protective call you will be penalized. While you do not lose your entire call premium of $1,000, there is the potential that this can occur. In this example you end up losing $850.

The same problem arises for the sold put. The put has to be bought back at the market's going rate. You initially collected a premium of $250, but you now have to pay $700 in order to get out of the position—making your put loss $450. This gives your corn position a total loss of $1,300 against a backdrop profit of $4,000. This leaves the corn position with a net profit $2,700.

Convert It The decision to put on a ratio spread can be difficult. There may be a feeling that the market will continue downward, but you don't want to expose your profits to any pullbacks, nor do you want to lock yourself out of any future short profits solely because you sold a put.

That is when the ratio spread comes in. If we look at Figure 14.6 we can see the nascent beginnings of converting from a collar to a ratio spread.

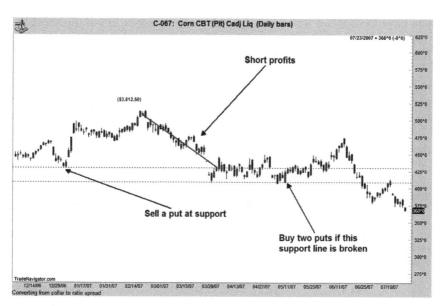

FIGURE 14.6 Converting from Collar to Ratio Spread
Source: TradeNavigator.com © 2007. All rights reserved.

Since there is a new area of support developing around the $4.10 level, we decide to take a portion of the profits and reinvest them into purchasing two puts. The intent is get all of our short futures profits locked into our account, while at the same time avoiding taking a loss on the put that we sold.

By holding on to the short futures position until it reaches $4.10 we eke out an additional thousand dollars, bringing our futures total to $5,000. By doing this we make sure that any potential losses incurred by the put we sold are covered between $4.30 and $4.10. It also gives us a little more capital to purchase the two put options at $4.10.

One put option continues to cover the put we sold, diminish our unlimited risk, and let us get out of our futures position. The second put is our moneymaker. For $900 we get to free up the equity in our account by eliminating corn's margin requirements, yet still participate in the drop in price and any potential chance at collecting the premium.

In Table 14.6 we see the trade fully exited: no call, no puts, sold or bought. The time it takes to get to that point is almost four months. This is definitely a position trade.

Risk There are a number of drawbacks in converting from the collar to this type of ratio spread. The first problem is the number of variables that you have to contend with leading up to the final execution of the short futures trade. If you hold on to the short futures position too long, the market has the opportunity to rebound on you and take back your profits.

A second problem arises in purchasing the additional two puts. While slightly out-of-the-money, they have the ability to be quite expensive compared to the premium you collected from the put. In fact, the expense may far outweigh the benefits of continuing the trade.

Finally, a trade that originally took only 26 days to profit now takes 103 days before you get all of your money, and the whole time you are not sure

TABLE 14.6 Corn Classic Collar Convert to Ratio Backspread

	Short Futures	Exit Call	Sell Put/ Premium	Buy Two Puts to Continue Short
Entry	$5.10	$5.10 (−$1,000)	$4.30 (+$250)	$4.10 ($450/each or $900)
Exit	$4.10	$4.30 (−$1,000)	$3.70 (−$2,400)	$3.70 ($2,000/each or $4,000)
Profit/loss	+$5,000	−$1,000	−$2,150	+$3,100

whether the trade will work. This is almost a quadrupling of your trading time frame with little guarantee that the market will continue down. If the market were to move against your two puts, you would lose the $1,100 in premium. This risk simply may not be worth it. That's why it is important to do your math before you execute a trade like this.

Comparison of Different Potential Returns   In 26 days or less you can walk away from the trade with a simple profit of $2,700 or you can simply hold on to the trade with little to no change and collect $3,000. Although you have an opportunity to make extra money in putting on a ratio spread, it doesn't necessarily mean that it always must be done. Depending on the circumstances, it may be better to take your profits as soon as possible. This can only be determined by the individual trader who is looking to hold on for longer time frames.

Hold it	$3,000
Walk away	$2,700
Ratio backspread	$4,950

Example 3: Short Strangle into a Synthetic Futures

In Chapter 14 we looked at the S&P 500 and used it as an example for a short strangle. We sold an S&P 500 1400 call for $1,250 and we sold an S&P 500 1325 put for $2,250. We collected a total of $3,500 in initial premiums. As the trade evolved we ended up losing money on our 1325 put, $250, and picking up a small profit of $950 on the trade overall (see Table 14.7).

In Chapter 14 we thoroughly looked at the unlimited risk exposure that short strangles have, along with the consequences of holding on to the trade too long and exiting the trade early. What wasn't explored was

TABLE 14.7   S&P 500 Strangle Position

	S&P 500 1400 Call	S&P 500 1325 Put	Total S&P 500 Option Values
Initial premium	$1,250	$2,250	$3,500
Offset	−$50	−$2,500	−$2,550
Profit/loss	$1,200	−$250	$950

the ability to convert the trade from an unlimited risky investment into a synthetic futures position.

In Chapter 13 we defined synthetic futures as a position that combines a short option position with a long option position. In this case we want to collect the premium on our call, the losing position, and buy a put option to catch the market's move down.

In Figure 14.7 we see the original position where we sell the call at 1400 and we sell the put at 1325. The market breaks past the 1325 target put price and has to be exited. A trader has to ask the question, "Why wait until it breaks past the 1325 level before exiting?" As the market moves up to 1400 and stalls out, only to collapse later, why can't you exit near the top, and attempt to collect as much premium as possible?

The reality is that nothing is stopping you from taking your signals early. There is no unwritten rule that says that you have to hold on to the sold option (put in this instance) until the market has broken through the support or resistance line.

Convert It   In Figure 14.8 we can clearly see the market has stalled out near the top, in the 1390 area. Not only is this confirmed by the price stalling

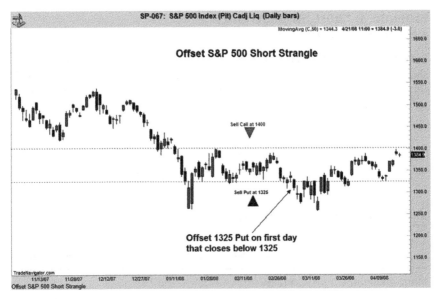

FIGURE 14.7   Offset S&P 500 Short Strangle
Source: TradeNavigator.com © 2007. All rights reserved.

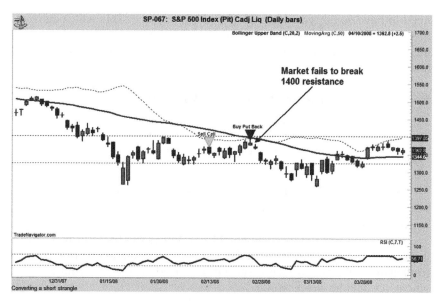

FIGURE 14.8 Short Strangle Convert to Synthetic Futures
Source: TradeNavigator.com © 2007. All rights reserved.

out, but three indicators are backing it up. The upper Bollinger band, the 50-day moving average, and the RSI are all screaming "overbought." This is the absolute end of the road for the rally in this market.

With all three indicators pointing downward, there is the ability to catch a profit on the sold option, then short the market to ride the market back down. In this instance the premium can be retained as a profit from the sold call. This particular conversion gives you three different sources of income from the execution of one trade (see Table 14.8).

Risk This is not without its own problems. You are now nakedly exposed to the markets, with the potential of unlimited loss as well as unlimited gain. If the market flips around on you and shoots past 1400, you will

TABLE 14.8 S&P Short Strangle Convert to Synthetic Futures

	Short Futures	S&P 1325 Put/Premium	S&P 1400 Call/Premium
Entry	$1,390	$1,362 (+$2,250)	$1,362 (+$1,250)
Exit	$1,260	$1,390 (−$1,400)	$1,260 (−$10)

need to have some type of protective setup in place. This will require either a stop or another option, and you will have to react for both the losing short position and the losing sold call. This is important to keep in mind.

Comparison of Different Potential Returns

Short strangle	$950
Synthetic futures (Emini position)	$8,590

The question that you must ask yourself is: "Is the potential, in this instance, to make almost 10 times as much, with all of the associated risk, worth the effort?"

If not, you must ignore the ability to convert the trade. If it is worth it, you have to take advantage of the signals immediately. If this type of trading dovetails directly with your ultimate trading goal and your temperament, it could be successful.

If you are going for slow and steady, then the simple income generation of a short strangle is perfect for you. But if you are looking to grab some outrageous profits every now and then, then you have to execute a synthetic futures when the opportunity is right.

Example 4: Short Strangle into a Covered Position

Now let's look at the same example from Chapter 14, but instead of converting it into a synthetic futures position, we leave the sold put position on, and we decide to put on a short futures position to cover any losses. Everything is identical: We sell the call at 1400, we sell the put at 1325, and when the market stalls out at 1390 we short the futures.

In Figure 14.9 we see all of the components of the trade.

There are only two actions that are different. First, we don't exit the sold put position; second, we identify a second level of support. This is our overall target for both the short position and our sold call. If the market penetrates through this level, 1260, it will be very difficult for the S&P market to turn around and reach the 1400 level anytime soon.

Convert It   There is no easy explanation on why you would want to convert a short strangle into a covered position. Unlike stocks that you may own for years on end, a futures contract is a finite instrument that can

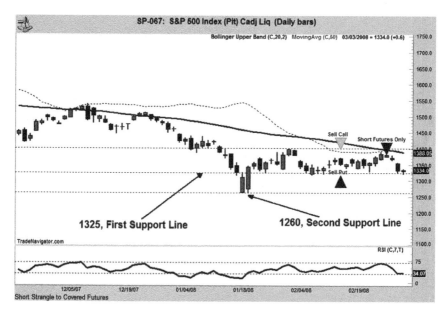

FIGURE 14.9 Short Strangle into a Covered Position
Source: TradeNavigator.com © 2007. All rights reserved.

be exited at any time. The only reason to convert a short strangle into a covered position is if you sincerely believe that a market will rebound and that it would be a mistake to give up the premium you collected because of a short-term retracement.

In the S&P 500 example, all of the indicators have lined up to show us that the longs have stalled out at 1390. By putting on a short futures position, we are able to capture the drop. Initially there may be no expectation for the market to penetrate the 1325 area; in fact, it would be ideal if it didn't. You could simply pick up profits between 1390 and 1325 (approximately $3,200 for an Emini S&P contract) and collect the premiums for both the sold option positions.

In Figure 14.10 we see that the market breaks through the 1325 area and eventually rebounds off of the second support line at 1260. This leads to the S&P 500 making a rally and eventually breaking through the 1400 level.

A fast-moving market can thwart your plans from catching the profits that build up in a sideways-moving market. In this case there were three up days before the S&P 500 slammed through 1325 and had three down days in a row. This would have given any trader little time to react and to exit the sideways trade, and would have forced the trade into becoming

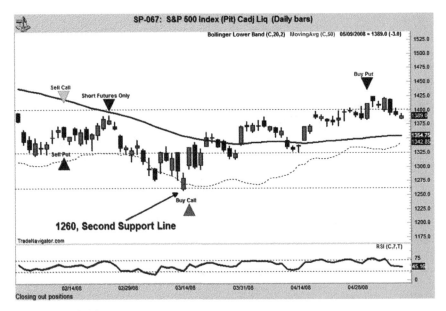

FIGURE 14.10 Closing Out Position
Source: TradeNavigator.com © 2007. All rights reserved.

a covered position. In this instance, that was not an altogether bad thing
(see Table 14.9).

Risk This position is not without its drawbacks. There is the possibility
that you will diminish your short futures returns because the market never
rebounds. Anything that the futures position makes past the strike price,
plus the premium you collected, is given up to the option buyer (for this
example a put buyer) once the option is exercised.

There is also the possibility that you will put on a covered futures position for the wrong option. In this case, while the indicators

TABLE 14.9 Converting a Short Strangle

	Short Futures	**S&P 1325 Put/Premium**	**S&P 1400 Call/Premium**
Entry	$1,390	$1,362 (+$2,250)	$1,362 (+$1,250)
Exit	$1,260	$1,425 (−$400)	$1,260 (−$10)
Profit/loss	+$6,500	+$1,850	+$1,240
	(Emini position)		

pointed to a potential short in the market, the market could have re-bounded and shot up. You would have lost on your futures position, along with the call you sold. Losses on both of these positions would quickly erode and quite possibly exceed the premium collected from selling the option.

Comparison of Different Potential Returns

Short strangle	$950
Synthetic futures (Emini position)	$8,590
Covered position (Emini position)	$9,590

This position just happened to work out. It was picked at random and the market operated in conjunction with the technical analysis, making each leg of the opportunity profitable. This is the benefit of 20/20 hindsight. As you trade you will have to make tough decisions. These decisions may drive you out of the market ahead of time, may make you second-guess yourself when it's time to put on trades, and may stop you from exiting a market when you know you have to. The reason for this example, along with all of the other examples in the book, is to show you what is possible when you apply these techniques. In the end all that matters is that you are prepared for the opportunities.

Example 5: Option Hedge into a Collar Position

In Chapter 6 we introduced options as an alternative to using a stop loss. The goal was to show the difference between a pure synthetic option, an at-the-money option and a futures position versus an option hedge, and an out-of-the-money option and a futures position.

Using an option as a hedge is a great way to lock in your money management strategy. But what happens if the market stalls out as it is heading in the direction of your underlying futures contract? You can exit the trade completely like we did in Chapter 6 or you can sell an option at or near the apex or the low and collect a premium. This will convert your position into a collar position and by default (if you don't exit the underlying futures contract) a covered option position.

We take an example from Chapter 6 and look at it more closely. In Figure 14.11 we have gold futures set up. Overall the market is bullish—it's above the 50-day MA. It has pulled back to a previous high, $860, which has become a short-term point of support. By purchasing gold on its way up, we get a fill at $883. If we had attempted to put on a synthetic

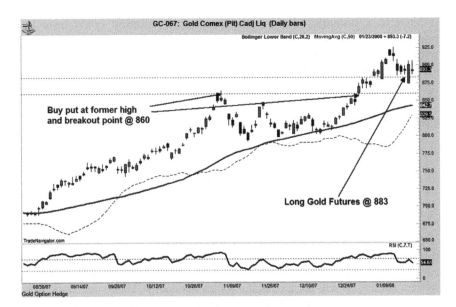

FIGURE 14.11 Gold Option Hedge
Source: TradeNavigator.com © 2007. All rights reserved.

option, an $885 put would have cost us $1,470, whereas a $860 put costs only $300.

The difference between $860 and $883 is $23 or $2,300. With a stop loss at $500, 5 percent of a $10,000 account, we have only $800 committed to our potential loss instead of $1,470. This decreases how much money we are paying for the intrinsic value of the option, particularly because we are only looking to diminish our loss and we are unambiguous about the market's direction (see Table 14.10).

Convert It In Figure 14.12 we see the market move up in value, only to collapse unexpectedly at $950.

With gold reaching unexplored territory, it is impossible to predict what height the gold contract could reach. It could go as high as $2,000 per ounce, but without any precedence at these lofty levels gold has

TABLE 14.10 Gold Option Hedge

	Long Futures	**Buy Protective Put/Premium**
Entry	$883	$860 ($300)

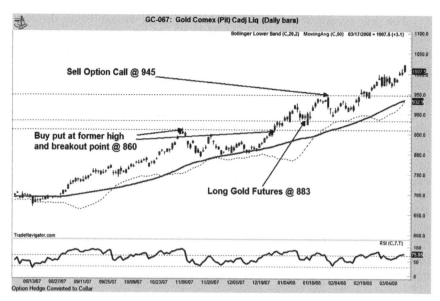

FIGURE 14.12 Option Hedge Converted to Collar
Source: TradeNavigator.com © 2007. All rights reserved.

developed intense volatility. This volatility struck on February 1, 2008, when gold dropped $30 in one day.

So while the gold market itself is still in a bull market, individual daily fluctuations cannot be ignored. In this instance we lose over $3,000 in profit form our futures position. The hope is that the market will retrace, but there is no guarantee. To make up for part of the losses, we sell a call at $945 for $620 in premium. This converts our position into a collar. Our put option is paid for, and we get an additional $320 to cover some of our losses.

We are still optimistic that the market will rebound; we just don't know when. In Figure 14.12 the market not only rebounds, but it exceeds $945. Our futures position returns $6,200 and we lose both the put and call premiums of $920 (see Table 14.11).

TABLE 14.11 Convert Option Hedge to Collar

	Long Futures	**Put Premium**	**Call Premium**
Entry	$883	$883 (−$300)	$945 (+$620)
Exit	$945	$945 (expired)	$945+ (exercised)
Profit/loss	+$6,200	−$300	−$620

The only reason we employ this strategy is so we can cover the cost of the put option, just in case our $500 stop loss is hit. The extra $320 will diminish our $500 stop loss to only $180. This is important, because while we may lose our profits on our futures position, we have set ourselves up for success on our put, and our account's principal of $10,000 is preserved. Our stop loss goes from 5 percent to only 1.8 percent.

If the market rebounds, as it did in this case, our option is paid for if the market doesn't exceed $951.20 (strike price plus premium); but if the market does exceed it, our original futures position is profitable enough to cover the $920 loss (cost of put and return of call premium), plus any exercise of the call will be covered by the futures position itself.

Risk   This type of conversion has few drawbacks. As with any collar trade, you will have to give up any of your futures contract profits that exceed the sold option's strike price. The put premium will be lost to you if your futures position is successful, plus your profit opportunity will be stuck between where you place both of your options.

CONCLUSION

Whether you are converting a collar trade into a ratio spread or you are selling options, your success is not because of how smart or clever you are; it is based on how well you follow the rhythms of the market. If the rhythm of the market dictates you can switch your original position or you can add onto your position, then do so without hesitation. If the rhythm of the market dictates that you exit a trade, then you must exit without hesitation. The worst actions that can be taken are to force a trade to become something it is not or to give up too early.

This chapter was designed to highlight just a few of the different types of conversions that are possible as you blend advanced and basic strategies together. In no way is this a comprehensive list of all of the different scenarios and possibilities. I could write an entire new book devoted just to that. This chapter is designed to highlight the fact that as you become comfortable with calculating your profit and loss potentials ahead of time, you give yourself the ability to trade in such a way that you can prepare for multiple opportunities while you are in the same trade.

CHAPTER 15

Analyzing Charts and Strategies

So much information has been given throughout this book that it might be overwhelming to get started. This chapter is meant to help you settle in and get used to playing around with the concepts of risk management. This cannot replace real world trading, but it can supplement your education.

The next several examples take a look at the five markets that we have been consistently reviewing. There are two charts for each example. The before chart has no technical analysis indicators and is representative of the trade setup. The after chart is overlaid with technical analysis information and shows where the market ended up. This setup encourages you to think critically about how you could have approached the markets using any one of the fifteen strategies in the book. I suggest that you photocopy and enlarge the charts so you can write on them.

The only rules that are associated with each of these charts is that you write up your risk/reward scenario based on particular capital constraints and the option prices presented to you. There aren't right or wrong answers. I then discuss how I would have approached the market, based on the same information.

Every trade you execute should undergo the same type of scrutiny. By taking the time to analyze the market, even if you are an active trader, you can create a myriad of possibilities for yourself. This type of critical approach prevents your capital from being unnecessarily lost. It also sets the stage for a more cerebral approach to the markets. Since our emotions of fear and greed tend to wreak havoc on our trading decisions, the more ways we have to cope with them the better off we are.

Let's begin.

S&P 500

There are two S&P 500 futures contracts. There is the full-size contract with a margin that can exceed $20,000 on any given day, depending on the volatility, and there is the Emini S&P 500 with a margin that hovers around $4,000. The Emini S&P 500 is therefore about one-fifth the size of a full-size contract. If you had a small account valued at $15,000, how would you interact with the following scenario? Would you use an option? How many? What if you wanted to trade the full-size contract—would a synthetic futures contract make sense?

Before

In Figure 15.1 it's obvious that the market has topped out. For those classical chartists, we have either a triple top or a head and shoulders pattern forming. How would you approach the market if you were assuming that the market was headed for some weakness?

Considering the option values in Tables 15.1 and 15.2, would it be worthwhile to put on a collar, a synthetic, or a bear put spread?

FIGURE 15.1   S&P 500 Index Before
Source: TradeNavigator.com © 2007. All rights reserved.

TABLE 15.1 Full Size Option Table

	Type	Strike	Cost	Amount
SPN8	Call	1600	$9.00	$2,250
SPN8	Call	1575	$13.80	$3,450
SPN8	Put	1525	$5.00	$1,250

TABLE 15.2 Emini Option Table

	Type	Strike	Cost	Amount
ESN8	Call	1600	$18.50	$925
ESN8	Call	1575	$20.50	$1,025

We can't determine by looking at the chart whether the market will flip around and go back up, nor do we have a lot of fundamental data that helps us make sense of the activity at the time. Nevertheless, two things are staring us in the face: the market seems to be at a top, and there is a double line of support around the 1525 price area.

If we were to execute a trade by shorting at 1575 and it reached the 1525 level, how much could be made? On a full-sized contract we make $12,500, and on a mini-contract we make one-fifth that or $2,500. Would this be a worthwhile risk?

After

In Figure 15.2, not only did the S&P drop, it broke through the 1525 level and kept going, causing new lows as far down as 1400 and 1425. In hindsight a synthetic option would have been the perfect vehicle; there would have been no capping of profits.

At the same time you have to ask yourself what if it had not kept going down? Would you be prepared to give the gains you made? Would a collar have worked just as well to cap off the risk of the market turning back on you?

In trading there is the constant second-guessing of both your decision-making process and your methodology. I would steer well clear of anyone who trades as if they are invincible. There will always be better ways you could have tackled a trade. The only thought you have to keep in your mind is that you acted 100 percent right based on the information you had at the

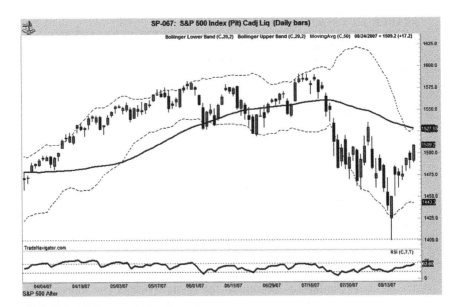

FIGURE 15.2 S&P 500 Index After
Source: TradeNavigator.com © 2007. All rights reserved.

time you made the decision. Does that mean you can't change your mind later? Of course not! With new information can come new decisions and actions, but, as with most things, you can only do the best that you can when you do it.

EURO

The euro currency trades in so many forms that it should actually have its own exchange. There is the euro cash market, for those with a lot of money. There is the euro spot market, for those who want to trade as if they have a lot of money. There is the euro futures market, for those who think they have a lot of money. There is the euro ETF, for those who believe they are nothing like the rest of the euro traders. Finally there is the euro options market, for those who wish they had a lot of money. And then there are the cross-currency euro contracts that have no relationship to the dollar: euro/yen, GBP/euro, euro/aud, etc.

The reality is that all these traders, no matter their market or exchange, are affected the exact same way, by the exact same charts, by the exact same news. While each one gains profits at varying levels and rates, and pay different types of commissions or spreads, at the end of the day long is long and short is short.

The artificial boundaries set between these various sectors of euro trading, and on a larger scale forex trading altogether, is fluidly traversed by professional traders looking for arbitrage opportunities. The imperfect system of having so many different products coming to bear on one currency exposes the absurdity of the situation. Nimble minds and nimble fingers are able to exploit these razor-thin discrepancies or at the very least apply their skill across the myriad of exchanges that are all trading the same instrument.

The following example is from the futures euro trading screen. It could have just as well been the forex euro screen, the cash euro screen, or the Emini euro screen.

Before

In Figure 15.3 we see the spot currency traded euro. It has recently gapped up and seems to be poised for a pullback. As a spot trader you are caught on a 24-hour timetable, so regardless of what the trend is, you typically find yourself forced to exit the market when faced with this kind of volatility.

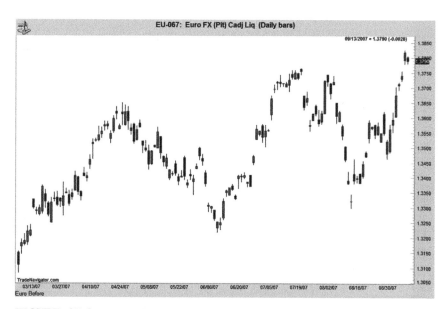

FIGURE 15.3 Euro Before
Source: TradeNavigator.com © 2007. All rights reserved.

What do you do to hold on to this trade? Do you believe this is the beginning of a much larger rally, or do you look to first catch any pullback in price?

There are a few choices available. A spot forex trader could decide to use an option as a hedge technique. For the most part, the trend seems to be long, but there is the possibility that a counter-trend is forming a possible short. There is also the possibility of creating a synthetic call option by purchasing a put at-the-money and riding the spot long.

After

In Figure 15.4 it can easily be seen that the gap up was the beginning of unprecedented price levels in the euro.

With the right tools in place, there was a tremendous profit opportunity. The success of a trader comes from his ability to take his nose off the canvas and look at the big picture. Since the euro's inception it has been a powerhouse of value in one direction—up. From its humble origins of being valued at less than a dollar to reaching parity to eventually outstripping the dollar for years.

This meteoric rise cannot last forever. Therefore, a systematic approach should be in place to manage both upside and downside risk for years to come. A sudden drop in price could start with an innocently small

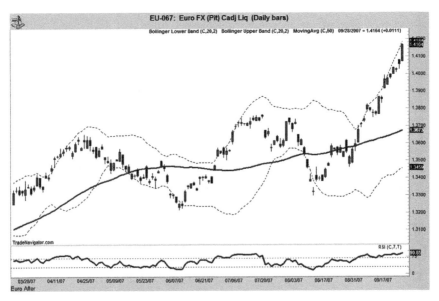

FIGURE 15.4 Euro After
Source: TradeNavigator.com © 2007. All rights reserved.

gap down, before it comes crashing down. Strategies that go beyond one marketplace or one exchange are a necessary component for anyone who hopes to succeed in the long run with forex trading.

GOLD

The use of gold as a storehouse of value has been around since ancient times and most likely will still be around when the book you hold in your hands crumbles to dust. That being the case, approaching gold investing intelligently is paramount to any trader's success. Failing to recognize the winds of change will most assuredly have you holding the bag when gold is no longer fashionable and missing out when it is.

Before

In Figure 15.5 we see gold attempting to reclaim territory by trying to break through resistance at former highs.

Can gold do it? The candlestick makes it appear as if gold may actually turn around. From an inverted hammer at the top, to a spinning top, to a

FIGURE 15.5 Gold Before
Source: TradeNavigator.com © 2007. All rights reserved.

hammer, the candlesticks are reflecting the market's volatility. Couple that with the collapse of the last rally, and the slow steady pace gold has had to get back, there is the possibility of a breakout to new highs. With so much uncertainty, would a straddle at 730 be wise? What about a strangle? Buy a call at 740 and buy a put at 720, just outside range, but well within the market's average true range (ATR). Would it make sense to sell a naked put and collect the premium under these circumstances?

In making a decision there are two potentials. If the market moves up, the next point of resistance is in the 800s and there is the potential to make $7,000; if the market drops, it apparently has support at 685 that would net you $4,200. So no matter which way it goes, you should not be risking more than $2,100 to $3,000. An outright futures contract may not make the most sense.

After

In Figure 15.6 gold drops like a lead balloon. It drops through the 50-day MA and falls back down to the 685 level of support and begins to turn around. A strangle, in two of the money options, would have probably been the best bet based on the risk/reward profile.

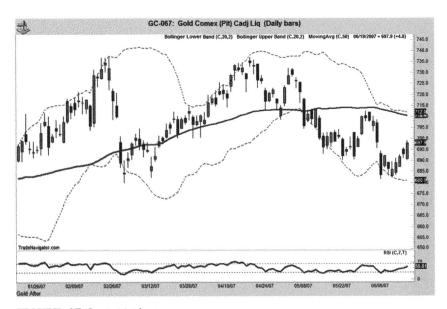

FIGURE 15.6 Gold After
Source: TradeNavigator.com © 2007. All rights reserved.

CORN

The dual life of corn has had a deep impact on the United States. Once thought to be a major commodity cash crop, corn has slowly evolved into an alternative fuel and not everyone is happy about that. From farmers to consumers, anyone involved with corn is beginning to feel the impact that this shift in consumption has created. Once it was an inexpensive commodity that could be purchased for a few dollars. All that changed at the beginning of the twenty-first century. Corn took the lead in one of the most aggressive grain rallies ever, actually doubling in price with the expectation that it could go even higher.

Before

In Figure 15.7 we see corn sitting on a sideways support at $4.10 after collapsing from a rally that reached $5.15.

The sideways support makes the trade perfect for an option as a hard stop. If it rallies back up from the current price of $4.36 to $5.15, there is a

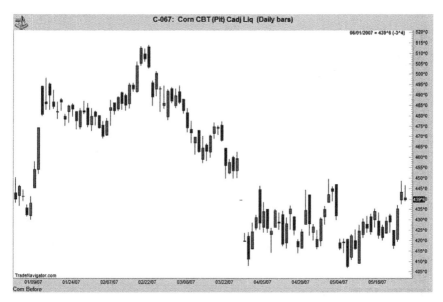

FIGURE 15.7 Corn Before
Source: TradeNavigator.com © 2007. All rights reserved.

profit potential of 79 cents or \$3,950. A stop loss can be placed at whatever money management target you may have.

A synthetic call could also work, or a ratio spread could be used to advantage of this trade for almost free. Whatever the case, it is important to make sure that a trade like this is not overlooked. Markets that move sideways for any significant period of time will be explosive, regardless of the direction. It is best to have all the necessary bases, long and short, covered in order to come out on top.

After

It appears this market did a little bit of both. In Figure 15.8 the market exploded to the upside, reaching as high as \$4.80, then collapsed in a beautiful fashion.

The corn drop took only four days before it was firmly below the 50-day MA, giving it a bearish trend. Depending on how nimble you are, you may be out of your primary position with a profit. The most likely outcome, based on the speed of the move, is that any long positions would have been breakeven, at best. The short position would have had to make

FIGURE 15.8 Corn After
Source: TradeNavigator.com © 2007. All rights reserved.

up all of the work, which in this case would not have been too bad since the corn market dropped to $3.78/bushel.

OIL

Black gold. The twentieth and twenty-first centuries have seen people die, kill, and lie to possess this commodity. While it has been the back of modernizing society, for the most part it has successfully helped ruin our environment and our intercontinental relationships. In spite of all that, one good thing definitely comes from the discovery of oil—the end of the killing of whales for their fat.

Before

Figure 15.9 shows with oil what classic chartists call a triangle formation, possibly even a pennant or flag.

This formation portends the potential for the market to explode upward. This would be one of the few times that using just a stop loss may

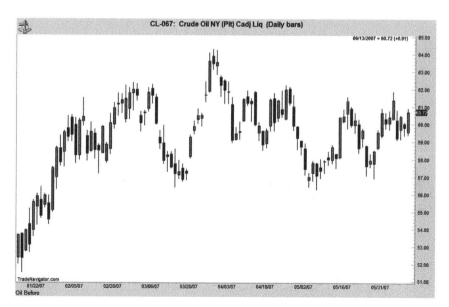

FIGURE 15.9 Oil Before
Source: TradeNavigator.com © 2007. All rights reserved.

be appropriate Or you could use an option as a hedge, or use this setup to sell puts and collect the premium. If your account can't handle the high margins that oil requires, then you could create a synthetic futures position of two options with a third option for protection.

After

In Figure 15.10 we see the flag proved itself and the oil market shot straight up.

This is a prime example of why paper trading or demo trading can be frustrating. According to the money management rules in *Winning the Trading Game* you would need $30,000 to trade one oil contract. There is always the possibility of trading the mini-oil contract, but it lacks a little of the same impact. When faced with a margin or capital intensive market like this and the trade setup looks just right, consider the ways you can reduce your margin expense. Whether you use a crack spread or put on a calendar spread to take advantage of contango or backwardation. Do not give up on figuring out an inexpensive way to participate in the trade.

FIGURE 15.10 Oil After
Source: TradeNavigator.com © 2007. All rights reserved.

CONCLUSION

By analyzing charts, whether in a paper format like this or in an online demo account, you have the ability to test your ideas and theories in depth. They say that practice makes perfect, but it is perfect practice that makes perfect. As long as you properly apply the principles and ideas you have learned throughout the book properly in your practice trading, then your actual trading will become more effective. This puts you leaps and bounds ahead of the majority of retail traders and that much closer to becoming a professional trader.

CHAPTER 16

Applying These Strategies with Stocks

T hroughout this book we have looked at futures and forex transactions consistently. Yet every strategy, beginner or advanced, can be applied to the stock market as well. Technical analysis is the same no matter the market. Unfortunately, many stock investors look at futures and forex trading and assume that there is some magical force working behind the scenes that makes trading more difficult than stock investing. The truth is a lot less magnanimous.

The misuse of leverage is the magical force that is misunderstood. The majority of stock traders believe that they have to use the 20-to-1 leverage of futures or the 500-to-1 leverage of forex in order to trade them, and that is not the case. Futures and forex can be traded just like stocks. The face value of a euro contract, U.S. $152,000, as of this writing, can be invested in euros and an investor can make or lose money in a EUR/US contract with a lot less volatility. The same can be said of a gold futures contract. The face value of a gold contract is $92,000. An investor can put up the entire $92,000, eliminating his leverage risk, and just gain or lose on the true value of gold going up or down.

Because leverage is the key factor that separates futures and forex trading from stock investing, it stands to reason that the majority of the other factors will remain the same, such as the daisy-chain effect and the strategies to exploit it. There are stocks, CFDs, single stock futures, and options, each one designed to protect the other. If you are holding on to a long stock position, like 97 percent of all stock traders, then you can protect yourself from a downturn in the stock with a CFD or a single stock futures position. If you are in a CFD or a single stock futures position, you could use either of these instruments to protect each other or use a stock option to protect the CFD, single stock future, or stock position. The mechanics are identical to the futures and forex market.

In this chapter we take a quick glimpse of a few popular stocks and how you can apply some of the strategies in the book to them. This chapter in no means is meant to be a complete tutorial on stocks. There are a number of great books out there that will give you an in-depth breakdown on analyzing a company's value. The goal here is to show you that once you have come to a decision to be long a stock there are ways to protect yourself. There is no need to watch your entire net worth evaporate while you helplessly stand on the sidelines, when there are actual tools that have been designed to help protect you.

When the dot-com bubble burst, over $7 trillion of wealth evaporated. The majority of investors could not afford to take such a loss. Any one of the strategies presented in this book could have either diminished their losses or eliminated their losses altogether, if they had just known they could do it. Trading is a zero sum game. Someone somewhere collected the $7 trillion, whether it was the corporations and their venture capitalists or sophisticated traders on Wall Street utilizing strategies to pick up the low-hanging fruit. It's time that you learned how to do the same.

STOCKS

Stocks represent ownership in a corporation. The history of stock ownership has been dated as far back as ancient Mesopotamia. Today, the trading of shares in corporations occurs in various parts around the world. From the famous New York Stock Exchange to the ever-popular Japanese Nikkei Stock Exchange, stock markets operate 24 hours a day, seven days a week, in some form or fashion.

While stocks are well-known, there is little about them that is truly understood. This leaves retail traders vulnerable to many of the stock market's inherent flaws. First and foremost, stocks are biased by nature. There are no stock companies that list their shares to raise capital that want to see the value of their shares drop. This leads to an overall market bias that encourages stocks be bought but not sold.

There are limitations on shorting stocks; brokers insist on clients' buying shares even when the value of the stocks are decreasing, and any bit of positive news has the ability to rally a stock. This overall tone has lulled stock investors into a false sense of security, to the point where companies like Enron and Worldcom can repeatedly tell their employees and shareholders to buy shares while they unload shares out the back door.

There is a level of sophistication when it comes to trading stocks that only professional traders are privy to. Proprietary stock-trading houses lend money to their professional traders far in excess of the 4-to-1 leverage that retail traders may be able to enjoy. Sometimes professional stock traders enjoy leverage as high as 100-to-1 from the prop firms they work with. Other professional traders are trained on how to short stocks to their advantage. Professional traders add all these capabilities to their knowledge of how to use stock options, single stock futures, and CFDs, and it quickly becomes apparent that while the industry rhetoric promotes buying stocks for the retail trader, professionals are doing something altogether different for themselves behind the scenes.

While you may not be able to enjoy the same leverage that professional traders experience, that doesn't mean you can't learn a little about how the various stock derivatives interplay with one another. In this chapter we will look at stocks, single stock futures, CFDs, and stock options and how you can intermingle all of them together to get optimum results.

Single Stock Futures

In 2000 the Commodity Futures Modernization Act (CFMA) lifted the ban on single stock futures and narrow-based security indices (security futures). Foreign countries such as Australia, Denmark, Portugal, and South Africa had become tremendously successful in offering security futures. At that time, the United States wanted to catch up with this new investment vehicle but had to come up with a mandate to unify the fractured regulatory environment that futures and stocks operated in. With the Internet economy changing the way people think, security futures were seen as a way to keep the momentum going. Unfortunately, they were held up for two years and interest in them waned.

The mechanics of single stock futures (SSFs) is pretty straightforward. They are standardized contracts between a buyer and a seller to exchange 100 shares of a specific stock in the future. While these contracts do not represent ownership, they do convey an obligation of physically delivering shares of a traded company if the contract is not offset before the expiration date. Each SSF contract represents 100 shares and has a minimum movement size of one cent/share that makes a tick worth one dollar ($1.00).

As with any futures contract, SSF traders enjoy the benefits of margin. The standard margin requirement for all stocks traded as security futures is 20 percent of the underlying value of the contract (initial and maintenance margin). This 20 percent minimum may be reduced for certain types of futures market positions, such as spread trading. There are also margin reductions for certain offsetting positions in stock options and cash securities.

Contracts for Difference (CFDs)

CFDs were extensively explored in Chapter 2. Developed in the 1990s in London, they are unique from single stock futures and stock options. They are an over-the-counter form of stock derivatives. CFDs have no set expiration date, unlike stock options and single stock futures. Yet they also enjoy the benefits of margin. Margin can be as low as 10 percent and as high as 30 percent of the stock's face value.

CFDs are illegal to trade in the United States due to various U.S. regulations against OTC stock trading. Since no laws against OTC stock trading exist in other countries, they are becoming increasingly popular around the world. A CFD is simply a contract between a buyer and seller where they agree to pay each other the difference between an asset's current value and its future value. This concept can be applied to stocks, commodities, bonds, and so on. As long as there are two counterparties to the transaction, a CFD contract can be executed.

Stock Options

Options on stocks are no different from options on futures or forex. They are contracts that grant the right to buy the underlying asset, but not an obligation to buy the underlying asset. They can come in two forms, calls or puts, and they have an agreed-upon strike price and option expiration date that the buyer and seller agree upon. Stock options are traded in minimum increments of 100 shares. In 1973, the Chicago Board of Option Exchange (CBOE) was formed to develop a centralized marketplace for stock option trading in the United States.

Stock Index Futures

In 1982, nine years after the establishment of a centralized options exchange, stock index futures were introduced. Two of the most powerful investment regulatory bodies were pitted against one another. The Securities and Exchange Commission (SEC), which traditionally had oversight of securities, felt that stock indexes were simply an extension of the stock market. The Commodity Futures Trading Commission (CFTC), the SEC's futures and commodities counterpart, felt that stock index futures were a completely new animal under their exclusive domain.

The two most powerful financial agencies in the United States had to make a compromise. The SEC was granted autonomy over stocks and stock options, while the CFTC was allowed to regulate stock index futures. Today there are stock indexes on the Dow Jones, S&P 500, NASDAQ, Russell 2000, and a myriad of foreign stock indexes around the world.

STRATEGIES

When it comes to the stock market, there are many ways to protect your trading position. You can purchase a stock that doesn't follow the S&P 500 and short the S&P 500. Single stock futures can be combined with stock options or stocks to create synthetic or collar opportunities. Stock options can be matched with CFDs to create hard stop opportunities. Everything discussed in this book can be applied to the stock market. The following four examples highlight how to take advantage of stock opportunities using a synthetic, hard stop, and a collar. These stocks were picked at random to show that the techniques can be applied in any market regardless of the industry it's in.

Synthetic

In this example we take a technical analysis look at Alcoa Inc. It's listed on the New York Stock Exchange and has a single stock future derivative listed on OneChicago. As we have discussed, a synthetic is when you go long or short a market and purchase an at-the-money (ATM) option to protect your position. This turns your position into a synthetic option position.

In this instance you have the opportunity to trade the actual stock for 100 percent cash or utilize two other options' SSFs, which will cost you 20 percent of the face value, or a CFD, if you are based outside of the United States, which will only cost you 10 percent of the face value.

Purchasing the Alcoa shares outright on May 5th, 2008 would have cost you $3,664 for 100 shares at $36.64/share. We pick that point because it crossed over from being a bearish market into a bullish market. As an SSF the Alcoa share would only cost you $732.80. The same 100 shares as a CFD would cost you $366.40. The primary reason you would not purchase the shares outright and look at the two other market places, SSFs and CFDs, is to save money up front and to make it easier to create a synthetic put by shorting stock shares.

By freeing up 80 to 90 percent of your capital on the front end, you make it easier to purchase the protective put option necessary to turn the position into a synthetic call. In Figure 16.1, it costs $1.55/share to purchase an Alcoa Inc. put option at a $35.00 strike price. These options move in $2.50 increments; this is the best choice for the situation at hand. The final put option costs totals $155.

The profit from Alcoa's move from $36.64 to $44.60 would have been $7.96. With 100 shares you would make $796. On an investment of $3,664,

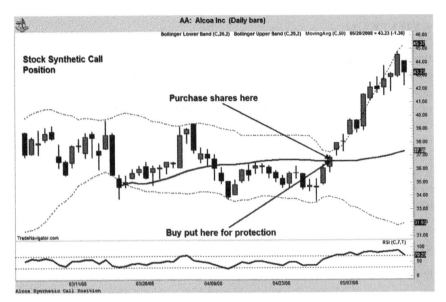

FIGURE 16.1 Alcoa Inc. Synthetic Call Position
Source: TradeNavigator.com © 2007. All rights reserved.

that would be a gross return of 21 percent. If you had traded it as an SSF, you would have a gross return of 108 percent. If you had traded Alcoa as a CFD you would have had a return of 217 percent.

The put option is designed to protect you in case the market moves in the opposite direction. No matter how you look at it, risking the $155 to insure your position is a small price to pay. Had the market moved in the opposite direction by 21 percent, 108 percent, or 217 percent, the put option would have been there to pick up the slack and protect you from potentially devastating losses.

Hard Stop

A hard stop is defined as a stop that you can pinpoint with accuracy, so that your losses will not exceed a particular price. Soft stops, that is, stop orders, are not able to guarantee that you will exit at the price you want. Hard stops, while similar to a synthetic trade, are a way of purchasing a less expensive option based on your money management rules. If you have a rule that sets your maximum loss at 2 percent on a position, a properly placed put option can achieve that goal for you. In addition, you can catch the move in the market as it drops, without being subjected to any particular shorting stock rules.

In Figure 16.2 we look at Coca-Cola Inc.

Coca-Cola is showing strength from February 22, 2008 to February 27, 2008. Three strong up days convinces us to purchase the stock at $60 per share. There is resistance at the $60.50 where it collapsed the previous week. Even so, it appears to have enough momentum to carry it.

The average daily trading range is approximately $1.50/share. Our money management rules set our stop loss at 2 percent or $58.80 cents. By purchasing a put option at the closest strike price of $57.50 we only have to pay $.20 per share. In this case in order to protect ourselves from the additional $1.30 loss, the difference between our money management stop loss and the available option strike price, we use a soft stop order at $58.80 to exit our stock and a hard stop at $57.50 to cover any losses.

In Figure 16.3 we see Coca-Cola drop in value by over $4.00. Half of that loss falls below our stop loss order of $58.80. As the market continues to drop, our put option gains in value. We paid $.20 to buy a put option at $57.50. Once the market price breaks below $57.50 our option contract shifts from an out-of-the-money option to an in-the-money option. This drives the value of the $57.50 option from $.20/share to $1.15/share. This $1.15 offsets most of the $1.20 we lost, $60.00 minus $58.80.

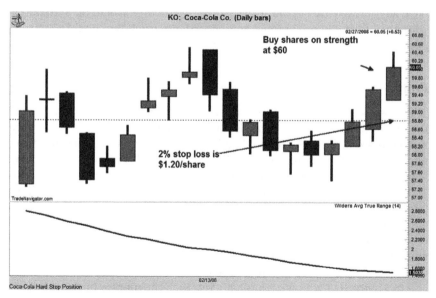

FIGURE 16.2 Coca-Cola Hard Stop

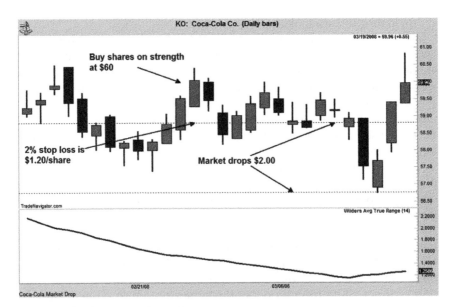

FIGURE 16.3 Coca-Cola Market Drop
Source: TradeNavigator.com © 2007. All rights reserved.

If you didn't have the put option protecting the position you would not have anything to offset your losses. Every 100 shares would be $120 out of your pocket. If you are holding onto an SSF contract, that could represent as much as 10 percent of your accounts margin value.

Collar

The most common option/stock relationship that traders are aware of is the covered call. A covered call is considered an income strategy for buy and hold stock traders. Covered calls are simple to conceptualize. If the market lacks momentum or volatility, you can sell options against your shares with a reasonable expectation that the options won't be exercised. If they are exercised you have the underlying shares to protect you from losing more than you invested.

A sister strategy to the covered call is the collar. In Chapter 7 we discussed collars in depth. The concept is effectively the same as the covered call. The difference is that you also purchase a put option to protect your stock position against any drop in price.

In Figure 16.4 we take a look at Tyco Inc. The market begins a bullish move on May 13th, 2008. To protect ourselves from a drop in price,

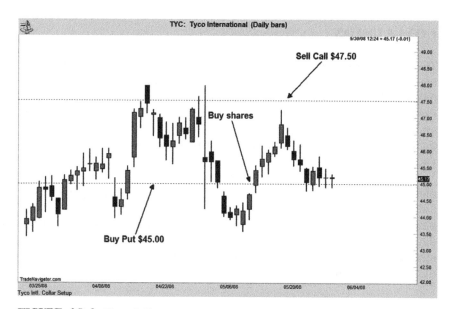

FIGURE 16.4 Tyco Collar
Source: TradeNavigator.com © 2007. All rights reserved.

we purchase an at-the-money put at $45 while simultaneously buying shares at $45. The cost of the option is $.90/share. To cover the cost of the option we then sell a call at $47.50, a price that Tyco shares failed to exceed throughout April. The $47.50 call brings in a premium of $.25/share, which means that your total option expense does not exceed $.65/share.

What makes this an attractive opportunity is that there are two ways to profit. The first is that you can make $1.85 in profits from the actual stock position itself, if the market moves in your direction but doesn't exceed the value of the sold call—$2.50 minus the cost of the $.65 in net option premiums. The second way to profit is if the market moves down against your shares and you gain the increase in value of the put option and the entire premium from the call.

This is no different than the collars we created for futures or forex contracts, yet it is a little-used technique. Depending on where you purchase your protective put, you could end up with a net-zero expense, depending on the amount of premium you collect on the call you sell. This is a versatile strategy that allows you to extend the buy and hold life of any stock that you want to keep in your portfolio.

CONCLUSION

The strategies in this book are universal. They are designed to help protect your principal while at the same time maximizing your profit potential. Whether you trade futures, forex, CFDs, or stocks, risk management is essential to your success. In today's sophisticated environment of swaps, swaptions, off-balance sheet derivative transactions, and interest strips, the information provided in this book has been a rudimentary look at what you can do to protect yourself.

Long gone are the days investors could stick to a particular investment type and expect to achieve the same results that they expected even a decade ago. With the telecommunication bubble burst, dot-com bubble burst, and the real estate bubble burst all happening back-to-back, everyday investors need to have a set of tools to help protect themselves. The strategies presented throughout this book have been designed to do just that, regardless of the market circumstances.

About the Author

Noble DraKoln is the founder of Speculator Academy, www .speculatoracademy.com, where he focuses on the development, management, and promotion of the company's core philosophy of "focusing on the trader, not the trading." Prior to this role, DraKoln served as a broker in the retail division of Royal Financial Inc., and as a professional sugar trader. DraKoln got his start in futures at the age of 17. He was an assistant to the top producer at a small futures firm. A short year-and-a-half later, he passed the Series 3 license exam—on his first attempt. At that point, he became one of the youngest practicing futures brokers in the nation. DraKoln speaks regularly at industry conferences in the United States and has also spoken at trading conferences in Romania, France, Germany, and China. He has written articles for *Forbes*, *Futures* magazine, *Technical Analysis of Stocks and Commodities*, *Traders* magazine, *Currency Trader*, *Cornerstone*, *Traders Journal*, *Pristine View*, and the eSignal newsletter.

Index

Printed and bound by CPI Group (UK) Ltd, Croydon, CR0 4YY

16/04/2025